Chicks on Film

VIDEO PICKS FOR WOMEN
AND OTHER INTELLIGENT FORMS OF LIFE

**GABRIELLE COSGRIFF, ANNE REIFENBERG,
and CYNTHIA THOMAS**

AVON BOOKS ◆ NEW YORK

GABRIELLE COSGRIFF:
For my children Michael, Carolyn and Claire.
You're better than any movie.

Anne Reifenberg:
For video lover Nicholas Arno Marks and all of
Connie Hill's grandchildren,
who have decades of movie watching ahead of them.

Cynthia Thomas:
For Sauce Boy.

AVON BOOKS, INC.
1350 Avenue of the Americas
New York, New York 10019

Copyright © 1998 by Gabrielle Cosgriff, Anne Reifenberg, and Cynthia Thomas
Front cover and inside back cover illustrations by Hal Just
Interior design by Kellan Peck
Visit our website at **http://www.AvonBooks.com**
ISBN: 0-380-79365-2

Library of Congress Cataloging in Publication Data:
Cosgriff, Gabrielle.
    Chicks on film : video picks for women and other intelligent forms of life / Gabrielle Cosgriff, Anne Reifenberg, and Cynthia Thomas.
        p.   cm.
    Includes index.
1. Motion pictures for women—Catalogs. I. Reifenberg, Anne.
II. Thomas, Cynthia, 1960–   . III. Title.
PN1995.9.W6C67   1998   98-10435
791.43'75'082—dc21   CIP

First Avon Books Trade Printing: July 1998

AVON TRADEMARK REG. U.S. PAT. OFF. AND IN OTHER COUNTRIES, MARCA REGISTRADA, HECHO EN U.S.A.

Printed in the U.S.A.

OPM   10 9 8 7 6 5 4 3 2 1

Introduction

Have you ever noticed that it's mostly guys who critique movies on TV, not to mention in newspapers and magazines? We have. That's why we started our cable TV show, "Chicks on Film," in Houston a couple of years ago, which then led us to write this book. Cynthia got us all together. She should be a casting agent—nobody else would have thought of this combination! There is very little we all agree on, including movies.

Cynthia is a thirty-something who wouldn't be seen dead in a dress and heels—she's way too cool for that. She's a tender soul who hates violence and artsy-fartsy pretensions in the movies. Anne, forty-something, is loud and cheerful and keeps her bags packed for the next adventure. She eats up that action-explosion-sweaty-biceps stuff with a spoon, and has a heavy hand on the FF button when it comes to anything that moves slower that a speeding jock. Gabrielle, a fifty-something feminist, never liked the word *Chicks* to begin with, but couldn't come up with a better equivalent for *Guys*. (*Women* goes with *Men*, but what goes with *Guys*? *Dolls*? *Dames*? *Broads*? She cratered.) But she still tries to pull that mature, worldly garbage—she sees it as refined and sophisticated; the others chalk it up to excessive exposure to subtitles and obscure Australian directors.

We're a motley trio. But we agree on one thing: Women need more options, and more voices, when it comes to the movies. As Mae West says in *I'm No Angel*, "Speak up for yourself, or you'll end up a rug." So we're speaking up, giving you our take on a few of the thousands of videos out there. We recognize that women are more complex than guys, who require only noise, cars, large firearms, and naked floozies on screen to be happy. We demand more from our movies. Sure, we crave romance and hunks and adventure. But we also need movies about sibling rivalry, nifty table-settings, rotten kids, great role models, and families even more dysfunctional than our own.

So we've organized our chapters to fit your various moods. What's the point of watching a witty, funny love story when you want to strangle your significant other? Just turn to the heading "He Done Her Wrong, She Did Him In" and pick your poison—metaphorically, or course. Or do you really want to watch TV sitcoms when your kid's just been expelled from military school, where you sent him after he'd been expelled from regular school? See our "I Will Survive" chapter and you'll feel better.

And don't worry, if you don't agree with a particular review, chances are that two out of the three of us didn't like it either. One of us writes a review, which is followed by the opinions of the other two Chicks—usually negative. (We figured that we all agree on a movie about 10 percent of the time.) So you get a three-fer on every review.

We want to thank some folks for making this book happen. First, Gabrielle and Anne want to thank Cynthia for bringing us all together on our TV show. We've all stretched and groaned—sorry, *grown* from the experience.

The three of us owe a lot to our swell director, friend, and cheerleader on that show: Sauce Boy, a.k.a. Caleb Solomon, a.k.a. Cynthia's husband. Applause also goes to our Chick-in-Wings, on-air substitutes Linda Barth and Elizabeth McMahon, Lindsay and Claire Heinsen; our intern Emily Medley; the folks at Access Houston; Landmark Theater's Sarah Gish; Audio-Video Plus; Louis Parks; Liz of Lizzard's Pub; and our families, friends, and colleagues, who put up with us while we were glued to the VCR. Gabrielle also thanks her friend and intrepid movie buddy Linda Friedman. Anne gives a high-five to Earl.

And finally, we thank you for choosing our book. We hope you enjoy it and we hope you enjoy our video picks.

Contents

one

SCREW THE PLOT:

Just Bring Me a Menu!

"As God is my witness,"
vows Scarlett in Gone With the Wind,
"I'll never be hungry again!"

"Oh, Beulah,"
yawns Mae West in I'm No Angel,
"peel me a grape."

Food in the movies, as in life, ranks up there with sex and breathing. And even in movies that aren't really about food, the food scenes are often what steal the show (see quiz below).

But chicks didn't cook in movies until the '50s. In the '30s, they were too busy pursuing careers, cracking wise, and enjoying sex. In the '40s, they paid for all that freedom by becoming bitches and gun molls or by contracting assorted diseases, preferably blindness. Then, in the '50s, they really got put in their place—the kitchen (except for Doris Day, of course). Even today, the apron is more often than not the mantle of virtue, and the business suit the cloak of Satan. (*Fatal Attraction,* anyone?)

Guys cook in movies, too. But, unless they're actually chefs, as in *Big Night,* they only get to cook in two kinds of scenes: One, for a kid (Dustin Hoffman in *Kramer vs. Kramer*), which proves they're sensitive; and two, for a chick they've just met (Jack Lemmon in *The Apartment,* page 203), in which case it's foreplay. Otherwise, Mom still cooks.

But the good news is, there actually are some movies about food that we can recommend. (Note that *Babette's Feast* is not one of them. This grim saga of a woman bankrupting herself to buy outrageously expensive ingredients and toiling over a stupidly intricate menu for a bunch of ingrates is no fun at all. I know, because I did that last Thanksgiving.)

So, whip up your favorite dish, break out your favorite nosh, send out for pizza . . . whatever lights your fire. Then put your feet up and enjoy. Bon appetit! **GC**

DELICATESSEN

1991. 95 min. Jean-Claude Dreyfus, Marie-Laure Dougnac, Dominique Pinon. Dir. Jean-Pierre Jeunet, Marc Caro. French w/subtitles

Cynthia says this brilliant, eccentric movie doesn't belong in this chapter. I really don't see why not. It's about a butcher, and people who crave meat versus vegetarian terrorists—it's definitely about food. People and food. Well, okay, people *as* food. And I suppose you *could* think of cannibalism—and murder and a nuclear holocaust—as unfunny, but that wouldn't be fair. Not until you've seen this movie.

It takes place in a postnuclear world that is low on people, and even lower on meat to feed them. But this butcher (Dreyfus) and his customers seem quite well fed. Pinon, playing a Chaplinesque ex-clown, applies for a job as the butcher's helper. (It hasn't dawned on him yet why the butcher goes through helpers at such a smart clip.) Pinon falls in love with the butcher's daughter (Dougnac), a saucer-eyed, gangly ingenue. It's a sweet, goofy romance, played out to the tune of murder, mayhem, and mincemeat.

The underground-dwelling vegetarian terrorists are hilarious—a geeky, bumbling bunch of sewer rats with code names like Artichoke Heart and Onion Swiper. The movie is shot in shades of brown—liver and gravy predominate—and bizarre camera angles pull faces into droll caricatures with bulging eyes and cavernous nostrils. The dialogue is witty and sly, and a number of supremely silly subplots keep the action spinning along. If you're a Monty Python fan, you'll feel right at home in this madhouse. If you're not, give it a whirl, anyway. What's at steak except a few laughs? **GC**

CT   And this from the woman who said after watching *Babe* that she'd never eat bacon again. Should that be in this chapter, too? Culinary debates aside, call me a pessimist, but there's just something about the postnuclear holocaust that depresses me.

AR Sick! But funny. ("I'm a butcher but I don't mince words. You just don't look cut out for the job.")

EAT DRINK MAN WOMAN
1994. 124 min. Sihung Lung, Kuei-Mei Yang, Yu-Wen Wang, Chien-Lien Wu, Sylvia Chang, Winston Chao. Dir. Ang Lee. Chinese w/subtitles.

Some films try harder to make the connection between the seductiveness of food and sex (*Tampopo*, anyone?), but I can't think of any that does it better than this one, a movie David Denby of *New York* magazine called "culinary porn." It's hard to imagine a cuisine better suited to such a genre, given the variety of foods, shapes, textures, and tools used in Chinese cooking. Chickens are baked in clay, dumplings steamed in baskets, oysters scooped out of shells. Vegetables simmer in clay pots, sizzle in woks, brood in broth. This is not only one of the truly great food movies, it's a really good movie period. It's the story of three sisters—the college student, the important executive in short skirts, and the virginal teacher—their father, and their loves. Their often-surprising romantic entanglements are revealed at the weekly Sunday dinner. When a sister says, "I have an announcement to make," get ready for another bomb to drop. The action, and the cooking, take place in Taipei, a city that still has little pockets of old Asia surrounded by the ubiquitous skyscrapers. A warning: I stuffed myself before watching this movie, and it didn't help. I still got major cravings, so keep the Chinese food delivery number handy. **CT**

AR A feel-good film. And Cynthia, have you tried the jumbo-size box of Milk Duds yet?

GC Okay, okay. It's a sweet movie, and yes, Chinese food is really good. But I thought the slap at *Tampopo* (reviewed by yours truly on page 5) was in extremely poor taste. There's no comparison. *Tampopo* is a satire, not a menu.

LIKE WATER FOR CHOCOLATE

1992. 114 min. Lumi Cavazos, Marco Leonardi. Dir. Alfonso Arau. Spanish w/subtitles

Reading Laura Esquivel's book was a nuisance, maybe because the recipes broke my concentration or made me think about cooking, which is almost always followed by cleaning up. So I went reluctantly to the movie. Then I saw it again, on a full stomach. Quail in rose petals! Oxtail soup! Sausage and sardine rolls! You'll need more than microwave popcorn to survive *Like Water for Chocolate,* and perhaps a hankie, depending on your reaction to fantasy stirred into romance with a tablespoon of tragedy.

The setting is Mexico in 1910. Cavazos is Tita, the youngest daughter of Mama Elena, and Tita is by family tradition bound to care for her aging mother rather than wed. It is cruel fate that she should fall in love with Pedro (Leonardi), who, to be close to his true love, marries an older sister. Tita, a supreme cook, is compelled to bake their wedding cake and weeps into the batter, and on eating the cake the wedding guests, seated outdoors at long tables in the grass, suddenly—no, you'll have to rent the video to find out. Don't you hate it when reviewers reveal too much? Just be assured that there is an outhouse scene to set you afire. *Like Water for Chocolate* is not only enchanting, it's the second-biggest-grossing foreign language film in U.S. history (*Il Postino* pipped it at the post). And ruled not eligible for the Academy Awards in 1993. Of *course.* Note of trivia: Director Arau, by the way, is married to author Esquivel.
AR

GC Funny, I loved this movie the first time around, saw it again and got indigestion. Too heavy on the magical realism, maybe. And no, Anne, I don't find it particularly enchanting when Tita's guy marries her sister, then Tita gets to nurse their baby, be everybody's good buddy, and generally get the short end of the stick. Reality's scary enough. Fantasies shouldn't be.

CT A magical movie is a rare thing. This is one. (I only watched it once.)

TAMPOPO

1986. 114 min. Nobuko Miyamoto, Tsutomu Yamazaki. Dir.
Juzo Itami. Japanese w/subtitles

It's no wonder *Tampopo* made twenty-three major top ten lists the
year it came out. It's a keeper. From the opening shot of a cool gangster's orgiastic snack to the closing frames of a blissfully nursing baby,
it's a giddy, sweet homage to the carnal pleasures of eating—and to
American Western movies. (It's been called the first noodle Western.)
  Miyamoto plays Tampopo, an ambitious young widow who runs a
small noodle restaurant in Tokyo. Yamazaki plays a truck driver—a
jeans-clad, aw-shucks-ma'am hero who moseys into her life and guides
her on her quest to create the perfect noodle soup—the top *ramen*.
Along the way, he and his trusty sidekicks send up American oaters
with a vengeance. And, yes, he tips his Stetson and rides off on his
metal steed at the end. In between, we are treated to the wickedest
food-and-sex scenes this side of *Tom Jones* (below). I didn't know you
could do that with an egg yolk—not a raw one, anyway.
  Director Itami's view of contemporary Japan is both satirical and
affectionate. (See his *A Taxing Woman,* also starring Miyamoto, his
real-life wife, for an equally hilarious take on the culture—and an
equally enterprising woman.) Embellishing the major story line is a
series of savory little sketches on the fatally seductive powers of
food. A totally satisfying movie. **GC**

AR   A loony Japanese export, and worth the duty.

CT   I figured, a movie about noodles, how could it go wrong?
      It's not that it ever went wrong, it just never went anywhere,
      except on and on and on. I wanted to scream, "Make the
      damn soup already and let the credits roll!"

TOM JONES

1963. 129 min. Albert Finney, Susannah York. Dir. Tony
Richardson

Finney complained that he was bored while making this movie. It
doesn't show. As Tom, a waif brought up by a country squire in
eighteenth-century England, he has a rollicking good time getting in

and out of a variety of petticoats while courting the squire's daughter (York) and eating a lot of greasy game and mutton. In a famous scene, he and a lady of questionable character enjoy a ribald dinner, making libidinous eyes at one another as they stuff their faces, licking fingers, caressing chicken legs, shredding bread, embracing wine chalices. Their table manners are appalling, but the result is probably the best food intercourse interlude in the history of cinema.

The rest of *Tom Jones* is a romp, too. I admit to not having read Henry Fielding's 1749 novel, which I think is about the size of *War and Peace,* but it just can't be as silly and impudent as the film, which won Academy Awards for best picture, best director, best adapted screenplay and best score. **AR**

CT   I understand why Finney was bored. I was too, except for the classic meat-ripping seduction scene, on which the whole reputation of this movie is based. Don't be put off by the book's length, it's *much* better.

GC   Finney is so young and cute and adorably randy. It's all sheer, naughty fun.

Tasteful Table-Setting Tips

Need to impress the hell out of the in-laws? Or just drool over magnificent table settings? Well, that's why God made Merchant-Ivory and their ilk. Martha Stewart, eat your heart out.

> *The Remains of the Day*
> *Howards End*
> *Angels & Insects*
> *Fanny and Alexander*

Name That Movie

- Female diner and "I'll have what she's having!"
- Paul Newman and hard-boiled eggs
- Humphrey Bogart and strawberries
- James Cagney and a grapefruit half
- Jack Nicholson and a piece of toast
- Joyce Redman, Albert Finney, a chicken leg, an oyster, a lobster . . .

(answers see p. 277)

two

I WILL SURVIVE

"We keep acomin'. We're the people that live.
They can't wipe us out. They can't lick us.
We'll go on forever, Paw, 'cause we're the people."
—Ma (Jane Darnell), in The Grapes of Wrath

As Duke Wayne would have said, if not for that pesky little Y chromosome: A chick's gotta do what a chick's gotta do. And, boy, have they done it in the movies. Anne Bancroft did it in *The Graduate,* Meryl Streep did it in *The River Wild,* Mia Farrow in *Rosemary's Baby,* and Barbra Streisand in *Yentl,* to name just a few. They did what they had to do to make it. Bancroft perked up her mangy, middle-aged life by swigging martinis and seducing the nerdy but horny Dustin Hoffman. Streep flexed her deltoids and ran those rapids and saved civilization as we know it—or at least her family and the dog—from evildoers. Farrow decided that, hey, he's a weird little devil, but he's *my* little devil. And Streisand, who always does it her way in real life, cross-dressed her way to a good education. Whatever it takes. Please note that this chapter does not contain any of the movies of the terminally plucky Sally Field resorting to vigilante violence in *Eye for an Eye,* or *Gidget Gets a Gun,* as the Chicks prefer to call it, or sobbing over her ruined manicure because she has to pick cotton (her own, mind you) in *Places in the Heart,* and accepting the Academy Award for that very performance with the immortal words: "You like me! You really like me!" No, no, no. We're recommending movies that we like, we *really* like. So get a grip, Sally. Which is just what the chicks in this chapter do. The envelope, please. . . . **GC**

THE ADDICTION

1995. 82 min. Lili Taylor, Annabella Sciorra, Christopher Walken. Dir. Abel Ferrara. b&w

This is a smart, funny movie, beautifully photographed, and with lots to engage your attention. When Kathleen (Taylor) is attacked by Casanova (Sciorra), a lovely female vampire, she reacts like any sensible NYU graduate student would. She reports it to the police, sobs, throws up, gets herself checked out at the infirmary and tries to get on with her life. No flickering candles and moldy caskets here, just fears about communicable diseases and getting that philosophy dissertation finished.

Kathleen is a good, moral person, concerned about the evil in the world, and being a vampire doesn't come easy. "What were you thinking about?" she lectures one of her early conquests, a young woman she's picked up in the library. But, hey, life—make that undeath—must go on, and she copes. It helps when she starts to meet other vampires, notably Peina (Walken), who's been around long enough to know the ropes. He urges moderation, cautioning Kathleen, "Eternity's a long time. Get used to it."

There's a lot of existential banter, and more philosopher quotes than you can shake a stick at. The climax, a faculty party to celebrate Kathleen's doctorate, brings together a motley assortment of professors and vampires, and things get hilariously out of hand. When the drinking stops, we know that Kathleen may not be headed for the career she had planned, but we know for sure she will survive. **GC**

CT Oh, please. If Gabrielle makes me watch one more pompous and killingly dull vampire flick, I'm going to bite *her* on the neck, assuming I haven't died of boredom first.

AR Too late for me. I did die, and within the first fifteen minutes.

ALICE DOESN'T LIVE HERE ANYMORE

1974. 113 min. Ellen Burstyn, Kris Kristofferson, Alfred Lutter. Dir. Martin Scorsese

So her husband dies and she hits the road with no money, no prospects, and a whiny, smart-mouthed kid to support. In real life that's a nightmare. In the movies, it could have been a soppy, simplistic, and irritating tearjerker. It's not. It's a gutsy, complex, and satisfying tearjerker. With Scorsese's powerful direction, a terrific cast, tasty dialogue, and vibrant New Mexico scenery, this movie delivers.

Burstyn, in the role of her career—it won her that little bald-guy statue—gives Alice a tough, realistic edge and a vulnerable warmth as she confronts her fears, makes her mistakes, and keeps on keeping on. Lutter, her pain-in-the-ass twelve-year-old son, Tommy, is completely believable, and Kristofferson makes a shaggy, decent-guy foil for the two of them. But there's more. Harvey Keitel shows up as a young, terrifying slimeball; a precocious Jodie Foster pops in to corrupt Tommy; and Diane Ladd shines in her supporting role as Flo, Alice's foulmouthed, tenderhearted cohort at Mel's Diner. (Yes, the very same, the one they based the television series *Alice* on.) Add it all up and you get a big bang for your buck with this movie. Plus a shot in the arm for any chick struggling to keep her head above water. **GC**

CT   With visions of TV's *Alice* in my head, I dreaded watching this flick. But I'm glad I did. It's a good stand-up-when-the-world-is-beating-you-down movie.

AR   There's nothing new about the story, which is as old as the grease on Mel's grill. But it's told in such a refreshingly tough-talking, seedy-looking, oh-*so*-'70s way that it works fairly well.

ALL THIS, AND HEAVEN TOO
1940. 143 min. Bette Davis, Charles Boyer. Dir. Anatole Litvak, b/w

Forget about *Mary Poppins* (page 59) and *The Sound of Music* (page 159). It's a good thing the only job for an educated but broke woman isn't "governess" anymore. She had to be the superwoman of the nineteenth century—smart, diplomatic, warm, and inspiring. And what did she get for this, other than a roof over her head and, maybe, enough to eat? She was dismissed as a mere servant by aristocrats who weren't half as smart or noble or charming. Bette stars as the upstanding teacher and role model who is beloved by the children under her care. She also starts looking a whole lot better to the children's father than the shrew of a wife he's married to. And Bette can't help but feel stirrings for Papa herself, played by Charles Boyer. A horrible crime takes place and our heroine is blamed, unjustly of course. Will she be found guilty? Will she ever be able to escape the slurs on her character? Does she remain a virtuous woman? Rent this movie to find out, and if you figure out what the title means, let me know. **CT**

AR   That a woman can have murder, love, *and* a full-time job? Whatever, rent it for the performance by Barbara O'Neil as the possessive wife (she was Scarlett's mother in *Gone With the Wind*.)

GC   One of the schoolgirls, hearing Bette's melodramatic story, sobs, "Oh please, Mademoiselle, don't go on!" My sentiments exactly. But she does.

ONCE WERE WARRIORS
1994. 103 min. Rena Owen. Temuera Morrison, Mamaenga-roa Kerr-Bell. Dir. Lee Tamahori

This is one of the most original and powerful movies I've ever seen. Set in present-day New Zealand, it tells the story of Beth, a Maori woman struggling to raise her children in a poor inner-city neighborhood. Married to Jake, an abusive, muscle-bound loser, Beth sees her family begin to disintegrate around her as her children drift into gangs and petty crime and are exposed to the escalating rage and hopelessness of her drunken husband and his lowlife mates. Gradually, painfully, and at a bitter cost, she comes to realize what she must do for herself and her kids. "Our people once were warriors," she says, ashamed and disgusted at her situation. By the end of this raw, vital movie, she persuades us that they can be again.

Owen, whose earthy sexuality and not-quite-beautiful features recall the young Jeanne Moreau, plays Beth with a blazing intensity, but she doesn't overshadow Morrison. His Jake—pathetic bully that he is—captures the blind, brutal frustration of an underdog ground down by poverty, racism, and ignorance. Another bonus for the viewer is that this movie, based on Alan Duff's novel—a best-seller in New Zealand—was made by a Maori director using Maori actors. It gives a rare, fascinating glimpse of contemporary Maori customs and culture, and the struggle for identity in an Anglo-dominated society. So, for Americans, it is at the same time exotic and all too familiar.

But this is no polemic. It's vivid, wrenching, and personal. See this movie. **GC**

CT   This is a very good movie about family dynamics that makes me want to learn more about Maori culture. It's also a major bummer. Don't watch it if your Prozac needs refilling.

AR   Tamahori doesn't flinch in storytelling, that's for sure. But he disappoints me in the end, with a too-pat, too-late awakening.

RUBY IN PARADISE
1993. 115 min. Ashley Judd, Todd Field, Bentley Mitchum, Allison Dean, Dorothy Lyman. Dir. Victor Nunez

There are so many coming-of-age movies for guys and so few for us chicks, but this is one of them, and a good one, too. It's about Ruby, who escapes the Tennessee hills before getting pregnant or beat up—which she considers no small victory—and heads for a Florida resort town she once visited as a kid. Arriving at the end of the tourist season, she gets a job at a store selling tacky souvenirs and tries to start a new life. Her aspirations aren't grand, her opportunities limited. She sleeps with two guys, one a pseudointellectual dropout (the good guy), and one a pretty boy with a fancy car and too many carefully placed blond streaks in his hair (the bad one). Each one has an impact on her, but a limited one. She's not letting a guy take over her life. With its slow and deliberate (but never boring) pace and its sometimes introspective dialogue, this film feels almost French (although not infuriatingly so). But *almost* is the key word. Eventually, something happens besides talk. Plus, Ruby's internal struggle takes place in an American context, where *job* and *career* aren't dirty words. *Ruby* could easily be a major snooze if it weren't for Judd's extraordinary ability to let us in on what's going on inside her. It's mind-boggling that she's the sister of one and daughter of the other of the famous country-singing Judds' duo. (See her also in *Smoke,* in the small but captivating part of a drug addict.) **CT**

AR   I sure would like to like a film with such good intentions, and such strong and believable female characters. But *arrggghhh!* To call this "slow and deliberate" is too kind. Try soporific.

GC   I agree with both Anne and Cynthia. It's a lovely coming-of-age movie, and it drags. Judd's character talks waaay too much, but hey, she's entitled. She's got a lot of stuff to sort out. So settle in and get to know her. She's one of the most appealing characters you'll meet at the movies.

THREE ON A MATCH

1932. 64 min. Ann Dvorak, Joan Blondell, Bette Davis. Dir. Mervyn LeRoy. b/w

Part of the reason politicians and old folks can get away with talking about how much better life was in the good old days is because when we think of the good old days we think of the good old movies, which have been cleansed of anything seemingly unseemly, like sex or drugs. We can thank Hollywood's Production Code for that. So it's a shock to see a film from 1932 with guys in fedoras wiping their noses to suggest someone's been hitting the cocaine stash. Especially when that someone is the mother of a mop-headed kid cute enough to be sidekick in a W. C. Fields movie.

Blondell, Dvorak, and Davis play schoolgirl friends who reunite as adults. At school Dvorak was the beautiful rich girl who "had it all," Blondell the juvenile delinquent, and Davis the brainy Goody Two-shoes. Dvorak evolves into a socialite with too much of everything to be happy, Blondell a burgeoning Broadway star, and Davis the stock hardworking girl. Dvorak takes up with the wrong guy and gets them all embroiled in one another's lives. In addition to making me wish there were more gritty old movies around, *Three on a Match* makes me miss that old convention of flashing newspaper headlines to show the changing times. If we think things are moving fast today, look what these three chicks went through in twenty years: women getting the vote, World War I, the Roaring '20s and the Depression. **CT**

GC   It's a fascinating movie with a wonderful cast. And I agree, Cynthia, as far as chicks are concerned, those really were the good old days.

AR   And Blondell is tremendous, heads above her costars. (If the movie title seems familiar, it's because television offered up a tiresome remake in 1987.)

TO LIVE
1994. 133 min. Gong Li, Ge You. Dir. Zhang Yimou. Chinese w/subtitles

Zhang Yimou really knows how to make movies. He knows how to irritate the leaders of the People's Republic of China, too. They didn't like the way he depicts the Communist revolution in the magnificent *To Live* and so refused to let him submit it for an Oscar. Then they didn't allow him to travel to Cannes for the film festival, where it won the Grand Jury and Best Actor prizes. And of course they missed the point entirely: *To Live* isn't about politics, though it does span more than three decades of political turmoil in China.

It's really a simple story, beautifully told, about people—in particular a family headed by husband Ge You and wife Gong Li—and you grow to care about them very much as they endure civil war, the nationalists, Mao, the Great Leap Forward, the Cultural Revolution, tragic deaths, and great happiness. They must adapt to survive, and in fact the husband's loss at the gambling table of the family fortune and mansion in the 1940s is a blessing, for the Communists later execute the new owner for the crime of being a landlord, and the mansion burns down. "Your family's timber was first rate," a local bureaucrat tells Ge You, who, having figured out which way the wind is blowing, quickly responds, "It wasn't my family's timber. It was counterrevolutionary timber." Funny, sad, sweet, moving, *To Live* is wonderful. **AR**

GC And if the crash course in Chinese history confuses you as much as it did me, fear not. Just enjoy the beautifully authentic settings and the glorious Gong Li.

CT Sensual and cruel images from this movie stick with me as if I had been in China myself.

WHAT HAVE I DONE TO DESERVE THIS?

1985. 100 min. Carmen Maura, Luis Hostalot, Chus Lampreave. Dir. Pedro Almodóvar. Spanish w/subtitles

You have to hand it to Almodóvar. His movies, good or bad, are unmistakably his. They are manic, garish, and outrageous, and it's the female characters he cares about and develops most fully. Luckily for us, this is one of the good ones. I rank it up there with *Women on the Verge of a Nervous Breakdown* (page 17). It's a bleak, black comedy with a soft center. And there's a plot. Sort of. (Almodóvar's plots are like clotheslines. He throws them out there and then hangs all sorts of colorful, mismatching scenes on them, but they all somehow come together. It's all in a day's wash, I think he's saying.)

Gloria, played by the divine Maura, lives with her husband, two children, and her mother-in-law in a tiny flat in a mammoth, faceless apartment block in Madrid. Her brutish, taxi-driver husband has a Nazi-songstress fetish, one son sells drugs, and the other sleeps with older men. Her mother-in-law plays arcade games, raps with the kids, and pines for her native village. Gloria cleans other people's homes and offices all day, and gets by with a little help from uppers, No-Doz, assorted nasal sprays, the occasional sexual encounter, and whatever else is at hand. When a druggist tells her it's against the rules to give her any more No-Doz without a prescription, we sympathize fully when Gloria asks, "What are the rules for an eighteen-hour working day?"

As life erupts untidily around her, Gloria hangs on, doing the right thing as she sees it. When the dust finally settles, and it does, we realize that love and hope can exist in the unlikeliest places. Oh, and watch out for the lizard. **GC**

CT   And the prostitute neighbor adds a certain spice to the mix, as if it needed any!

AR   Plot? Almodóvar's movies leave me feeling disheveled, though, I admit, not completely unentertained.

A WOMAN'S TALE
1991. 93 min. Sheila Florance, Gosia Dobrowolska. Dir. Paul Cox

A slow-moving, slightly grim tale of a dying almost-eighty-year-old woman doesn't sound like gripping entertainment, but this touching film from Australia is just that. It's also something to pop into the VCR when you feel your priorities getting all screwed up. Think of it as a visit to a moral chiropractor. (It's sure to send those guilty of ignoring their elders on a serious guilt trip.) That's not to say *A Woman's Tale* is dull by any means. This rare cinematic peek at the lives of the elderly is rich with both the sense of loss and of the joys of life. Martha, played by Florance, wants simply to live whatever time she has left as a functioning human being in her own apartment without being thrown into an institution to wither away slowly. A common enough story in real life, but not on film. Florance is a formidable Martha, the kind of old broad I'd surely like to be. This is not a movie about staying alive. It's about *being* alive. **CT**

GC   I think of it as a lovely, inspiring movie about a gutsy woman. And it's all the more striking because Florance herself was terminally ill as she played Martha. She died of cancer a few days after winning the Australian Oscar for Best Actress for her role.

AR   Was it really only ninety-three minutes long? It seemed to go on forever, though I was passably pleased to have stuck it out.

WOMEN ON THE VERGE OF A NERVOUS BREAKDOWN

1988. 88 min. Carmen Maura, Antonio Banderas. Dir. Pedro Almodóvar. Spanish w/subtitles

When I watched this on video recently it took me awhile before I realized, oh my god, that's Antonio Banderas! He's such a dweeby guy here—kind of a Spanish Clark Kent—that it's hard to picture him as the smoldering sex symbol we all know and love. So what happens in this wacky soap opera? Well, let's see, television actress Pepa (Maura) tries furiously to find the lover who just dumped her, a friend who abetted terrorists shows up and wants to hide out in Pepa's apartment, a young couple drops by to look at the apartment, which is on the market, and one is accidentally drugged by spiked gazpacho Pepa had in the fridge. . . . All the while, Pepa's unaware that her lover's wife, fresh out of the loony bin, is tracking her down. All this culminates in what is probably the only chase scene I've ever liked. This movie is so original, it leaves an impression for a long time. Images from the movie keep popping up in your head. It's the kind of movie that makes you want to be a director. **CT**

GC Especially a director who bleaches his hair bright yellow and drives a cab that's a cross between a drugstore, a bar, and a bordello, as Almodóvar does in this movie. I love it. It's an acid jolt from the smashing opening credits all the way through.

AR Okay, I take it back about Almodóvar always leaving me feeling disheveled. In this case, I was out of breath. A fast-paced hoot.

Oy, the Things Chicks Go Through Just to Stay Alive

Match the movie with the obstacle these chicks had to over-come—or at least tried to overcome. (Hint: All the movies are in this book.)

1. Addiction to cocaine

2. Addiction to No-Doz

3. Addiction to candy bars

4. The Toronto Police

5. Being in charge of a kid with no father

6. Being in charge of a kid with no father and spending life on the run . . . in high heels

7. Violent father

8. Murderous ex-boyfriend

9. Paralyzed husband

10. Dead lover

(answers see p. 277)

three

GROWING PAINS

"When I was a child, I used to race rats."
—Julian Beck, *in* The Cotton Club

If you find yourself gazing jealously at the tot bundled up and strapped snug in her stroller, or suddenly awaken from a cozy daydream about Jane and Spot, or realize you've been carting around for the past seventeen years the plastic tiara you wore at the dance recital in junior high where Tina Callis high-hipped you during your solo and propelled you upended so that all the boys in the first row spied your tulip-patterned underwear—*desist*. It is time to rent one of the videos recommended below. Prepubescence wasn't nearly as comfy as your selective memory would have you believe, now that you're in your dotage. You were, as a kid, too young to appreciate most everything that matters in life and too guileless to know what you were missing and too short to see over the adults who hogged the curb at the Thanksgiving Day parade. We suggest you pop a few iron pills, apply a mud mask, soak your tired dogs in a seltzer footbath, and remind yourself why you're thankful you're not a kid anymore. **AR**

BEAUTIFUL GIRLS

1996. 107 min. Timothy Hutton, Matt Dillon, Uma Thurman, Mira Sorvino, Rosie O'Donnell, Natalie Portman, Martha Plimpton. Dir. Ted Demme

Some poor schmucks never get out of high school. They spend their adult lives replaying the highs and lows of what they think were their best, most exciting years. That's the case with the twenty-somethings in this snowy New England town who just have to travel down the street to attend their ten-year high school reunion. The only one who went on to a new life was Hutton, and all he became was a two-bit piano player, but at least he's a two-bit piano player from *Manhattan*. He returns home to find that an irresistibly charming 13-year-old girl has moved in next door, and he's smitten. Okay, it *sounds* weird, but it's really not. Plus, the Lolita in question is played by Portman, who has one of the most brilliant screen presences I've ever seen. She's been compared to a young Jodie Foster because of her obvious smarts, but to me she has more the luminescence of Audrey Hepburn. She glows. While Hutton ponders his somewhat illicit attraction, his buds, who shovel snow for a living, obsess about dating women like Elle Macpherson. The ludicrousness of this prompts a great riff by O'Donnell—as she tears through a drugstore tossing necessities into her basket—on the differences between real women and models. The performances by the young Hollywood pack make this better than the standard ten-year-reunion reexamine-your-life movie. Plus, Portman alone is reason enough to watch. **CT**

GC The good news: fresh talent Portman, Hutton resurfaces, O'Donnell's Spike Lee-type monologues. The bad news: everything else. Nobody was interesting enough for me to care.

AR Gee, I thought they were *all* interesting. The way it explores normal lives and normal relationships, it reminded me a bit of *Nobody's Fool,* which is a compliment.

BROKEN BLOSSOMS
1919. 95 min. Lillian Gish, Richard Barthelmess. Dir. D. W. Griffith. Silent.

Watching *Broken Blossoms*—particularly the color-tinted version—is more like watching a series of ethereally beautiful paintings and photographs than what we think of as a movie today, and much more exquisite because of it. That's not to say there's not a lot of emotion, drama, and violence in this story told with fairy tale simplicity. Gish plays ''The Girl,'' a 15-year-old who gets regular beatings from her violent father. (As a matter of fact, Gish suffered so many blows in Griffith's films, one movie critic said he was going to form the Society for the Prevention of Cruelty to Lillian Gish.) The film opens with an exotic setting in the Orient where the "Yellow Man" talks to Buddha and has a dream "to take the glorious message of peace to the barbarous Anglo-Saxons." He ends up in a London ghetto and soon loses his idealism to the opium den. But his gentle side is awakened by seeing the girl who's palpably sad as she goes about her day. After one thrashing she collapses in the Yellow Man's shop, and he takes care of her until her father finds out. Another reminder of how sophisticated films could be—even silent films— before Americans decided censors were a good thing and movies should uplift society. **CT**

GC   I did okay with "all night long he crouches, holding one grubby little hand," and even "breathing in an amber flute to this alabaster Cockney girl her love name—White Blossom." But I lost it at, "What makes you so good to me, Chinky?" Too sophisticated for me.

AR   The way for fidgety late-twentieth-centuryites to view this is while walking on a treadmill or riding the Exercycle you bought fifteen years ago and have been meaning to dust off. When I watched it this way, with the sound off, I got into it.

GLORIA
1980. 121 min. Gena Rowlands, John Adames. Dir. John Cassavetes

Gloria's a New York broad with mob connections, a quick draw, and no soft spots for children, thank you very much. "I hate kids," she tells a neighbor who asks her to take the kids for a while, "especially yours." But the neighbor's kind of desperate because she and her family are about to get blown away by mob goons and the only way she can save her children is to send them out the door with Gloria. So the reluctant Gloria ends up with Phil, a skinny six-year-old topped by a head of curls. It turns out that it was Gloria's friends who killed the kid's family and they still want the kid, which puts her in sort of a bind. So she and Phil spend a lot of time running through the streets of New York and hopping in taxis to evade the gangsters on their tail. If a mobster gets in her way, she just shoots him, until even the kid notes: ''You can't just go shooting everybody that goes knocking on your door.'' Eventually they realize they can't go on like this forever. It's not the type of movie that usually appeals to me, having an abundance of mobsters and gunplay and chases, but, okay, maybe the fact that it's a little different than most given that a chick is the major player here has something to do with it, and then there's that irresistible little kid. **CT**

GC   For me, it's Gloria who's irresistible. Rowlands becomes so completely Gloria that it's hard for me to take anyone else seriously.

AR   Rowlands is fantastic, but the movie is too long. Worth it if you use FF.

THE LAST EMPEROR
1987. 160 min. John Lone, Joan Chen. Dir. Bernardo Bertolucci

Unwitting Pu-Yi was but 3 years old when it was decided, in 1908, that he would sit on the Dragon Throne as emperor. Poor kid. How could he, or the mother who relinquished him with pride to the blessed mystery of the Forbidden City, know that he'd wind up decades later an impoverished gardener in Communist China? What transpires between his bizarre ascension and ultimate end is, as told in flashbacks by Bertolucci, surely among the most beautifully filmed epics ever framed by Hollywood (or ever scored—the soundtrack is *stunning*). The passive Pu-Yi is batted about through a half-century of arresting history by a succession of power-hungry men and powerfully pathetic women, including the marvelous Joan Chen as an exquisite bride-turned-opium-addict, and Maggie Han as a lesbian spy.

All that occurs is absorbing, but it is Pu-Yi's sorrowful childhood, one that denies him his mother, refuses him friends his age, and bars him from riding his bicycle beyond the Forbidden City gates, that resonates later. One scene lingers: The chubby little boy, bored with the attention from servants who tend to his every need, jumps up from his too-big throne and runs to the doorway, where a billowing silk curtain is being buffeted by the wind—and opens to reveal thousands of bowing eunuchs in the courtyard below. You know this kid hasn't a chance for a normal life, and later you *almost* thank the

Communist nutcases for forcing him into something resembling ordinariness. *The Last Emperor* won nine, count 'em, nine Academy Awards, including Best Picture and Best Director. **AR**

CT   Probably the most visually stunning movie I've ever seen, so much so that I almost didn't notice how the movie drags toward the end.

GC   This is one of the very few movies on my almost-perfect list. It's a glorious feast, almost too much for the senses to grasp at times.

LITTLE NIKITA

1988. 98 min. Sidney Poitier, River Phoenix. Dir. Richard Benjamin

If you rent this, you'll mourn all over again that Phoenix was dumb enough to die the way he did at the age he did. But *Little Nikita* is well worth it. It's part thriller, part family tragedy, big part coming-of-age drama. And, oh! How wonderful to watch Poitier in a good role!

Jeff (Phoenix) is a typical San Diego teenager, happy at home, beloved by his parents, kind, middle-class Americans who run a nursery. All is well until his application to the Air Force Academy places him in a surreal situation no one his age, any age, should have to face. With Poitier as an FBI agent who rents the house across the street, he has a chance to save himself and those he loves, but only after he confronts some grown-up truths about loyalty. And history. The secrets in the plot are buried so well and so deeply that to say anything more about the story line would be doing a disservice. Trust me that it is exhilarating, charming, and intelligent, and that the title will make sense before the end. **AR**

GC   I think *My Own Private Idaho* (1991) is an infinitely better monument to Phoenix's talent. He's stunning in that one. The only one who held my interest here was Poitier. But, then, he could always hold anything he wanted of mine.

CT   Despite Phoenix and Poitier, it had the slick, flimsy feel of a TV movie of the week, and I was bored by the tired Russian spy plot.

LITTLE MAN TATE

1991. 99 min. Jodie Foster, Dianne Wiest, Adam Hann-Byrd. Dir. Jodie Foster

Foster makes her directing debut with this flick as well as plays a cocktail-waitress mother trying her darndest to do right by her son, a genius in a little boy's body. Hann-Byrd is irresistible as Fred, the boy who's too smart for school but befuddled about how to make friends. Mom doesn't know what to do with Fred's smarts, but she's convinced if he just makes an effort he can fit in with the other kids. In one scene Fred bravely passes out handmade invitations to a Mom-mandated birthday party. The kids accept them, but then the bell rings and the invitations scatter across the school yard as his classmates run off to class. Can it get more heartbreaking than that? The future picks up for Fred when he gets to hang with other child prodigies at a school for near geniuses, but he doesn't necessarily see a fairy tale future. Fred's too smart to believe in happily ever after. With its somewhere-in-America set and fall-like colors, the film looks as if it takes place somewhere between a 1990s urban street and an Edward Hopper painting. It feels a little gritty, sad, and lonely, but infused with a glow nonetheless. It's also refreshing to watch an unusual protagonist—not a slacker, a gangster, a spinster, or a home breaker—but an extraordinary little boy. It can't be easy to carry a movie at that age (never mind, at any age). **CT**

GC   Nice movie. And what a sweet hero. But he doesn't have to carry the movie alone. He has a gifted, sensitive director and a wonderful costar in Foster.

AR   Hann-Byrd is extraordinary. Doesn't he remind you of Foster when she was a kid in Hollywood?

MY LIFE AS A DOG

1985. 101 min. Anton Glanzelius, Melinda Kinnaman. Dir. Lasse Hallström. Swedish w/subtitles

This is a sweet, honest movie about the pains and pleasures of childhood. It's 1959, and young Ingemar lives with his dying mother, his obnoxious older brother, and his beloved dog. Terrified and guilt-ridden that he is somehow responsible for his mother's illness and eventual death, he desperately fixates on anybody and anything worse off than he is. "You have to compare," he tells himself over and over. The space race is gearing up, and he obsesses about Laika, the Russian dog in space. She's definitely worse off than he is.

But things improve when he is sent to live with his uncle for the summer. He plays soccer, meets other kids, and finally enjoys a stable home. He still worries about his mother and his dog, but as the movie progresses he comes to terms with life, thanks to his loving uncle and the eccentric goings-on of the neighbors in the village. Glanzelius, with his homely features and awkward manner, makes a most endearing and totally believable kid. We really want him to be happy.

Hallström's sense of place and time is flawless. My memories of this movie are as real to me as many actual memories. I remember the crunch of the snow, the welcome heat of the furnace in the factory, and how much I liked those people, especially that little worrywart Ingemar. In my book, that's the mark of a terrific movie. **GC**

AR   Charming! But are all 12-year-old boys so obsessed with sex, or is it just those crazy Swedes?

CT   Surely one of the best movies about childhood ever made. I'd put this high on my list.

SALAAM BOMBAY!
1988. 113 min. Shafiq Syed, Hansa Vithal, Nana Patekar, Aneeta Kanwar. Dir. Mira Nair. Hindi w/subtitles

Nair takes her cameras into the bowels of one of the most crowded, polluted, and vibrant cities on earth for her first film, which she directed and produced, and which focuses on the struggles of street kid Chaipau (Syed), a modern-day Oliver Twist who has one of the most expressive, unforgettable faces I've ever seen on screen. This scrappy, resourceful boy is heartbreaking in his hustle for every rupee he can get, skinning chickens, cleaning out their cages, or delivering tea to the pimps, prostitutes, and drug addicts in his neighborhood. Surrounded by heartless adults and cruel children, he becomes enamored (he must be all of 11 years old) with a girl the local brothel brought in from the country to sell as a virgin. He in turn is idolized by young Manju (Vithal), the daughter of a prostitute, with the beauty of a young princess in a fairy tale. Chaipau's search for human connections in the squalor of Bombay and his attempt to earn enough money to return to his village are haunting. **CT**

GC I liked it fine, but it doesn't hold a candle to Indian director Satyajit Ray's brilliant *Apu* trilogy, about a young boy's life: *Pather Panchali, Apur Sansar* (aka *The World of Apu*), and *Aparajito*.

AR Oh, Shafiq! What a sweetie. He breaks my heart, as intended.

WELCOME HOME, ROXY CARMICHAEL
1990. 98 min. Winona Ryder, Jeff Daniels. Dir. Jim Abrahams

This has a reputation as a bad movie, and I don't care. It's not that I like it even though it's a bad movie, I just don't think it's a bad movie. Nobody does smart but dysfunctional teenagers like Ryder. And she's at her brow-knitting, incredulous best as Dinkie, a teenage nihilist with no social skills and very bad shoes. She keeps possible friends away with bad hygiene and shuts out her adoptive parents behind a multibolted and chained door. If the kids pay attention to her at all, it's only to throw stuff at her or knock her off her bike. And yet there's something noble about Dinkie, despite her name, something that puts her above the petty concerns of the residents of her small Ohio town. As the town awaits the return of Roxy Carmichael, the town's most famous former resident, Dinkie becomes convinced that Roxy is her mother and she's coming back to rescue her.

There aren't many movies that do justice to teenagers, girl teenagers in particular. In most teen movies, girls (who can play either the slut or the wallflower) are merely the appendages of the boys. So I like this movie, and I love Ryder. She's the master of the killer teenage stare that lasers through the hypocrisy of adults. **CT**

AR On top of all that, *Roxy* is funny, too. And members of the supporting cast—Daniels in his typically inept-male role, Frances Fisher as Dinkie's sexpot mom, all the gals at the beauty parlor—are just as good as Ryder.

GC *Au contraire,* y'all, this is a bad movie. Really bad. Maybe John Waters—director of such poor-taste classics as *Pink Flamingos* and *Polyester*—could have made something of it, but even he had enough taste not to touch it. Neither should have anyone else. It's trite and it's sexist. As if all Dinkie needed was a guy, a shower, and a pink dress to straighten her out. Please.

THE WINDOW
1949. 73 min. Bobby Driscoll, Barbara Hale. Dir. Ted Tetzlaff. b&w

'Fess up. At least once in your youthdom, you told a fib. So you'll empathize with nine-year-old Tommy (Driscoll), whose frequent little lies embarrass his folks, as when he brags to buddies that his family is moving to a big ranch Out West from a tenement on Manhattan's Lower East Side, which gets Mom and Dad into trouble with the landlord. It's not until he witnesses a murder from the fire escape, where he finds refuge on a hot summer night, that he learns his lesson—but is it too late?

Poor Tommy, lucky video viewer. Tetzlaff worked as a cinematographer for Hitchock before striking out on his own and offers up a sooty, steamy, swarming working-class New York that makes Tommy's proclivity quite understandable. Anyway, what's a kid to do when in time of crisis he can't trust his parents or the police or, certainly, the creepy Kellertons who live across the way? Notes of trivia: *The Window* is so fine, it was made twice again—as *The Boy Cried Murder* (the name of the original novella) in 1966, and as *Cloak & Dagger* in 1984—and was featured in *Crumb*, the weird documentary about the equally weird cartoonist. **AR**

GC Loved the kid, who was believable. Hated his parents, who were not. They looked and talked like Ward and June, but

left the boy alone at night, locked him in, and came across
as plot devices, not people.

CT   Nice, scary flick. Too bad Driscoll died a poor drug addict
at age 31.

WISH YOU WERE HERE
*1987. 92 min. Emily Lloyd, Tom Bell, Geoffrey Hutchings.
Dir. David Leland.*

What a treat to see this lovely, debut performance by the sixteen-
year-old Lloyd as Lynda, a willful, dirty-mouthed, and promiscuous
girl in an English seaside town in the early '50s. Grieving for her
dead mother and at odds with her stiff, undemonstrative father
(Hutchings), she scandalizes the town. She flaunts her reckless, naive
sexuality, runs through boyfriends—and jobs—at breakneck speed,
looking for love in all the wrong places. Predictably, she ends up
pregnant by her father's seedy friend, Eric, played to lecherous perfection by Bell—whose slimy guts I will hate forever. (If he looks
familiar, it's probably from his role as the cynical sergeant in Helen
Mirren's terrific BBC series, *Prime Suspect,* aired on PBS in the
United States, and available on video.)

Lloyd, a dead ringer for Drew Barrymore, is bracingly funny and
cheeky; her comic timing is great. She's also heartbreakingly vulnerable. The scenes between Lynda and her father, especially, convey a
silent, tongue-tied world of anger, loss, and love. This movie marks
a great directorial debut, too, for Leland, who also wrote the script.
(He cowrote the fine *Mona Lisa* a year earlier with that movie's
director, Neil Jordan.) And there's a slew of those wonderful British
players, headed by Hutchings, who excel in bringing their small-
minded, small-town characters to life.

This is a rare bird—a movie that brings us a fresh, bright talent,
and that treats what could have been a clichéd wild-girl-pays-for-
her-sins story with warmth, originality, and respect. **GC**

AR   I wished I were anywhere but. Particularly at the end, with
its wrongheaded message.

CT   I know I'm supposed to care for the foul-mouthed tramp. . .
but I just don't. Or about the movie.

And, Speaking of Childhoods, Name These Kid Stars

a) Born Natasha Gurdin, in 1938, she starred in a slew of
movies, including one beloved holiday perennial. She was
one of the few to make the transition to adult star *(West
Side Story, Bob & Carol & Ted & Alice)* before her
untimely death in 1981.

b) Born in 1963 of famous parents, she made one very big
hit at the age of ten, a few minor ones, married a big
sports star, and pretty much stayed home to raise her kids.

c) Born in 1928, she was a big star by the age of 4, America's Sweetheart . . . oh, this one's too easy. But something
you may not know: She was probably the first public
figure to reveal she had had a mastectomy, and encour-
aged other women with breast cancer to have the surgery.

d) She started her career in commercials at the age of two
in 1964, got her big break, and a Best Supporting Actress
nomination in 1976 in a Robert De Niro movie, and went
on to make her mark as an adult in both acting and
directing (and she's still in her 30s!).

e) This enormously successful child actor was born in 1937
and starred in such movies as *Music for Millions* (1944),
The Secret Garden (1949), and *Little Women* (1949). She
didn't make the transition to adult roles and went to work
as a still photographer.

(answers see p. 278)

four

IF WE DIDN'T HAVE FAMILIES, WE'D HAVE TO FIGHT WITH OUR FRIENDS

"I shall repair to the bosom of my family, a dismal place, I must admit." —W. C. Fields, *in* The Bank Dick

We're born into them, sometimes give birth to them ourselves, frequently wonder how we possibly could be akin to them, and usually can't resist returning to them. Novelists and playwrights—not to mention women and men throughout history—have provided enough out-of-kilter kith and kin fodder to keep Hollywood busy for generations. And watching movies about eccentric families not our own is probably better therapy than what's available at a headshrinker's. It's definitely a lot cheaper, plus you don't actually have to lie on the couch. So put your crazy uncle back in the basement and toss the family photo album into the grate: Kick back and escape into the combustion of relations between relations. We promise that viewing our recommendations will prove cathartic, or at least relieve you of the notion that your clan is the most abnormal ever conceived. **AR**

CRIMES AND MISDEMEANORS

1989. 107 min. Woody Allen, Martin Landau, Anjelica Huston. Dir. Woody Allen

This sold me on Landau, and erased from my memory chip the principal image of him as the former husband of Barbara Bain and the sharp operative in television's *Mission: Impossible.* Oosh, what an actor! He is Judah, an ophthalmologist whose mistress, Dolores (Huston), is threatening to ruin his life if he fails to divorce his wife. Judah's underworldish brother (Jerry Orbach, in one of those grand Jerry Orbach roles) suggests that he have Dolores killed, posing the solemn question that frames a delicious Allen morality tale: What is worse, public humiliation and the disintegration of family, or murder? And will the doors to heaven be closed either way? Says Judah at one point, "I remember my father telling me, 'The eyes of God are on us always.' The eyes of God—what a phrase to a young boy! What were God's eyes like? Unimaginably penetrating, intense eyes, I assumed. And I wonder if it was just a coincidence I made my specialty ophthalmology."

It's serious business, but lightened by a comical subplot involving Clifford (Allen), who is hired to make a glowing documentary about his irritating brother-in-law (Alan Alda), who personifies everything Clifford despises. Clifford and Judah don't meet until the movie's end, in a rather chilling scene, when they reveal to one another their struggles with right and wrong, with what is moral and what is not. The acting all around is fantastic, and the writing is intelligent. And the music ain't bad, either. **AR**

CT Chilling, you say? Try Arctic. It'll leave you shuddering for days.

GC I liked this movie a lot, very meaty and thought-provoking. Interesting, too, in that it's not a typical, intimate Allen movie. The navel-gazing here is on a bigger, more expensive scale than usual.

DOUBLE HAPPINESS
1994. 100 min. Sandra Oh, Frances You, Callum Rennie. Dir. Mina Shum

Movies about a first-generation Chinese woman's struggle with being an independent American woman while remaining a good Chinese daughter don't come along every day—or decade. To keep her family happy, Jade (Oh) must live at home, do the dishes, keep her father supplied with red bean buns, his favorite, and trot off on dates

with every Chinese man her parents fix her up with. They want her
to give up the notion of being an actress and settle down with a nice
Chinese man with a good income and respectable job. Jade doesn't
want to hurt her parents, but she has other ideas—some pretty sala-
cious ones, too, when she thinks about the blond masters' degree
candidate she met outside a club (Rennie). He happens to be a good
enough actor to convince us he could actually be a nerd even though
he's very handsome in a wash-and-wear sort of way. She keeps her
Anglo-lust secret from her parents as long as she can, until the
inevitable happens and they threaten to disown her. This is a refreshing new look at an old story: the nice Jewish girl or the nice
Catholic girl or the nice Latina girl . . . who wants to be her own
person without having the ancestral wrath of centuries caving in on
her head, accusing her of destroying her culture. *Double Happiness*
also has some biting scenes that remind us how few roles there are,
still, for Asians in "the biz." **CT**

AR   Too lethargic to make my big hit parade, but it did make
        me smile. And it's wonderful to see Asian life in the movies.

GC   This is a good chick movie, and Oh is a delight. Her Jade
        is a smart, sympathetic character, and the cultural arm wres-
        tling is entertaining and honest. Of course, she does say at
        one point, "I grew up wondering why we could never be
        the Brady Bunch." But, hey, nobody's perfect.

THE LION IN WINTER
*1968. 134 min. Katharine Hepburn, Peter O'Toole. Dir. An-
thony Harvey*

Hepburn, as the conniving Eleanor of Aquitaine, nabbed her third
Best Actress Oscar for *The Lion in Winter,* making her the first in
history to have that many on her mantel. O'Toole, a comparatively
young man playing a middle-aged Henry II, was nominated for Best
Actor and should have won. So beyond-adjective good are the two
of them together and apart in this erudite (do *not* read "boring")
movie that it seems a waste of ink to go on about the plot. But, of
course, I will.
Though Henry usually keeps Eleanor imprisoned in a faraway cita-

del to protect his empire from her wiliness—she did, after all, support their sons in their unsuccessful revolt against him ten years earlier— he deigns to invite her home for Christmas in 1183, along with three of their sons (including Anthony Hopkins as Richard the Lion- hearted). Also present for the festivities are Henry's mistress and her brother, King Philip of France, well disguised as that fleeting James Bond-pretender Timothy Dalton. What ensues on the banks of the Thames suggests that this clan might have been the genesis of the custom of linking "dysfunctional" with "family." Their enthralling squabbles take place in drafty castle quarters that put off such a chill, you feel like wrapping a blanket around you on the couch; the beauty of the cutting words spoken might send you running for that vocabu- lary-building primer accumulating dust behind the romance novels on the bookshelf. But push the pause button first. **AR**

CT   This movie's just one great line after another: "He was 18 when we met and I was queen of France. He came down from the north to Paris with a mind like Aristotle and a form like mortal sin. We shattered the commandments on the spot." And this one: "I know. You know I know. I know you know I know. We know Henry knows, and Henry knows we know it."

GC   One of the many reasons I love this movie is that it comforts me to see that wealth, power, and noble birth are no guaran- tees of family harmony. These royals are every bit as ugly to their relatives as regular folks are.

QUEEN OF HEARTS
1989. 112 min. Vittorio Duse, Anita Zagaria, Joseph Long, Eileen Way, Vittorio Amandola. Dir. John Amiel

Fans of *Cinema Paradiso* will love this less-well-known gem by first-time British director Amiel. (And as a bonus for the subtitle- averse, it's in English.) The opening sequence is stunning, with two young lovers racing to be together—despite the wishes of their fami- lies—through the tower-filled Tuscan hill town of San Gimignano. Love beats all, and the young pair move to England to find their fortune. In many ways this movie covers familiar territory: the tale of an immigrant Italian family told through the big brown eyes of one of the sons. The couple open a café, have a brood of children, and thrive. For a while, that is, until an old family nemesis appears in town and threatens to shatter their happiness. The characters are pretty much stock: the crabby mother-in-law, the jocular grandpa, the stoic mother, the father with big dreams. But it's so sincere and so beautifully filmed—and splashed with magical and comedic touches—that it outshines its own material. The mother-in-law, played by Eileen Way, has one of the most dominating presences I've ever seen in a film. And she gets to say this great line: "I'm his mother-in-law, he don't have no secrets from me." **CT**

GC This is a warm, intriguing movie, not at all sappy or manipulative, as the subject might suggest. The family is so tightly knit and caring that when Eddie, the ten-year-old, describes heaven, he says, "It must be like coming home."

AR Now *that's* Italian, or what I imagine it would have been like to grow up in a zesty, cappuccino and pasta, several-generational family from Tuscany. The movie's the next best thing.

SWEETIE
1989. 97 min. Genevieve Lemon, Karen Colston, Dorothy Barry, Michael Lake. Dir. Jane Campion. Australian

"This family's coming apart like a wet paper bag," opines Flo. She's right, and it's all too clear who's to blame. It's her daughter, Dawn, otherwise known as Sweetie. As a child, Sweetie was cute enough, mildly talented, and would tap-dance and sing for her doting family. But she's way past that now. She's grown into a dangerously volatile, out-of-control woman who terrorizes her patient but weary parents, Flo and Bob, and her sister, Jan (Colston).

This movie has a garish, gritty feel to it, and Sweetie, played in no-holds-barred style by Lemon, is a most unsettling character. After leaving the family blessedly alone for several years, she returns and disrupts their lives so severely that Flo (Barry) runs away from home, "Out West" to find a new life. Bob (Lake) and Jan aren't far behind.

They follow her and together they at least begin to acknowledge what they face as a family.

Sweetie isn't an easy movie to watch sometimes, but it's original and tough, and in many respects quite beautiful. Jan narrates parts of the story, introducing poetic, original thoughts and images that would be difficult to convey otherwise. The photography is superb. Many scenes remain painted on my memory. One is where Sweetie is up in a tree and refuses to come down. It's harrowing. Another takes place Out West, where the jackaroos (cowboys) on an isolated station are dancing alone, or with each other, while Flo sings along with the boom box under a vast, lonely sky. It's a beautiful image. And the music in *Sweetie* is gorgeous and haunting. It's by Martin Amiger and The Café of the Gate of Salvation Choir. **GC**

AR Oooo, it's kind of creepy. I'm not a big Campion fan, but I stuck with her here, and didn't mind so much in the end. The scenery, of Sydney and the outback of New South Wales, helped a lot.

CT Tedious. I *tried* to stick with it . . . then I gave up.

TRUST

1991. 105 min. Martin Donovan, Adrienne Shelly. Dir. Hal Hartley

If you're a fan of director/writer Hartley, you already know this movie. If you've never heard of him, you'll either love it or hate it. Here's a test. This pregnant high school dropout has just unwittingly killed her father, her mother is threatening to kill her, and her sister doesn't like her much, either. She meets a brilliant loner whose ethics just got him fired from his assembly-line job and who carries around a live hand grenade and is terrorized by his father. There's a subplot about a stolen baby, and more dysfunctional family members than you can shake a stick at. And this is a comedy.

If you like the sound of it so far, you're in for a treat. Like all of Hartley's movies, this one deals with rage and repression, misfits and the walking wounded, and the agonies of communicating with other human beings. The humor is black, the dialogue is droll, and everybody is exceedingly polite—unless they're being violent. (Example: "You'll probably get pimples from all that makeup you're wearing." "Makeup hides my pimples." "Sorry.")

Hartley does well by his female characters. They're always interesting and usually smarter than the guys. No wonder chicks are his biggest fans. Donovan, who stars in most of Hartley's movies, is hilariously deadpan, an iceberg covering a volcano. Shelly gives a wonderful performance as a young woman suddenly slapped in the face by life who has the guts and the brains to slap it right back. **GC**

AR   Actually, you don't have to either love it or hate it: You can be entertained by the well-orchestrated quirkiness and grin at the black humor one-liners and then be thankful Hartley had the sense to yell "cut" after ninety minutes.

CT   Hear, hear, Anne. Consider me completely neutral on this one. I'll say this for it though. It's unmemorable.

WHAT'S EATING GILBERT GRAPE?

1993. 117 min. Johnny Depp, Leonardo DiCaprio, Juliette Lewis. Dir. Lasse Hallström

Despite the fact that Depp is sort of void as an actor—I keep waiting for him to have an expression—this is still a sweet little movie. Gilbert works in a sad-sack grocery store that's slowly dying while customers head to the glitzy new Food Town supermarket. He has two sisters, a mentally disturbed brother, and an extraordinarily large mother who hasn't left the house in seven years. She's so heavy, she can hardly move, period. The only excitement in Gilbert's life comes courtesy of a lonely housewife, played by Mary Steenburgen, who wants him to deliver more than the groceries. So you get the idea: small town, young man, no hope for anything other than a little nooky in the afternoon. That's until a snowbird heading south in a silver Airstream gets stranded by a bum carburetor, and her spunky granddaughter, Lewis, sets her sights on the soft-spoken Gilbert. Yes, this is a love story. It's also a movie about the slow death of small towns and how they cope with their homegrown oddballs, eccentrics, and outcasts. Lewis always adds a sort of alcoholic punch to the films she's in, and DiCaprio is so convincing as the crazy brother that it's hard to imagine him going from that role to becoming a matinee idol. **CT**

AR Good, low-key movie. But, hey, Cynthia: With those sleepy-eye looks, Depp doesn't *need* to have an expression!

GC Whoa, you two! Johnny Depp a void? No expression? Not only is he the best thing about this dark little movie, he's also just about the most intriguing, original presence in Hollywood, period. *And* a pretty face. And he has the guts to go for the offbeat challenges, as in this movie, and in *Edward Scissorhands* (page 66), *Dead Man, Ed Wood, Donnie Brasco* . . . so give him a break, okay?

A WOMAN UNDER THE INFLUENCE

1974. 155 min. Gena Rowlands, Peter Falk. Dir. John Cassavetes

First, a confession: I'm crazy about Gena Rowlands. She's a class act. And I like the intimate, home-movie directing style of her husband, John Cassavetes. I know, he's self-indulgent and lollygags around, but he's brave and true to himself, much like Rowlands is as an actor. I bet they made a dynamite couple (he died in 1989). I see this movie as his *hommage* to his wife—a showcase for her tremendous talent and for that of her costar, Falk, one of Cassavetes's best friends.

Rowlands plays Mabel, mother of three kids, wife of Nick, a blue-collar guy who works for the city. Mabel is coming apart at the seams, losing it. She desperately wants to please everybody, to be a good wife, a good mother, cook spaghetti at a moment's notice for Nick and all his hard-hat buddies. "Tell me what you want me to be," she implores Nick. "I can be that." But Nick—terrified, angry, and embarrassed by this slovenly, strange-acting woman—can only say, "Be yourself."

Okay, the movie is long, but so is life in these circumstances: a woman who is slipping into madness, and a husband who can't help her. She has no identity of her own. She tries to be all things to all the people in her life and she can't cope. And all Nick can say is, "Be yourself." That's what's driving her crazy.

Both Rowlands and Falk are superb. (This role earned Rowlands a Best Actress Oscar nomination.) And while the movie is harrowing to watch, it's also uplifting to see these actors make Mabel and Nick and all their problems so real that you hurt for them. **GC**

AR   I'm a Rowlands fan, too, but I also adore Falk. And here we get to see him *without* the rumpled raincoat—he's so talented, he was almost ruined by *Columbo* on TV. But, jeez, why are all Cassavetes's flicks so darn long?

CT   I'd watch it just for Rowlands's performance as the loony-bin-ready Mabel, but don't you get the feeling that today a bottle of Prozac might just have fixed all of her problems?

Name These Real-life Movie Dynasties:

1) Grandfather: Beloved screen actor for half a century, nicknamed One-Take.
   Children: One son, who made his mark as Captain America. One daughter, who won accolades in movies, brickbats in politics.
   Grandchild: If you're a single white female, this could happen to you.

2) Grandfather: Lovable TV character
   Son: Little-known but busy character actor (*Waiting for Guffman,* 1995).
   Grandchildren: Five siblings—three male, two female—all in movies. The sisters' movies include *Desperately Seeking Susan* and *Flirting with Disaster.*

3) Grandfather: Distinguished, titled, mostly stage acting.
   Children: Two sisters, one a star and politically left-leaning, the other a demistar, mostly humorous roles. One brother, a lesser light.
   Granddaughters: Three up-and-coming actresses.

(answers see p. 278)

five

HEAVING BOSOMS AND THE MEN IN LACE WHO LOVE THEM

"I keep remembering things—all the old things.
Everybody was sweet and pretty then, the whole
world. A wonderful world. Not like the world today."
—Joseph Cotten, *in* Shadow of a Doubt

What is it about a guy with an English accent that makes American women swoon? Put him in lacy cuffs and ruffled shirts, and he's just about irresistible—even if he does have the world's biggest nose (*Cyrano de Bergerac,* page 42). Or the heart of a sadist (*Dangerous Liaisons,* page 43). These aristocratic gents in doublets are always surrounded by women wearing the eighteenth-century precursor to the Wonderbra, and great nightgowns. These flicks offer a retreat from the twentieth century and a feast of cinematic excess: beautiful clothes, beautiful scenery, and beautiful people, all catered to by platoons of uniformed footmen in wigs. So turn off the fax, hide the pager, turn on the answering machine, and pop one of these babies into the VCR. **CT**

THE AGE OF INNOCENCE

1993. 133 min. Daniel Day-Lewis, Michelle Pfeiffer. Dir. Martin Scorsese

From the director who brought you *Taxi Driver, Mean Streets, Raging Bull,* and *GoodFellas* comes a richly filmed rendering of Edith Wharton's novel about the circumscribed social world of wealthy New Yorkers in the 1870s. There are bustles, chandeliers, multicourse dinners (gee whiz, how did those women fit into their corsets?), high collars, and concealed bosoms that heave, though they certainly aren't supposed to. And, of course, much of the heaving is incited by Day-Lewis as upper crusty Newland Archer, engaged to the vapid (at first) May Welland, nicely portrayed by Winona Ryder.

What's the fuss? Well, consider that Scorsese called this his "most violent" movie. It's not at all bloody, but it is emotionally vicious. Newland falls for his fiancée's cousin, the Countess Olenska (Pfeiffer), unconventional for the era and a social outcast, to boot, seeing as she's separated from her husband. There can be no hope for this romance, can there? Watch and see—and watch to see one of the most passionate scenes ever filmed, and all straying no further than handholding. Beautiful. **AR**

CT   Plus it wins the prize for the movie that could have gone in most of our other chapters, including hunks, cads, families, interiors, food, weepies, chicks who did it their way, clothes, old-fashioned romance, and of course, lust.

GC   Okay, it's beautiful, but Day-Lewis is *so* gloomy, and Ryder is *so* dull, and Scorsese is *so* reverential that I was glad to see it all end so I could get back to The Age of I Want It All And I Want It Now.

ANGELS & INSECTS
1995. 117 min. Mark Rylance, Patsy Kensit, Kristin Scott Thomas. Dir. Philip Haas

When I first saw this movie I was so taken by the look of it, its gorgeous, original costumes and settings and its elegant language, that I'd been out of the theater a couple of hours before it dawned on me how downright funny and outrageous it was.

The setting is England in the 1860s, and William, a young naturalist, played by Rylance, has returned after ten years in the Amazon. He has survived a shipwreck in which he lost most of his rare specimens, and is dependent on the wealthy Alabaster family for his living. He soon marries the daughter, Eugenia, played by Kensit, and is drawn into a sticky web of family rituals and relationships.

Darwin is all the rage at this period, and the family studies the animal kingdom avidly. The humans mirror the insects: The women's gowns are encrusted with flowers and fruits, and their hair is braided to suggest antennae; Mrs. Alabaster gorges like a queen bee; and we gradually discover other interesting family traits. Thomas, still relatively unknown—this was just before *The English Patient* (page 86) bowled us all over—is a delight as Manny, the smart, poor relative. There are some surprisingly graphic sex scenes, and the payoff, though it takes a while to get there, is a doozy and well worth waiting for. **GC**

CT   I liked this movie okay when it came out, but Gabrielle's right. I do find myself thinking about the wonderful weirdness of it, all those entomologically inspired costumes, not to mention the perverse sexual couplings.

AR   A very fine, very strange film. Thomas is tremendous, even better than she is in the desert (page 86), and I applaud the ending.

BARRY LYNDON
1975. 184 min. Ryan O'Neal, Marisa Berenson. Dir. Stanley Kubrick

You might have caught yourself wondering what Ryan O'Neal did after *Paper Moon* and *What's Up Doc?* and before the big break-up with Farrah. If that's so, you might want to consider getting a life. But before you do, sit down for three hours (don't *panic*) of Kubrick interpreting William Makepeace Thackeray. After I saw this in college I dashed out to buy the sound track, full of Irish folk music and Schubert, beautiful background to the unlucky life of the social-climbing Lyndon, quite nicely portrayed by O'Neal. Kubrick went to nutty extremes in abundantly re-creating the eighteenth century— the costumes are to die for, and he used all-natural light, including in one scene just candles, throughout. His efforts are much appreciated by those few of us who've observed the entirety of his product.

I'm a big critic of the overlong movie, but I was hooked by the storytelling of this one. I like it more than ever now, since FF is at my fingertips. But use that function wisely—poor Barry goes through much that is interesting and prettily rendered in three hours, including

Berenson, two wars, sword fights, large meals, muddy carriage rides, several countries, would-be fortunes, countless ruffled shirts . . . you get the idea. It's fun. **AR**

GC One of my faves—a mammoth romp, full of stunning detail. And O'Neal, who usually ranks below Jean-Claude Van Damme in my ratings list, does a fine job. Go figure.

CT Bored outta my mind. Plus, I don't know how anyone who turns her nose up at Hugh Grant thinks she can get away with lauding mushy O'Neal.

CYRANO DE BERGERAC

1990. 135 min. Gerard Depardieu, Anne Brochet. Dir. Jean-Paul Rappeneau. French w/subtitles

Need a beautiful, swooning, swashbuckling romance? Check out Cyrano, a man who's both soldier and poet. Brochet is a rapturous Roxane, who runs around in lovely white nightgowns and falls for the handsome but facile soldier Christian de Neuvillette, played by Vincent Perez. Depardieu is Cyrano, of the legendary schnoz, who gives voice to the beautiful but witless Christian. Roxane falls for the dashing soldier, believing the poetry he sends her to be his. The production is gorgeous, with lush scenery and costumes from the age when women were damsels and men were musketeers. But for all its romance and beauty, it still has a certain realistic bite to it, like the starving soldiers willing to risk their lives for a bit of pork. *Cyrano* is perfect to rent when it's raining out and you're feeling out of sorts with the 20th century, when the whole notion of poetry is a little absurd. Go back in time to an era when people still believed in the concept of great men (and who knows, maybe even great women, provided they were saints). The last scene is a little, well, operatic. Don't get up and make popcorn in the last half of this movie. Without the continuity, the end tests our endurance for such unabashed romanticism. But watch straight through and it's a several-hankie movie. **CT**

GC I agree, it's a lush, romantic extravaganza. And there's another plus: The subtitles, written by author Anthony Burgess *(A Clockwork Orange),* are unusually beautiful and poetic.

But, like Cyrano's nose, the movie's ending would have been a lot more appealing had it been shorter.

AR Too darn long. The movie, not the nose—I *like* the nose.

DANGEROUS LIAISONS
1988. 120 min. Glenn Close, John Malkovich, Michelle Pfeiffer, Keanu Reeves, Uma Thurman, Swoozie Kurtz. Dir. Stephen Frears

Despite being loaded with stars, you easily forget you're watching Uma and Keanu, and Michelle and Malkovich as you get sucked into the villainous intrigues of Vicomte de Valmont and the Marquise de Merteuil. Filmed in France and directed by Frears, of *My Beautiful Laundrette* fame, it opens with one of the best getting-ready scenes in movie history. Getting Close, the marquise, into her gown is as laborious as preparing a dinner party for eight people who don't like each other. The seductive details of the aristocrats' *toilette* are filmed so lushly that you can almost choke on the powders they pat themselves with in their obsessive preening and perfuming. Gilt and chandeliers and landscaped gardens surround these eighteenth-century narcissists whose hearts are as cruel as their environs are beautiful. Malkovich, in embroidered velvets and lace, has the bloodless, feral look of a vampire as he sets out to shatter the innocence of two pure young women—just for sport—played by Thurman and Pfeiffer. ("Monsieur Valmont never opens his mouth without calculating what damage he can do.") His cohort Close is as scary as she was in *Fatal Attraction*. The moral? Men are scum . . . and women are, too. **CT**

GC Scarier, for me, because in this movie she's not crazy. She's evil. So is Malkovich. And the authentic fabrics and furnishings are magnificent.

AR A must-see that raises many questions, including, how did women make their breasts do that back then? Didn't it hurt?

RESTORATION

1995. 122 min. Robert Downey, Jr., Meg Ryan, Sam Neill.
Dir. Michael Hoffman

This is a riotous film, chockablock with wretched excess. Which
is absolutely fine, because the period it's set in is the very epitome
of wretched excess. It's England in the 1660s, the Restoration period
(as in restoration of the let-it-all-hang-out monarchy after the austere,
no-fun-at-all Cromwell years). It's big hats and feathers and curly
wigs and velvet and satin and lace—and that's just the guys. Downey
plays the lead, Merivel, a talented, serious physician who is seduced
by the perks of sucking up to the royals and throws away his career
to wear ostrich feathers and take care of King Charles's spaniels and
his mistress.

Of course, restoration doesn't just apply to the monarchy, it also
refers to Merivel's rehabilitation as he hits the highlights of the
seventeenth century—and what a busy century it was! He wises up
after a year or so of debauchery (and I must say, it's some of the
wittiest, prettiest debauchery I've seen in a while), leaves the court,
runs into a scary, saintly David Thewlis and a bunch of Quakers,
teams up with the scruffy but ever plucky Meg Ryan, and wanders
through the great plague and the great fire of London.

I adore the sets in this movie. You've heard of actors chewing the
scenery; well, in this case the scenery just up and chews the actors.
Think Merchant-Ivory on hallucinogens. The scenes at court are deliri-
ously ornate, with everything gilded and bejeweled out the wazoo.
And Merivel's wedding to the king's mistress is a hoot—opulence
gone mad. Even the apocalyptic tableaux of plague victims—mud
and grime and panic in the streets—are teeming with vitality and
detail. There's just no way to take it all in at one viewing. This is
a video you need to buy. **GC**

CT   *Buy* it? Get real. If you can't catch everything in this movie
         the first time around, so what? That's not to say it's not
         worth a rental.

AR   Great fun! And Neill is adorable in waist-length curls.

Dated Definitions

Unscramble these old-fashioned words and their meanings:

Peruke	Evil
Jade	Maid
Pox	Carriage
Popinjay	Ruffle
Furbelow	Corset
Wench	Whore
Quaff	Dandy
Stays	Wig
Four-in-hand	Drink

(answers see p. 278)

six

CHICKS IN CHARGE

*"She shouldn't try to be top man. She's not built for it.
She's flying in the face of nature."*
—Ray Milland, *in* Lady in the Dark

Old Ray said that back in 1944, when Hollywood wasn't supposed to know any better. Okay, it *still* doesn't know any better most of the time, but then society in general remains so astoundingly unenlightened about chicks that we're not shocked. Consider the media's emphasis on the divorce, motherhood, and attire of Madeleine Albright when she was named the first female secretary of state. It's not that the personal stuff isn't fascinating, it's just that it's not usually included in reports about male secretaries of state (though it must be noted that Henry Kissinger did get ink for dating aging starlets). But fortunately for this important chapter, there are moving-picture exceptions to the rule of Men Rule. In real life, women manage to be tough, savvy, smart, muscular, and powerful without worrying about the impact that strength and influence might have on their femininity. And sometimes that happens on screen, too. **AR**

ALIEN
1979. 117 min. Sigourney Weaver, Tom Skerritt. Dir. Ridley Scott

When I saw *Alien* for the first time, in 1979, I thought I'd died and gone to heaven. Here, finally, was an ordinary chick, just trying to do her job and get home and take a shower and forget about work for a while, who didn't set out to be a hero but rose to the task when she had to. Guys in movies had been doing it forever. It was about time.

Sure, the action takes place on a spaceship and involves a grotesque, slimy alien creature, but in its own way, *Alien* is a down-to-earth, realistic movie. The ship is a patched-up, deep-space mining ship, the crew are blue-collar workers who grumble about their working conditions and the food, and the only reason they even stop to investigate the strange signal that starts all the trouble in the first place is that their pay will be docked if they ignore it.

There's not much of a plot. In *Ten Little Indians* fashion, the crew are serially bumped off by an alien creature until it's just Weaver and the alien, *mano-a-mano*. Oh, yes, and the cat. But the movie never loses its edge, thanks to a stellar crew that includes Harry Dean Stanton and British heavyweights John Hurt and Ian Holm, with the usually low-key Holm in hilariously ghoulish, over-the-top form. *Alien* was a launching pad for the visual wizardry of director Scott, who had mostly worked on commercials up till then. He went on to direct the stunning *Blade Runner* (1982) and the Chicks' *raison d'être*, *Thelma & Louise* (page 62).

And just look at what it did for Weaver. It became a cult favorite and spawned three more *Aliens* as of 1997, the last of which earned Weaver a cool $11 mill. And just two years before the first *Alien*, in 1977, she was paid fifty dollars for her six-second screen debut as one of Alvy's dates in *Annie Hall*. Now that's what I call a Chick in Charge. **GC**

AR   I get a bigger kick out of the sequel (page 121). And this one comes with a warning: Do not rent if pregnant.

CT   I'm sorry, those slimy-fanged aliens gross me out. Can't watch it. Call me a weenie, I don't care.

BORN YESTERDAY
1950. 103 min. Judy Holliday, William Holden. Dir. George Cukor

You're thinking, "I need to watch another dumb blonde movie like I need another gray hair." But this is not just another dumb blonde movie—it is *the* dumb blonde movie. And, anyway, Holliday as Billie Dawn, in a role she first teetered into on Broadway, ain't so dumb. In fact, she's the smartest cookie in the cast. "As long as I know how to get what I want, that's all I want to know," she tells Holden's character. He's a handsome hunk of a freelance reporter hired by her boyfriend, shady junk dealer Broderick Crawford, "to learn her how to talk good" for her sojourn in Washington, where the blowhard is busy buying himself some favorable legislation from fairly inexpensive politicians. The result is a delight.

The back-and-forth between the trio played by Holliday, Holden, and Crawford is brisk and funny and sharp. The scenes of the nation's capital in the '50s are splendid. Even the corny stuff—as when Billie's democratic eyes are opened during educational visits to various monuments—isn't too musty for jaded viewers of today. Fact is, you might get to thinking that Washington hasn't changed all that much in the last fifty years. The real treat, though, is Holliday's Billie Dawn, who refuses to let men or corruption run over her or her spike heels. Though they don't realize it until it's too late, her loudmouth boyfriend and his tractable lawyer don't stand a chance against her guileless honesty and guts. Holliday won the Oscar for Best Actress for her performance, beating out Bette Davis in *All About Eve* (page 243) and Gloria Swanson in *Sunset Boulevard.* **AR**

GC   It gets a little preachy, but Holliday is so magnificent, you'll overlook the heavy-handed civics lessons. All blondes—and brunettes, and redheads—should be so dumb.

CT   It's a hoot. And when Crawford calls Holliday from another room in their oversize hotel suite and she shouts, "Whaaaa?" it sounds like glass and gravel going through a grinder and cracks me up every time.

THE INN OF THE SIXTH HAPPINESS
1958. 158 min. Ingrid Bergman, Curt Jurgens. Dir. Mark Robson

The more Ingrid Bergman movies I see, the more I want to watch. In this one she's a dowdy missionary (or at least as dowdy as someone with that bone structure can be) in China in the 1930s. After a rocky start—the Chinese didn't take too well to "foreign devils" and didn't much like being preached to about Jesus Christ—she earns a place of respect in a remote mountain village. When war breaks out with the Japanese, the inn she runs becomes an orphanage, and Bergman must lead her children on a two-week trek to safety. As they hike across beautiful mountains, it looks like an Asian *Sound of Music* (page 159) without the music, except for the "Paddywhack" song the children sing to take their mind off the hard journey with little food and rest. There's a love story here, too, with Bergman falling for a half-English, half-Chinese soldier (Jurgens)— they called them half-breeds in those days. But the real interest is in the heroic star turn of Bergman. And I must say she cuts a far more heroic figure than the perky yoddle-le hee Julie Andrews (not that I don't love *The Sound of Music*). *Inn* falls into the man-against-all-odds genre, except that it's woman against all odds, which means there are no shoot-outs and no chases. It's also an interesting snapshot of pre-Communist China. **CT**

GC   And it's based on a true story, the life of intrepid English missionary Gladys Aylward. So it gives me a warm glow to know people like that really exist. And Curt Jurgens gives me an even warmer glow.

AR   It's the best of the missionary-in-China movies. Rent it along with 1937's *The Good Earth*, and, perhaps, *The Last Emperor* (page 22) for an evening's worth of the old China.

JOHNNY GUITAR
1954. 110 min. Joan Crawford, Mercedes McCambridge, Sterling Hayden. Dir. Nicholas Ray

Crawford plays Vienna, a frontier saloon keeper who isn't ashamed of the way she earned her money (back in the days when she was *supposed* to be ashamed) in this unintentionally campy and often forgotten Western classic. With her tight pants, prodigious eyebrows, and determination to cash in big time when the railroad comes through, Vienna makes all the gun-totin' men around her look like silly little boys. 'Course that's not so hard when they all have names

like Turkey, Dancing Kid, and Johnny Guitar. Vienna's only real
threat is Emma (McCambridge), the other major chick—and full-
time party pooper—in town. Seems Emma and the townspeople don't
like the outlaws who hang out at Vienna's saloon. The flick builds
up to a final, pistol-packin' confrontation between Emma and Vienna
on a mountain. The first time I watched this I found it silly, but it
grew on me. Images from the movie keep popping in my head. If
someone said name your favorite Western, I'd pick this one because
one, why not pick one with a chick in charge, and two, I hate
Westerns. **CT**

GC   The camp is slathered on pretty thick to be unintentional. I
         think the director had a seriously kinky sense of humor.
         Whatever, it's pretty hilarious. But I'm sorry to hear you
         hate Westerns, Cynthia. There are some gems in all that hay.
         And for a great chick role in a western, check out *Destry
         Rides Again,* where Marlene Dietrich, in fishnet tights, stands
         on the bar and belts out "See What the Boys in the Back
         Room Will Have."

AR   One of those so-bad-it's-good flicks, and therefore highly
         recommended. As is the theme song, written by Victor
         Young and Peggy Lee and warbled by Lee herself.

A LITTLE PRINCESS
*1995. 98 min. Liesel Matthews, Eleanor Bron, Vanessa Lee
Chester. Dir. Alfonso Cuaron*

Warner Brothers was so sure of *A Little Princess* that it dispatched
it to theaters twice, first in May 1995, and again three months later.
The adaptation of a children's novel penned in 1888 didn't draw the
audiences the studio had hoped for in the spring. And thank you
Warner for the rerelease. It was more enthusiastically received the
second time round and now is destined to become a classic, a magical
fantasy with a little chick as heroine.
    Plucky Sara Crewe, deposited in a dreaded boarding school by her
handsome and fabulously wealthy father when he goes off to fight
in World War I, has what it takes to endure against the odds, even
the very big odd of a forbidding headmistress named Miss Minchin,

played with marvelously snobby sternness by Bron. Matthews's Sara
has *imagination,* and so does this movie. Sara is prized by her classmates for her inventiveness and by Miss Minchin for her father's
money, until cruel fate intervenes and Sara finds herself locked in
the attic with Chester as the servant Becky, the only black girl in
the school. But even then, Sara doesn't let reality get her down: Cold
and hungry, she and Becky fall asleep fantasizing about food and
awake to discover a banquet awaiting them in the sun-washed attic.

A *Little Princess* brims with a sense of wonder, and of what can
and should be right in the life of an intrepid schoolgirl. The bonus
is that it's gorgeously filmed. **AR**

GC   Amen to all of the above. And a big hand for the drop-dead
gorgeous Indian fantasy scenes.

CT   A classic that all parents should buy for their little girls.

PAPER MOON
*1973. 102 min. Tatum O'Neal, Ryan O'Neal, Madeline Kahn.
Dir. Peter Bogdanovich*

On the one hand you could say this is just another two-cons-on-
the-road story, except for the fact that one of them is a nine-year-
old girl with the face of an androgynous angel and the mind of a
professional lock picker. Small-time con man Moses Pray (O'Neal
père) shows up at the funeral of his onetime lover and gets rooked
into driving her orphaned daughter Addie (Tatum) to her aunt's house
in St. Joe, Missouri. After Addie catches Moses running a scam, she
insinuates herself into the next one, and the two become a con pair
extraordinaire, bilking widows and hapless clerks out of tens and
twenties. When they try to launch even bigger scores, though, they
get in over their heads. Shot in black and white amid a Dust Bowl
Midwest with the tinny '20s music on the sound track, this movie's
a delight. Tatum won an Oscar for this role, although for some
infuriating reason she took home the statue for Best *Supporting* Actress, even though she carried the whole movie. Addie's a great role
model for young girls—okay, so she's a crook and smokes cigarettes,
at least she's smart and motivated, and not waiting for some daddy
figure to take care of her! **CT**

GC I found the movie manipulative, but Tatum is great and the music is a trip. And I agree, that was a dumb Oscar, although I don't think she was up to a Best Actress award. Why don't they go back to the special children's Oscar they used to award when a kid performance warranted it?

AR Hey, what about O'Neal senior? Something happened in the '80s, but in the old days he showed an awful lot of talent (and an awful lot of handsomeness), and Bogdanovich knew how to bring it out.

TERMINATOR 2: JUDGMENT DAY

1991. 135 min. Linda Hamilton, Arnold Schwarzenegger. Dir. James Cameron

A lot of inattentive, uninteresting, and wrongheaded people like the 1984 original better. They are, in case I didn't mention it, blockheads. The sequel dances hoops around the first, and that is due almost entirely to Hamilton's take-no-prisoners character. Consigned to a mental institution after the evil time-traveling Schwarzenegger in the inaugural *Terminator* drove her into a state that narrow-minded psychiatrists diagnosed as nuts, she spends her days pumping iron. By the time she outwits her dim captors, her biceps are the size of my thighs, and a heck of a lot firmer. It is exhilarating (not to mention refreshing, since she's a chick and all) to see her tote large firearms, flex muscle, drink right out of the bottle, and sweat and swear with no whining. Of course, she *is* a mother protecting her child, but you get over that early on. Schwarzenegger here is a more friendly version of the T-800 android from the earlier film, and Robert Patrick is the creepy, updated T-1000 model—able to assume the appearance of anything it comes into even fleeting contact with. The special effects, extraordinary for their high-techness back in '91, are still wondrous today. For good reason, *Terminator 2* garnered an Oscar for best sound effects editing and nominations in the cinematography, sound, and visual effects categories. To top that, this movie is witty. (And you thought Arnold didn't have a sense of humor, no doubt because you've been trying to judge him solely on the basis of *Kindergarten Cop*. Stop that. If you don't believe me, rent *True Lies*.) **AR**

GC   Funny, a sweaty, muscle-bound chick has about as much appeal for me as a sweaty, muscle-bound guy. But, hey, Anne, you're right in saying that anybody who liked the 1984 original better is wrongheaded and a blockhead. They're both awful. As is the utterly sexist and manipulative *True Lies*. Get over him. He's no good for you.

CT   You'd have to be a T-800 with no human parts to enjoy this movie, which is kind of scary given the numbers of people who went to see it, not to mention Anne.

seven

ÜBER-CHICKS

"You've got some foolish idea about me. I'm no
trembling little rabbit full of smoldering, unsatisfied
desires. I'm a woman, full grown, very smart . . . and
I expect to live at the top of my head without help
from you."
—*Joanne Woodward, in* The Long Hot Summer

They're the women we most want to be like: the ones who set the standards we all try to follow, from Marcia Brady to Hildy Johnson. Mary Poppins is an über-chick—she makes things happen with magic and a song. *Fargo*'s Marge is an über-chick, the first pregnant crime solver in a major motion picture! Madonna's the ruler of a multimillion-dollar enterprise, not to mention setter of hairstyle trends and symbol of sexual liberation. Mrs. Miniver, über-chick, inspired millions of World War II–era women to cope with death and destruction with dignity. Marcia Brady, '70s shiny-haired teen über-chick extraordinaire, proved you could be perfect, pretty, and nice! And let's not forget the pair who inspired *Chicks on Film,* launched a national debate, and paved a new path for chicks in the movies: Thelma and Louise. **CT**

BARBARELLA
1968. 98 min. Jane Fonda, John Phillip Law, Marcel Marceau, Milo O'Shea. Dir. Roger Vadim

I love this movie. It's campy, corny, soft-porn pap. Its culinary equivalent would be extra-gooey macaroni and cheese made with that penis-shaped pasta that I would never be caught dead buying. Based on a bawdy French comic strip, it chronicles the adventures of a futuristic Wonder Woman, Barbarella, played by Fonda. As the opening credits roll, Barbarella establishes the tone of the movie with a slow striptease, floating weightless as she peels. She meets a blind, beautiful angel (Law), who has lost the will to fly, and sets off with him on a series of exploits, most of which turn out to be sexual in nature.

It's all charmingly low-tech and slightly perverse. There's now an orgasm pill, so sex is obsolete. But that doesn't phase our heroine. She drops her skintight, synthetic-fiber pants at every opportunity and even blows the fuse on a death-by-orgasm machine. The dialogue is refreshingly hokey: "Why would anyone want to invent a weapon? It would shatter the peace of the universe." "What have you done with the positron ray?"

Vadim obviously gets off on the Pygmalion act, manipulating his then-wife, Fonda. But I won't rag on him, or her. I'm still too full of ersatz '60s peace and love. And just in case you're wondering if this movie made any discernible contribution to culture as we know it, the answer is yes. O'Shea's character is named Duran Duran. Yes, *that* Duran Duran. **GC**

AR   I hadn't seen this and thought GC was nuts to review it, but I get her point. Fonda is at her psychedelic best. When first issued, it had an R rating, but has since worked its way down to PG.

CT   Gabrielle claims she's not a fan of Fonda, then she recommends this piece of penis-shaped macaroni and cheese. Go figure.

THE BRADY BUNCH MOVIE
1995. 90 min. Shelley Long, Gary Cole. Dir. Betty Thomas

Surely one of the icons of twentieth-century American girlhood is Marcia Brady, with her perfect teeth, flawless complexion, and most of all, that long straight shiny hair. Most of us can relate more to Jan, the average-looking middle child stuck in Marcia's shadow. This hysterical send-up of the early '70s sitcom makes the Bradys look as weird as the Addams Family. The Brady house and backyard remain unchanged from their '60s suburban cookie cutout, but '90s America lurks just outside their yard: a landscape of tattoo parlors, car-jackings, and grunge. The Bradys are about to lose their home thanks to a corrupt neighbor, who yells at little blond-curled Cindy, "Why don't you go back to the Swiss Miss package where you belong?" And the Brady kids go to work to save their family from ruin. Those of us who grew up watching the show won't be disappointed by the new cast, and many of the old cast members make cameo appearances, including Alice (Ann B. Davis) as a rather butch truck driver. A great scene features RuPaul as a guidance counselor: "What can I help you with?" she asks Jan. "Teen pregnancy, bulimia, suicidal tendencies?" And Jan whines, "It's my stupid *glasses*." **CT**

GC   Don't even think about it. Life's too short to watch inane movies based on inane '70s sitcoms. And Cynthia, nobody *ever* grew up watching *The Brady Bunch*. They're guaranteed to retard growth.

AR   Well, I would have grown up watching the TV show if I hadn't been so busy with *Gilligan's Island,* which was far more sophisticated. Come to think of it, reruns of *Gilligan's Island reruns* are better than *The Brady Bunch* movie.

FARGO
1996. 98 min. Frances McDormand, William H. Macy. Dir. Joel Coen

It warmed the cockles of my heart when McDormand won the Oscar for her portrayal of Marge, the very pregnant, very ordinary, small-town sheriff who sails with equal aplomb through grisly murders, howling blizzards, and the all-you-can-eat buffet line. She may lose her lunch occasionally, but never her sangfroid. She's a beautifully realized character.

I was already a big fan of the smart, inventive Coen brothers, Ethan and Joel. (Joel directed, both of them wrote and edited the movie, Ethan produced, and Joel is married to McDormand.) Their movies are always worth watching (*Blood Simple; Raising Arizona,* page 69; *Miller's Crossing*), but this one is damn near perfect. It's audacious, it's offbeat and, in its own deadpan way, funny as hell. It tells the story of a Minneapolis car dealer who arranges the kidnapping of his wife to collect the ransom money, and then things get out of hand.

Life is wonderfully, weirdly out of kilter in *Fargo*. Everything looms toward us out of a blinding white field of snow and ice, so we are disoriented and on edge all the time. Its stars are not really stars—McDormand; Macy, as the nerdy, nervous car dealer; and Steve Buscemi and Peter Stormare as the fatally inept bad guys—and the action doesn't take place in Fargo, but in Minnesota. Scenes of placid, predictable, middle America alternate with sudden, horrific murder and mayhem. The effect is stunning. *Prairie Home Companion* meets *Reservoir Dogs*.

And the cinematography is superb. I'll never forget those images. It's so satisfying to be able to say that about a movie. **GC**

CT   There are certainly some images I *want* to forget—stump grinder, anyone? But mostly I agree. Plus it has one of the best damn chick characters ever.

AR   Marge clearly came from hearty, pioneer Scandinavian stock, which is among the best kind; hats off to my maternal grandparents. She's a pillar of near normalcy in a sea of weirdness.

HAROLD AND MAUDE
1972. 90 min. Ruth Gordon, Bud Cort, Vivian Pickles. Dir. Hal Ashby

Something of a cult favorite, black comedy *Harold and Maude* is a love story, but maybe not the one you see on the surface. Harold, played by Cort, is 20, a lonely, rich kid obsessed with death, whose only discernible pastimes are attending strangers' funerals and faking his own suicide. Some of the most hilarious scenes in the movie are his staged deaths—usually in front of his unimpressed mother, played with delightfully deadpan hauteur by Pickles.

Maude (Gordon) is hell on wheels, pushing eighty, a force of nature, a law unto herself. She enjoys funerals, too, so she naturally meets Harold, and thus begins his education in life, love, and his favorite, death.

It's a terminally '70s movie, with music by Cat Stevens and acres of loud polyester. But the humor and the values are eternal, and

Maude embodies everything I'd like to be when, and if, I grow up—
except maybe for the tie-dye. **GC**

AR   Excuse me, but the Cat Stevens sound track is the only
memorable thing about the movie, which wears about as well
as hot pants I thought were so cool in ninth grade.

CT   I've always wanted to like this movie . . . but I never have.
I'm just not hip enough, I guess.

HIS GIRL FRIDAY
*1940. 92 min. Cary Grant, Rosalind Russell, Ralph Bellamy.
Dir. Howard Hawks. b&w*

This is one of the smartest, funniest movies ever, a frantic, antic
romp with two classy, great-looking stars. Grant plays Walter, a fast-
talking, devious newspaper editor, and Russell plays Hildy, his
equally fast-talking, equally devious ex-wife and soon to be ex-star
reporter. She's retiring today to marry a nice, normal guy and live
a nice, normal life. But, first . . . there's a particularly juicy murder
story to cover, and the dueling duo can't resist.
   This is the only movie Grant and Russell ever made together,
more's the pity. They're a perfect match, trading barbs at breakneck
speed, scheming and conniving to the end. The dialogue sparkles. "I
intended to be with you on our honeymoon, honest." "You have an
old-fashioned idea that divorce is for life." Grant, the master of cool,
is hilariously manic, but it's Russell who dominates. She's nothing
short of smashing as she swaggers and wisecracks her way through
the newsroom. What a woman. What a movie. No wonder the Library
of Congress, in 1993, declared *His Girl Friday* a national treasure.
GC

AR   Russell can do no wrong for me in the movies, and she's in
top form here. If I'd seen it when I was wondering whether
I should become a newspaper reporter, I'd have made the
decision in a snap.

CT   Hildy Johnson, what a woman! An inspiration for us all.
Why can't they make movies like this today?

MADONNA: TRUTH OR DARE
1991. 118 min. Madonna. Dir. Alek Keshishian

Except for the masturbation scenes, the conical breasts, and sometimes heretical subject matter, Madonna's essentially an old-fashioned song-and-dance woman (doesn't have the ring of song-and-dance man, does it?) in this documentary that follows her world tour of 1989. When she's not spraying her throat, hurling the F word, or fixing her makeup, she's dealing with the daily dramas caused by the likes of the Toronto police, who threatened to arrest her for public lewdness if she left certain bawdy scenes in (she did, of course), and the Pope, who didn't want her coming to Italy at all.

But best of all is seeing the behind-the-scenes maneuverings of the people around her, particularly crotchety Warren Beatty, the only one to question Madonna's inviting the camera to follow her everywhere from the ladies' room to the doctor's office. There's also an amazing conversation with her dad (who sounds like a character out of *Fargo*). He says he'll come to the show whenever it's convenient, and she's trying to get across the fact that it's *her* show, he can come whenever he wants. Madonna produced this flick, so you get the feeling that even when we see her looking bad, it's carefully lit bad. But for a view of what it's like inside the magic bubble of fame, it's aces. **CT**

GC Oh, say it ain't so, Cynthia! Surely you can enter the magic bubble of fame and not be as narcissistic and cruel as Madonna. I for one am glad that her particular bubble seems to have burst. This was a tacky exercise in self-promotion.

AR Bleeeeech.

MARY POPPINS
1964. 140 min. Julie Andrews, Dick Van Dyke. Dir. Robert Stevenson

Andrews was mighty ticked when Hollywood rejected her in favor of Audrey Hepburn (and someone else's singing voice, no less) for the lead in *My Fair Lady,* and she rather unenthusiastically took the role of commander in chief of the nursery in *Mary Poppins,* thinking it was second prize. Instead, it landed her an Oscar for Best Actress and launched a national craze for using supercalifragilisticexpialido-cious in conversation. That was annoying. But the movie isn't, even after you've grown up, unless, of course, you've grown up to be an old poop.

Though some of its special effects don't seem so special anymore, *Mary Poppins* is still packed with can't-get-them-out-of-your-head tunes, magical characters, delectable gags (remember what happens every time Uncle Albert goes into one of his laughing jags? Or when the retired addled admiral next door checks his watch?), and very nice dance steps from Van Dyke and his chorus line of chimney sweeps. The tea-serving penguins, in one of Disney's earlier meldings of animation and live-action, are a hoot. And Andrews as the "practically perfect in every way" take-charge nanny is marvelously unaustrianantinazinunlike (four fewer syllables than the annoying word). She rules the roost, outwitting mother, father, and kids, and teaches them lessons along the way. Ordered by the father to explain what's happening in his house, she responds, "First of all I would like to make one thing perfectly clear." "Yes?" says the father. Continues Mary, "I never explain anything."

Watching Andrews, you are delighted to be reminded that she did something other than *The Sound of Music*. So skulk into your video store, make like you have a gaggle of kids waiting in the car, and rent this movie. The embarrassment will be worth it. **AR**

GC   Sweet revenge for Andrews and a timeless delight for the rest of us.

CT   To this day I can't look at the tops of buildings without expecting to see Van Dyke dancing on them, a sidewalk chalk painting without seeing it open up into another world, or a carousel without envisioning the fabulous flying penguins, not that this movie had an impact on me or anything.

MRS. MINIVER
1942. 134 min. Greer Garson, Walter Pidgeon, Dame May Whitty. Dir. William Wyler. b&w

In December of 1941, when the Japanese attacked Pearl Harbor, *Mrs. Miniver* was in production. Recognizing it as a great national morale booster, President Roosevelt urged MGM to get it into theaters as soon as possible. Never mind that *Mrs. Miniver* was about life in a small English village; it was *Hollywood*'s idea of life in a small English village. Roosevelt was right. The movie was a smash hit, and garnered Academy Awards for director Wyler, Best Picture, screenwriting, and cinematography. And Greer's Mrs. Miniver became a powerful symbol of courage and grace.

The movie begins in 1939. The war clouds are gathering, but for now it's still garden parties and flower shows and chats with the vicar. Mrs. Miniver's major preoccupations are new hats, her perfect children, and adoring hubby. Then comes the war. Son Vince joins the air force, hubby helps with the evacuation of Dunkirk, and tragedy shatters the Minivers' idyllic lives.

It's all manipulation, clichés, and simplistic patriotism. But it's also fascinating and stirring, with a great cast and lovely photography. And Garson is superb. I want to be on her team next time. **GC**

CT   Dynamite flick. And when the family is hunched in a bunker listening to falling bombs whistle on their way down and wondering how close to them they'll fall, you feel your heart starting to pound, too.

AR   Churchill loved it, too, but then he had the Nazis breathing down his neck. Otherwise, he would have noticed that it's heavy-handed and hackneyed. I, for one, ended up wanting to slap Garson, not hand her an Oscar.

QUEEN CHRISTINA
1933. 97 min. Greta Garbo, John Gilbert. Dir. Rouben Mamoulian. b&w

This is a smashing movie, with Garbo at her most beautiful and regal, and with magnificent sets and costumes. In seventeenth-century Sweden, the king raises his daughter Christina as a boy and teaches her the manly arts, the better to prepare her to ascend the throne on his death. When that time comes, Christina can stride and ride with virile grace, and even has a little thing going with one of her ladies-in-waiting, kissing her on the mouth and promising a weekend in the country (this was Hollywood B.C., before censorship). When her adviser urges her to marry, saying, "You cannot die an old maid," she parries with, "I have no intention to, Chancellor. I shall die a bachelor."

But all that changes when the dashing Spanish ambassador, Gilbert, breezes into town. In a lovely, erotic scene in a country inn, after they have spent the night together, Christina caresses the furnishings in the room and fixes them in her memory forever. She goes back to the royal court a woman in love, and it's off with the pantaloons and on with the jewels and décolletage.

Christina is an intellectual, worldly monarch, which gives weight to her struggle between heart and crown and makes her surprisingly contemporary. And her wardrobe is to die for, from her well-cut boots to her velvet gowns. The closing scene, as she faces her destiny and makes her choice, is one of the most breathtaking in screen history. **GC**

AR   Yowza! So *that's* what all the fuss was about Garbo! (She initially wanted Olivier for the role played by Gilbert, but she and Sir Larry didn't hit it off during rehearsal.)

CT   I love this movie and the fact that Garbo looks much better in equestrian drag than she does dolled up as a queen.

THELMA & LOUISE
1991. 130 min. Susan Sarandon, Geena Davis, Brad Pitt. Dir. Ridley Scott

This is the movie that planted the seed of an idea for our *Chicks on Film* TV show—not the movie itself, but the reaction to it. When (male, of course) critics called it "male bashing," my jaw dropped to my knees. Even though women get bashed and beaten in movies by the hundreds, nobody ever suggests that there's something the least bit wrong with this. What do they call movies where chicks are stalked and slaughtered? "Thrillers." So, anyhow, *Thelma & Louise* is a cathartic revenge flick for chicks who have been hooted at as if they were desperate bimbos ready to jump out of their undies for any yahoo with a beer gut and musky scent.

Thelma, an Arkansas housewife, and her savvy waitress friend, Louise (who both have a history of getting kicked around by yucky men), set off on a rare weekend getaway. When the guileless Thelma is attacked in a parking lot, Louise shoots the about-to-be-rapist, and thus begins an unintentional crime spree across gorgeous Western scenery. The harder they try to stay out of trouble, the more they find. Still, if they do find themselves in the position of holding a gun to a state trooper's head, they apologize profusely.

And we can't forget Pitt, who makes his memorable debut as J. D., hitchhiker/robber with flame blue eyes and the cutest butt this side of the Mississippi. (For this reason this movie could also go in the lust chapter for the scene between him and the sexually naive Thelma, after which she says, "I finally understand what all the fuss is about.") Written by first-time screenwriter Callie Khouri, this is *the* pivotal movie for chicks in the movies. **CT**

GC This has been called the first chick buddy movie, à la *Butch Cassidy and the Sundance Kid* and the *Lethal Weapon* string. But there's one important difference. Unlike their reckless, violence-addicted counterparts, Thelma and Louise actually agonize over killing somebody, over breaking the law. They weigh the consequences, so that their last defiant act is not a cop-out, it's a deliberate "fuck you" to society and its sexist demands. I love it.

AR And furthermore, after the one act in the parking lot, these chicks don't do anything all that naughty to the men they come upon. From the reaction, you'd have thought they went around bopping stray males on the head for grins. And not only that, but there's a couple of good *guy* roles to ease the fellas' pain. Boys, it's time you got a grip.

The Über-est

Katharine Hepburn is the über-über-chick—a chick who did it her way all the time. As aviatrixes, suffragettes, newspaperwomen, faith healers . . . or even debutantes or actresses or wives—she played the parts with intelligence, spunk, and chutzpah. She was a chick in charge of her own life, too—whether it meant getting fired from stage productions for talking back to the directors early in her career, to asking for absurd amounts of money—and getting it—to carrying on a twenty-seven-year affair with a married man and practically daring anyone to say something about it. And let's not forget, no one could get that chick in a skirt. She was a pants pioneer and a tough-talkin', pull-yourself-up-by-your-bootstraps kinda gal. Listen to her in the book *People Will Talk,* by John Kobel: "The tougher you are in life, and the more you blame yourself, the better off you'll be." She won three Academy Awards (for *Morning Glory, Guess Who's Coming to Dinner,* and *The Lion in Winter,* page 32), and got eight more nominations. Here's a Hepburn sampler; you really can't go wrong with any of them, not even *The Iron Petticoat,* with Bob Hope:

> *Little Women* 1933
> *Christopher Strong* 1933
> *Morning Glory* 1933
> *Stage Door* 1937
> *Bringing Up Baby* 1938
> *The Philadelphia Story* 1940
> *Woman of the Year* 1942
> *State of the Union* 1948
> *Adam's Rib* 1949
> *The African Queen* 1951
> *Pat and Mike* 1952
> *Summertime* 1955
> *The Rainmaker* 1956
> *Desk Set* 1957
> *Suddenly Last Summer* 1959
> *Long Day's Journey Into Night* 1962
> *The Lion in Winter* 1968
> *On Golden Pond* 1981

eight

STOP! REWIND TO THAT DARLING LOVE SEAT!

"What a dump!" —Bette Davis, in Beyond the Forest

Are you as sick as I am of Martha Stewart and *This Old House?* They and their kind have a lot to answer for—making sideboards out of old sweat socks and lamp shades out of pigs' ears, remodeling and redoing like there's no tomorrow and making the rest of us look like cave-dwelling troglodytes. Who needs the guilt trip? It's far more constructive to watch a movie, and if anybody asks you can tell them it's research. So curl up with these videos and check out the coolest Southwest decor (*Waiting to Exhale,* page 71), funkiest retro look (*Edward Scissorhands,* page 66), and best English country—any Merchant-Ivory production, but start with *Howards End* (page 179). Pay close attention to the flower arrangements. Warning: If all of this inspires you to rent out a couple of those newly decorated rooms, don't rent them to Michael Keaton. He's a bad risk. **GC**

DISCLOSURE

1994. 127 min. Michael Douglas, Demi Moore. Dir. Barry Levinson

Yes, this is about gender in the workplace—and what a workplace! The glass-and-brick Seattle headquarters of the computer company where Tom (Douglas) and Meredith (Moore) work is ultra Northwest trendy, with individual offices at various levels suspended seemingly in midflight. There is ergonomically correct furniture, filtered sunlight, and walls that are floor-to-ceiling windows, so that almost everything everybody does is on public display (except for the laughable harassment scene that takes place in a dark, out-of-view office undergoing renovation). In sharp and oh-so obvious contrast to the high-tech grooviness of the workplace is the old-fashioned, spacious comfiness of the home Tom shares in the leafy-green suburbs with his ridiculously supportive wife.

The film itself is entertaining as a virtual reality whodunit and as commentary on man's inability to control his libido and the importance of wearing black garters to work. It also reminds us of why Donald Sutherland still gets supporting roles. But the primary reason to rent *Disclosure* is because Moore, who probably can't act, is probably *not acting,* and in the end gets what she deserves. Quite satisfying. And the set is out of this world. **AR**

GC Make the set the only reason to rent it, AR. With sexual harassment a pervasive problem for women in the workplace, you'll have to forgive me if I don't feel Douglas's pain. And we've already seen his decent-white-guy terrorized-by-predator-female shtick in *Fatal Attraction.* Enough, already.

CT Demi, Michael, and their cyber-yuppie headquarters give me the creeps. And spare me another movie where the wife tromps around in potato sacks while the Other Woman kicks butt in miniskirts and high heels.

EDWARD SCISSORHANDS
1990. 98 min. Johnny Depp, Winona Ryder, Dianne Wiest, Alan Arkin, Vincent Price. Dir. Tim Burton

It's been a slow day for Peg, the Avon lady, so she decides to pay a call on whoever lives in that mysterious, craggy castle on the hill that towers over her pastel-painted, cookie-cutter suburb. That's how she meets Edward Scissorhands, a young man whose inventor died before giving Edward hands, leaving Edward digitally challenged, with huge scissors where his fingers should be.

So kindly Peg adopts Edward and takes him home to her family.

It's the '60s—in spades—and director Burton (*Beetlejuice, Pee-wee's Big Adventure,* two of the *Batman* movies) is in his element, dishing up bizarre happenings in banal settings. It's all here: capri pants, Bermuda shorts, plastic earrings, and candlewick robes; ducks in flight across fireplace walls; swag lamps; and Tom Jones on the LP. It's kitschy, colorful ambiance is accentuated by the atmospheric, moody flashbacks to the castle, to the rickety, Rube Goldberg-like workshop of Edward's well-meaning but wacky inventor, played endearingly by Price.

Depp makes the perfect Edward, poignant and childlike, but with unsettling potential. Wiest's Peg is a joy, maternal instincts firing on all cylinders as she champions her oddball foundling. Ryder waltzes through her role as Kim, Peg's daughter and Edward's love interest, and Arkin does a nifty turn as the sunny, oblivious dad.

The neighbors are a wonderful, motley lot. One of the funniest themes is their delighted exploitation of Edward's skill with his scissors: As the movie progresses, lawns sprout increasingly intricate topiary trees, and the coiffures of all the women, and their dogs, become ever more bizarre. It's all great fun and a feast for the eyes, and surprisingly touching. Having scissors for hands is not that different from coping with other physical challenges, and if you're really lucky the Avon lady might ring your bell. **GC**

AR   Depp is fetching, even with his pincers. I'd let him hug me, to heck with the tailor's bills.

CT   Another Johnny Drip movie. Not for me, thanks.

LA CAGE AUX FOLLES
1978. 91 min. Ugo Tognazzi, Michel Serrault. Dir. Edouard Molinaro

One of my favorites of all time—joyously campy and funny as hell. Renato (Tognazzi) and Albain (Serrault) own La Cage aux Folles, a popular Saint-Tropez drag club on the Côte d'Azure. Renato runs the place, and Albain is the tempestuous star of the show. Renato's son, from a brief and unusual liaison, shows up and announces he's getting married. Renato and Albain get over the shock that their son's marrying a *girl,* then find out they have to prepare for the arrival of the fiancée's family, including her father, a conservative politician. Obviously it won't do to introduce the ultraconservative secretary of morals to the cross-dressing gay couple, so various schemes are concocted to either get Albain out of the way or butch him up and pass him off as an uncle. They have to butch up their apartment too, which involves tossing such haute transvestite accent pieces as the butt-shaped vase. I also liked the 1996 remake, *The Birdcage,* with Robin Williams and Nathan Lane, but a big flaw in the '90s version is that there appears to be no love between the two men, whereas in the original their relationship is obvious, touching, and sweet. *La Cage* bonus: beautiful if brief shots of the south of France that could include it in our travel section. **CT**

GC   No contest. The original is head and shoulders (cross-dressed or no) above *The Birdcage.* Serrault is sublime, not only funny but poignant, as he proves that love is love, whatever the wardrobe.

AR   Was *The Birdcage* even related? *La Cage* is the real thing.

PACIFIC HEIGHTS
1990. 103 min. Melanie Griffith, Matthew Modine, Michael Keaton. Dir. John Schlesinger

This black comedy stars Griffith and Modine as an earnest young couple who invest everything they have to buy an old San Francisco house, fix it up, and rent out a couple of rooms to help with the mortgage. Sounds reasonable. It's a lovely gingerbread Victorian, ocean view, with great potential, high ceilings, and hardwood floors, and the couple sand and buff their little hearts out. But they didn't bargain on a diabolically deranged Keaton as their tenant. You get the idea he could be difficult when you first see him playing with a cockroach and a razor blade. Things deteriorate fast, and the movie speeds us through a crash course in every landlord's worst nightmare, and then some.

Under Schlesinger's deft direction *(Midnight Cowboy, Marathon Man),* this mordantly funny tale of a yuppie twosome pushed to the limits covers all the baseboards. And Griffith definitely wears the coveralls in this household. Not only does she spackle and saw with the best, she goes after the villain and nails him—really nails him—in the end. **GC**

AR   It has the feel of a made-for-TV movie, and besides, the couple wouldn't get into all the trouble if they weren't such nincompoops.

CT   I didn't like the movie much at all, and I can't help noting that Leonard Maltin's video guide called making Griffith the stronger and Modine the weaker character the "cleverest touch."

RAISING ARIZONA
1987. 94 min. Nicolas Cage, Holly Hunter. Dir. Joel Coen

Ahh, those Coen brothers. After *Blood Simple* and before *Fargo* (page 56), there was *Raising Arizona,* which gives new meaning to the phrase "trailer trash." In fact, the yellow mobile home in the middle of the Arizona desert—an arty version of the Arizona desert—is the most normal prop, or person, in the movie. Will you get decorating tips? Let's hope not. But you'll have fun. A clumsy crook by the name of H. I. (Cage) marries cop Edwina (Hunter) after meeting her during one of his many bookings. They long for a child to join them in the trailer, and so they kidnap Nathan Arizona, Jr., one of the quintuplets just born to a furniture baron (in keeping with the interior design theme). Along the way, the happy family is visited by a pair of H. I.'s escaped con buddies—named Evelle and Gale, of course—who throw out some of the best lines in a ninety-four minutes full of them. Evelle: "We released ourselves on our own recognizance." Gale: "What Evelle means to say is, we felt that the institution no longer had anything to offer us." And later, Evelle offers the new parents advice: "You don't breast-feed him, he'll hate you for it later. That's why we wound up in prison." H. I. has a few pearls, too, as when he's robbing a convenience store. "I'll be taking these Huggies and whatever cash ya got. And make it quick—I'm in dutch with the wife." The whole affair is as fun and weird as the dialogue. Note of trivia: The role of Edwina was written specifically for Hunter. **AR**

CT What a treat to see Hunter and Cage together as the comically manic couple, and John Goodman as one of the post-prison cons.

GC I never tire of watching this movie. It's smart, it's goofy, it's adorable.

THE THIN MAN
1934. 93 min. William Powell, Myrna Loy. Dir. W. S. Van Dyke

If you think you've seen this classic too many times to rent the video, think again. Not that it isn't worth watching over and over. But if you're like I am, you'll realize you've really only caught snippets of it here and there on late-night television and have forgotten the plot and some of the glorious repartee, delivered in lazy, top-of-the-world style by Powell, as detective Nick Charles, and Loy, as Nora Charles, Nick's wealthy, definitely-her-own-woman wife. Reading the papers the morning after a gunman has wounded Nick, the detective crows that he's a hero: "I was shot twice in the *Tribune.*" Loy responds, "I read you were shot five times in the tabloids." Says Nick, "It's not true. He didn't come anywhere near my tabloids." Hah!

There's so much of this great back-and-forth, it's hard to keep track of the plot, from the novel by Dashiell Hammett. And the plot is really quite fine. But it hardly matters, for *The Thin Man* is, after all, really a drinking chick's comedy. Rarely does so much ice clink against glass on-screen. The talk is a lot about boozing, too. Powell asks a guest, "What are you drinking?" The guest says, "Oh, nothing." Powell says, "That's a mistake." A visitor asks Loy if her husband is working on a case, and Loy says, "Yes—a case of scotch." Prohibition had recently been repealed when this came out, and audiences absolutely drank it up. They still do. **AR**

GC Anne is right. This is a charmer that never gets old. Same again for me, please. Cheers.

CT Me, too, make mine a double. That tabloids joke gets me every time.

WAITING TO EXHALE

1995. 121 min. Whitney Houston, Angela Bassett, Loretta Devine, Lela Rochon. Dir. Forest Whitaker

Black women flocked to this movie. Because it was such a great movie? Um, probably not. But it *is* a movie about black women, which is not something that comes along every day (unlike movies about, say, boys who grew up in mob families, disaffected white suburban kids, or gun-totin' guys in the hood). In this novel screenplay (based on Terry McMillan's best-seller) four friends in Phoenix, who have varying degrees of success in their careers, commiserate about their rotten, two-timin', no-good men. And they don't just exhale, they vent! Which, of course, caused men across America to contract into the fetal position and whimper "male bashing" once again. Guys *do* get it good, girlfriend, particularly in some humiliating between-the-sheets scenes, which should go a long way toward improving the sex lives of women everywhere. This movie will also make you want to move to the desert, drink martinis, and subscribe to *Elle Decor*. From swanky hotel bars to sleek sepia-toned bedrooms that look out on cactus-dotted hills, the scenery is oh-so-cool yet honey-warm, just like the sound track. I'd like to see more of Devine in the movies; she has a lively presence that fills up the screen and makes you want to nestle next to her on the couch and just listen to her talk. **CT**

GC   This is a handsome, shallow soap opera, which could be just fine and dandy if it were one of many movies about black women. But, as you say, Cynthia, they don't come along very often. It is worth watching for decorating and fashion tips.

AR   Thin stuff, as Gabrielle says, though there is an extraordinary insight offered: Not only can Houston not act, she can't dance, either.

Still Need Help? Check out the Following:

Horse-farm wealthy, but scuffed and comfy: *Something to Talk About*

Filthy rich: *Sabrina* (the original, with Audrey Hepburn)

Mafioso moderne: *Married to the Mob*

In-your-dreams Manhattan apartment: *Green Card*

Tastefully messy and lived-in-by-somebody-far-more-intelligent-than-you Manhattan apartment: Any Woody Allen movie

nine

REVENGE OF THE UGLY DUCKLINGS

"The Ivy League stinks. All they got there is those
ugly, intellectual girls with Band-Aids on their
knees from playing the cello."
—Anthony Edwards, *in* The Sure Thing

Let's face it. Most truly beautiful women are boring (with a few stunning exceptions, to be sure). Guys don't know this. They think they're fascinating just because they're beautiful. We know better, which is why we'd much rather watch movies about misfits with unruly hair and expanding waistlines. Not because we don't feel threatened, but because they tend to be more dimensional than your average Julia Roberts character. . . . An Ugly Duckling is by definition the antithesis of what we call Stick Chicks, actresses who stand there and look good but don't do much else. (See Renée Zellweger in *Jerry Maguire*.) An ugly duckling doesn't always transform into something beautiful. And that's fine by us. **CT**

A DANGEROUS WOMAN
1993. 102 min. Debra Winger, Gabriel Byrne, Barbara Her-
shey. Dir. Stephen Gyllenhaal

Martha has a big problem. She's mildly retarded, which is no picnic, but that's not the big problem. The big problem is that she's completely honest, without guile, and therefore a menace to society, a dangerous woman. As everybody knows, the lies and pretenses are what grease the wheels of daily living.

It's an interesting premise, and Winger, as Martha, has one of the meatiest, and most overlooked, roles of her career. She's in good company, too, with Byrne as Mackey, an alcoholic, itinerant handyman, and Hershey as the loving but exasperated aunt with whom Martha lives. When Martha's honesty causes her to lose her job and her only friend, she turns to the weak, no-account Mackey for comfort, with disastrous results.

Martha is no prize, however you figure it. She's awkward and unattractive, causes everybody headaches, and is not an easy person to like. Winger, to her everlasting credit, makes her hard to forget. **GC**

AR   Winger is every bit as good here as her reputation of old said she was. Some of the plot turns are almost laughable, but she's watchable enough to overcome them.

CT   I agree with Gabrielle. It's also an odd sort of love story that keeps you wondering what you really think about this kind of love story.

FRIED GREEN TOMATOES

1991. 130 min. Kathy Bates, Jessica Tandy, Mary Stuart Masterson, Mary Louise Parker. Dir. Jon Avnet

I find this movie as irresistible as the candy bars Bates's Evelyn hides all over her house. There are two stories going on here—one, the search by ugly-duckling Evelyn to find an identity of her own and her friendship with nursing-home blue-hair Mrs. Threadgoode (Tandy). The other tale takes us back fifty years, through Mrs. Threadgoode's memories, to the friendship between a young tomboy (Masterson) and her sweet and timid friend (Parker), who run the Whistle Stop Café in a small Alabama town. Bates is hysterical as a frumpy, overweight, undersatisfied housewife who sets out on a '70s-like quest for self-actualization. She tries many paths to redo herself inside and out and to save a boring marriage (Saran Wrap is involved). One of my favorite scenes of all time is Evelyn screaming at two twinkies in shorts in a parking lot who've just beaten her to a parking space. "We're younger and faster," they say when she yells they stole her space. And then Evelyn backs up and bashes into their twinkmobile, hollering, "I'm older and better insured." This is a funny, sweet look at the problems of women fifty years ago versus today. The melodramatic flashback scenes with Masterson and Parker are nostalgic of small-town American life. I'd also recommend reading the book by Fannie Flagg. **CT**

AR   Bates and Tandy are what make this fly. When they're not on-screen, I miss them.

GC   I know movies don't have to be faithful to the book. In fact, some, like *The English Patient* (page 86), give us a brilliant variation, but this one strikes me as a cop-out. In the book, the friends are a young lesbian couple. Apparently their problems haven't changed much in fifty years.

THE HEIRESS

1949. 115 min. Olivia de Havilland. Montgomery Clift, Miriam Hopkins, Ralph Richardson. Dir. William Wyler. b&w

Poor Catherine. She's not so bright, she can't dance, she has no social skills. Her wit's dull, her face plain, and her only talent needlepoint. She's also loaded, so charm bedamned, there's sure to be some swain willing to make a play for her. Clift—who has a Brad Pitt glint in his eye—ignores her constant bumbles, flatters her inarticulation, and promises true love and marriage. The hot pursuer is possessed of many charms, but little dough. When Catherine's papa finds this slick pauper moving in on his daughter, he threatens to disinherit her so the scheming lover won't get his paws on her money. But is Papa right in his estimation of his character, or could Clift really love her? (Haven't we all wondered at some point what one person sees in another?) Will the marriage take place? Will someone get dumped? The snippy father and easily duped Aunt Lavinia liven up the joint with his snobbiness and her dippiness. Shot in classic black and white, the film is based on the novel *Washington Square*, by Henry James. I'd do both. **CT**

GC   De Havilland won a well-deserved Oscar for her performance, and Richardson, who played her father, should have. He still makes my blood boil.

AR   Powerful, and featuring one of my favorite chick lines, spoken by poor Catherine: "Yes, I can be very cruel. I have been taught by masters."

MURIEL'S WEDDING

1994. 105 min. Toni Collette, Bill Hunter, Rachel Griffiths. Dir. P. J. Hogan

What's a dumpy, horse-faced wallflower from a family that's collectively dumber and dumpier to do? Especially when she tries to hang with genetically pert, chemically coifed—and need we add horrifically popular—cheerleader types? Turn off those Abba songs and get out of Porpoise Spit, for one, which is what our Muriel does. Muriel's attempts to create a new persona for herself in the big city of Sydney can be excruciating. She doesn't know not to wear black leather pants. She hasn't figured out how not to look gooney when she smiles. And she has this little obsessive-compulsive problem about trying on wedding gowns, but we're in her corner all the way. As the movie starts, Muriel's venal friends are demanding she relinquish the bridal bouquet she caught and give someone else a fair chance, because who would marry *her?* This is not your typical revenge of the ugly duckling movie. It's better than that. But it's a real catharsis for anyone who's ever been picked on by superficial popularity terrorists. (And does Muriel really end up marrying the Aryan-looking swimmer with the buff bod?) Watching this Australian flick also lets you soak in the bubbles of those silly Abba tunes, a vice more shameful than eating fat. Also, Muriel's bridal magazine fetish is probably more common that your average working girl would want to admit, but you didn't hear that from me. **CT**

GC   Don't you just love it when some average-looking chick is made to look really dumpy at first so that she can look almost beautiful when they clean her up at the end? (See Barbra Streisand's *The Mirror Has Two Faces*—the woman has no shame.)

AR   Yes, *excruciating* is the word. I was torn between being insulted and bored, and settled on the latter.

NOW, VOYAGER

1942. 117 min. Bette Davis, Paul Henreid, Claude Rains, Gladys Cooper. Dir. Irving Rapper. b&w

You know when you see the close-up of the frumpy black shoes she's wearing that Davis's character, Charlotte, is overdue for a major makeover. She's a mess, plain and timid, cowed by her dominatrix Boston mother, and teetering on the verge of a nervous breakdown, which she conveniently succumbs to while the doctor, played by Rains, is visiting. Whisked off to his sanitarium, she is, in a remarkably few feet of celluloid, transformed into a poised, sophisticated fashion plate in high heels. She heads off on a South American cruise, where she meets and falls in love with the married but available Jerry (Henreid).

Thus begins one of the most unconsciously hilarious wooings in screen history. And it's all done with cigarettes. Yes, I know, cigarettes were always portrayed as sexy in movies of this era, but this one is over the top. When Jerry sticks two in his mouth and lights them at the same time, Charlotte almost has an orgasm on the spot. I counted four of these incendiary moments, but I was laughing so hard, I could have missed some.

There's more business about Jerry's daughter, Charlotte's mother, and such, but it's the cigarettes that make this a must-see. And one wonderful, soppy line as the story ends: "Oh, Jerry, don't let's ask for the moon. We have the stars." That's just the way I felt. **GC**

AR   Nobody but Davis could have played Charlotte. Producer Hal B. Wallis wanted Irene Dunne for the role, but Davis talked him out of it. She runs the show.

CT   That's because Davis is the archetypal ugly duckling—just as believable homely as she is beautiful.

A SPECIAL DAY

1977. 105 min. Sophia Loren, Marcello Mastroianni. Dir. Ettore Scola

The desirable Loren as a dowdy housewife? The gloriously macho Mastroianni as a suspected homosexual? In *A Special Day,* the actors, usually teamed up in steamy love stories, take on these uncommon roles so beautifully that they'll darn near break your heart. In a sack

of a housedress and with dark circles beneath her eyes, Loren greets
the dawn of the special day in Rome in 1938 by rousing her six
children and ungrateful husband and sending them off to the big
rally celebrating Hitler's state visit. The bands are already playing,
and the radio announcer's voice already blaring importantly from
loudspeakers outside, when she meets, by chance, a lonely neighbor,
played by Mastroianni. A busybody neighbor whispers that he's a
damnable anti-Fascist, and hints that he might be something even
more abhorred. But the housewife is drawn to him nonetheless, and
he to her. The few hours they spend together as the radio announcer's
voice drones on outdoors are meaningful and touching and a little
bizarre for each, for different reasons. Mussolini's Italy has marred
them, and it's easy to imagine as the credits roll that it's going to
get worse before it gets better. Stick with this movie during its rather
languid beginning, and you'll never forget it. Loren is so good a
performer that she, of all people, is absolutely convincing as an
unattractive woman who learns what beauty really is. **AR**

CT   I agree. I stuck with it through a very bad dubbed version
         that needed subtitles and was really glad I did. Who woulda
         thought Sophia could do dowdy?

GC   What a strange, but affecting, movie. And "dowdy" is the
         least of it. That's just makeup, or lack of it. What Loren and
         Mastroianni deliver is great acting and a beautiful rapport.

SUGARBABY
*1985. 87 min. Marianne Sägebrecht, Eisi Gulp. Dir. Percy
Adlon. German w/subtitles*

She's Marianne, a mortuary attendant, large and plain and pushing
forty. He's Eisi, twenty-five, married, drives a subway train, and looks
like a Greek god. She sees him, and *pow!* It's love at first sight, for
her, anyway. "Sugarbaby," she sighs under her breath. She wants this
guy, and sets about getting him with awesome efficiency. Before she
even speaks to him, she transforms her little flat into a satin-sheeted
love nest, invests in sexy lingerie, good liquor, and five-inch heels.
    Unlike most of the timorous, cowering plain Janes in movies,
Marianne grabs for the gusto, and she's wonderful to behold. It's
great fun to go along with her on this adventure, and—as in all fine

adventures—we find some unexpected treasures along the way. Not only do we discover what makes Marianne tick, we learn a few important lessons about life and love. And all in eighty-seven minutes. Such a deal. **GC**

CT Anything with Sägebrecht is great, and I think this is my favorite. I love watching her set her trap like an ace hunter and snaring her very adorable prey.

AR Eighty-seven minutes is a good thing. Beyond that, I can't recommend it. I didn't give a hoot for the characters, except maybe the corpses.

Anatomy of an Ugly Duckling

Ugly duckling flicks are great fun for the backward makeover. Get a nice-looking actress, then turn her into a mouse: At the movies, we can learn what *not* to do.

Hair: parted in the middle or pulled back in a bun. Vital to the ugly-duckling character so it can later be let down, curled, or swept up in a seductive fashion.

Glasses: a must. The thicker the better, both lenses and frames.

Eyebrows: must be thick *and* woolly

Posture: Nothing says ugly, dumpy, and uninteresting better than bad posture.

Bad shoes: I hate to say it, but nothing says U.D. better than clunky shoes (my personal favorite).

Feeling too lazy to put makeup on and go out, let alone look at yourself in the mirror . . . pop some of these babies in the VCR and feel the self-esteem soar.

It's all in the posture
Dorothy McGuire is supposed to be so homely she actually frightens people in *The Enchanted Cottage* (1945). Poor Dorothy, somehow she made this work even though she wore hardly any makeup. Although, come to think of it, without makeup, I recall scaring quite a few people myself.

Deborah Kerr's so mousy she reaches ugly duckliness in *Separate Tables* (1958), a quirky and highly enjoyable flick about a remote British inn full of eccentrics, spinsters, one studly rake and Rita Hayworth.

Before there was Julie Andrews in *My Fair Lady* on Broadway, or Audrey Hepburn in *My Fair Lady* on screen there was Wendy Hiller with the starring role in *Pygmalion* (1938). The George Bernard Shaw script (on which those other *Ladies* were based) won an Oscar for best screenplay. Hiller does the transformation trick primarily through posture, pronunciation, an attitude shift and a change of hat.

Wanna-bes

Remember *Sabrina* (1954) when Audrey Hepburn was supposed to be a nothing little snippet of a school girl that no one ever looked at her? *As if!*

Hmm, let's see, you need a nerdy, timid type for the chick ensemble piece *Steel Magnolias* (1989), and long-legged, long-blond-locked Daryl Hannah springs to mind? It is a Hollywood tradition, though, many a good bone structure has been obscured with bad hair and shoes (everyone from Sophia Loren, pages 144–45 to Ingrid Bergman, pages 48–49). But Daryl looked like Lady Godiva in geek glasses.

Babes-or-nots

Minnie Driver can be babe or non-babe. She put on extra weight to play the non-babe who falls for Chris O'Donnell in *Circle of Friends*. (In *Good Will Hunting* she got to be babe and Harvard med school student, an excellent combination!)

Lili Taylor, the queen of sardonic loners with dark circles under their eyes, wins the contest of the ugliest date to be brought to the party in *Dogfight* (1991). Could you just rip my heart out right now or what?

Barbara Streisand in *The Way We Were* (see page 267) has very bad fashion sense when the movie opens and very bad common sense later on (when she irons her hair, but you know, it does look marvelous that way). She transforms from socialist wonk in bad shoes to glam Hollywood socialist wonk with ironed hair in this classic weepie.

Ultimate teen nightmare

Sissy Spacek in *Carrie* (1976) and Heather Matarazzo in *Welcome to the Dollhouse* (1997). Don't watch these alone or without lots of pig-out food handy. Häagen Daz ice cream, Entenmann's donuts and roast beef sandwiches are what we used to eat at St. Mary's Residence in Manhattan.

FALLING IN LUST AGAIN

"Love is a romantic designation for a most ordinary biological, or shall we say, chemical process, and chemically we are quite sympathetic."
—*Greta Garbo, in* Ninotchka

Every now and then the argument over sex and violence in the movies will flare up, and fuddy-duddies will go on TV to crab about how there's too much of both and it's ruining our country blah blah blah. Violence, sure. But, sex? Are they kidding? What movies are they watching? Coming up with good movies with really steamy scenes isn't that easy—and they don't have to be explicit to get the ol' heart rate up (*The Age of Innocence,* page 39, anyone?). There's more bare skin in an episode of *NYPD Blue* than most movies. And that's not even considering the fact that some of the big video chains edit out the most juicy parts for fear of offending someone or another! Which, ironically, is oddly reminiscent of *Cinema Paradiso,* where the post–World War II small-town Sicilian priest orders the movie projectionist to snip out all the kisses and embraces in the films shown at the local theater. But looking at our lust list, from *William Shakespeare's Romeo and Juliet* to *The English Patient,* it seems many of our sexy movies started out as great works of literature. Maybe the assumption is if it's *literature,* how dirty can it be? **CT**

BABY DOLL

1956. 114 min. Carroll Baker, Karl Malden, Eli Wallach. Dir. Elia Kazan. b&w

Lust, greed, jealousy, revenge, crumbling mansions, and lemonade. Now that's what I like about the South. And *Baby Doll* has it all—and more. This is the movie that so scandalized the Catholic Church that to see it was a mortal sin and you were headed straight for hell. Irresistible.

The screenplay, by Tennessee Williams, is set in the steamy Mississippi Delta and tells a gothic tale of Baby Doll, a thumb-sucking, sleeps-in-a-baby-crib teenager (Baker), her sweaty, balding husband, Archie Lee, and a mustachioed Sicilian stud, Vaquero. The reason Archie Lee (Malden) sweats so much is that when he married Baby Doll, a year ago, she promised that he could claim his conjugal rights on her twentieth birthday—tomorrow, in the movie. Enter Vaquero, played by Wallach, and this is where the nasty fun begins.

Directed by the legendary Kazan (*On the Waterfront, A Streetcar Named Desire, East of Eden,* etc.) *Baby Doll* captures the decaying South with a sly, devastating wit. The actors are superb. Baker's Baby Doll grows up before your eyes, Malden makes you smell Archie Lee's lecherous desire, and Wallach, in his first screen role, exudes enough sexual energy to light up Savannah. And Mildred Dunnock, in a supporting role as Aunt Rose Comfort, will knock your socks off.

The only dated aspect of this 40-odd-year-old movie is that Baby Doll is almost 20. Today she'd be 12. But, all things considered, this is still a blistering, juicy movie. As Aunt Rose Comfort says, when the dust finally settles: "Oh, my. Oh, my." **GC**

CT Ugh. Whiny Baby Doll and desperate Malden make up one of the most irritating screen couples I've ever come across. So sexist, bleak, and depressing, I had to quit watching halfway through. It was that or jump off a bridge.

AR Critics of the '50s didn't much like it, either—it was reviewed as a "dirty movie"—but I found it too amusing to be truly foul.

BETRAYAL

1983. 95 min. Jeremy Irons, Ben Kingsley. Dir. David Jones

The strange and compelling thing about this little movie is that it's a doomed lust story told *backward*. I'll admit I was confused for the first ninety minutes or so (just kidding), but the tack really works. As you watch the affair unfold in reverse, you know what Irons, Kingsley's best friend, and Patricia Hodge, Kingsley's wife, don't—or at least won't for a while. This makes for strange reactions as you see graves being dug before the people involved even realize they've got shovels.

The story starts where it would, conventionally, end, with the once-passionate lover and the wife meeting in a pub years after their affair has ended. Then it takes you back, one year, two years, and further, to the end, where a movie would, customarily, start. You'll wonder at one point or another why they bothered getting into one another's knickers—but, of course, you know things they can't possibly glimpse. The result is a remarkable downside up observation of love. And Kingsley is stunningly good, to the point of being on occasion scary in his self-possessed yet really ticked-off persona (makes you want to run out and rent *Gandhi* so you'll be comfortable with him again). *Betrayal* is topsy-turvy entertainment. **AR**

GC I really wanted to like this movie; great play, great cast. But I didn't. I found it stilted and contrived. But I did love what Quentin Crisp said about it in *Halliwell's Film Guide:* "Occasionally I pined for a little zest—perhaps a nude lesbian chariot race on ice."

CT Whatever you do, don't make the mistake of renting the *Betrayal* with Lesley Ann Warren. I spent thirty terribly long minutes wondering where Jeremy Irons was before I realized I had the wrong flick. After that, I didn't need nude lesbians; Irons and Kingsley were diverting enough.

THE BIG EASY

1987. 108 min. Ellen Barkin, Dennis Quaid, Ned Beatty, John Goodman. Dir. Jim McBride

Barkin plays Anne Osborne, a sexually frustrated assistant D.A. who has a sort of Clark Kent manner to her—with big glasses that keep slipping down her nose, and a tendency to bump into things. Quaid is Remy McSwain, a smooth-talking detective in New Orleans, where corruption is so much a part of the history of the force that the cops hardly see anything wrong with asking businesses to contribute to their "widows and orphans fund." Osborne comes in on a routine wise-guy murder, but also starts looking into the corrupt cops situation. Well, the charming if corrupt detective gets her into bed—and might I say, what a torso on that guy—anyhow, things get pretty steamy, and then she gets entangled, too. He starts wondering if this way of life he grew up in ain't so, well, you know, moral. These two are perfect together, except for the fact that they're on separate sides of the law . . . or are they? This movie does such a good job of re-creating the steaminess of N'awlins (not to mention the steaminess between the two leads), you'll want to crank up the A.C., order a bucket of crawfish, and suck off their heads. **CT**

GC   Oh, yes. Spicy plot, tasty music, delicious scenery, and yummy Quaid. I sure worked up an appetite.

AR   And whenever Quaid croons, "Just relax, darlin'. This is the Big Easy. Folks have a certain way a doin' things down here," I call my travel agent.

BREAKING THE WAVES
1996. 156 min. Emily Watson, Stellan Skarsgård, Katrin Cartlidge. Dir. Lars von Trier

When Bess talks, God listens. Mind you, he's the only one who does. (And, yes, in this curiously compelling movie, set in northern Scotland, a god as dour and sexist as this one *has* to be male.) Bess is a bit slow, naive, and childlike, except when it comes to God—and, later, to sex. She converses with God, and he talks back.

When Bess falls in love with an offshore oil-rig worker, Jan (Skarsgård), a big teddy bear of a man, and marries him, her strictly religious sect—in which women are decidedly second-class citizens—is less than pleased. A virgin before the ceremony, Bess isn't by the time the reception ends. She is so crazy for Jan, and so thrilled to discover her own sexuality, that she can't bear the thought of them being apart when he has to go back to work. So she asks God to send him home early. God does, but at a terrible price. Jan is flown home paralyzed after an accident on the rig.

Now impotent, Jan uses Bess's newfound, burning sexuality to live vicariously, as he urges her to embark on a dangerously escalating series of sexual encounters. It's an amazing, horrifying journey, and Watson carries it off magnificently. (This role won her a 1997 Academy Award nomination.)

Watson is so electrifying as Bess that it would be easy to overlook the other actors, but the cast is uniformly strong, with outstanding performances from Skarsgård and from Cartlidge, who plays Bess's sympathetic, practical sister-in-law. Another wonderful element is the photography. The story is presented in a series of chapters, each one opening with a gorgeous set piece, like a living painting. And the '70s rock sound track, featuring the likes of David Bowie and Leonard Cohen, is terrific. **GC**

CT   Wow, what a movie. At first it was so frigid and depressing, I didn't know if I could make it through, but I hung on. What a touching portrait of pure, undying, obsessive, almost pathological, love.

AR   Watson makes Bess unforgettable, but the film totters into such ridiculous territory that she couldn't hold it together for me.

CAT ON A HOT TIN ROOF
1958. 108 min. Elizabeth Taylor, Paul Newman. Dir. Richard Brooks

Tennessee Williams wrote the play, so you know what to expect: hypocrisy, suggestions of homosexuality (vague, in this case; no surprise considering the year of release), pent-up passion, and a coterie of screwed-up southerners who wish they'd been born late enough to enjoy central air-conditioning. Taylor is Maggie, and Newman is Brick, unhappily married but near to bursting with a strange sexual chemistry that has real trouble getting out of the lab. The patriarch, played by Burl Ives, is called Big Daddy, and boy is he. Dame Judith Anderson does a dandy turn as Big Mama. There's even a chick called Sister Woman. The whole cast has a great time overacting and playing with accents they reckon are southern. But Taylor's gorgeous. And Newman ain't so bad, either. Note of trivia: Taylor's husband at the time, Mike Todd, died in a plane crash during filming. Can you see her pain? **AR**

GC   The sexually frustrated Maggie, the cat on the hot tin roof, asks Buck, "Why can't you please get fat or ugly or something, just so I can stand it?" Luckily for us, he doesn't, which is one of the few reasons to watch this overripe drama.

CT   Larger-than-life performances by both. But, boy, Williams's play is so depressing, I suggest popping *The Sound of Music* (page 159) in the VCR as soon as it's over.

THE ENGLISH PATIENT
1996 160 min. Ralph Fiennes, Kristin Scott Thomas, Juliette Binoche. Dir. Anthony Minghella

Mom said honesty is the best policy, and so: The book by Michael Ondaatje is better than the movie. But the fact that higher marks go to Ondaatje's prose says more about the complexity of his novel, and about the thankfully true fact that some thoughts and emotions cannot be transferred from one medium to another, than it does about the movie. And the movie is a sweeping, extravagant romance to die for, not in the least because Fiennes, even burned to a crisp, is one of the sexiest and most charismatic fellows ever captured on film. Oooooh, when he rips open the bodice of Scott Thomas's pure white dress—well, you just have to *see* it.

The whole of the movie is like that, visual and robustly passionate, though so much of what occurs is history being played in Fiennes's mind as he lies near death in a bombed-out Italian monastery during the final days of World War II. Binoche is his Canadian nurse, and almost as sad as he. The extremely fetching Naveen Andrews is Kip, a Sikh bomb-disposal expert with whom Binoche falls in love, and Willem Dafoe is a thumbless thief who thinks he knows the true identity of the English patient, horribly burned in a plane crash in Arabia, who perhaps is not English at all. The Canadian nurse and the Sikh, the English patient and the Canadian nurse, the Hungarian count and the married British woman—too many relationships for a two-hour-plus movie? Not at all. You'll find yourself wanting more as you push "eject" on the VCR. Or you might push "rewind" for the chance to see it all again.

Tip: If you've neither read the book nor seen the movie, rent the video first, then crack open the book. That way, you'll relish both. **AR**

GC   I loved the book so much, I was almost afraid to see the movie. I needn't have worried. The movie is superb in its own right. Fiennes and Thomas make an incendiary couple, and the desert photography is the most beautiful since *Lawrence of Arabia*.

CT   The movie can't even begin to compare to the book, but only because the book is so great, no film can touch it. The movie itself? Super.

THE HUNGER
1983. 97 min. Catherine Deneuve, David Bowie, Susan Saran-don, Dir. Tony Scott

This movie is spooky, stylish, erotic, and more than a little sick. What more could we ask? John and Miriam (Bowie and Deneuve) have been lovers for ages—okay, make that centuries. They're vampires. Now he's fading, and she needs new blood.

I was sorry to see John go—not that vampires ever really go—because they made such a stunning couple. Great casting. And John's accelerated aging has to be the most awesome makeup triumph since Dustin Hoffman turned 100 years old in *Little Big Man*.

As he starts to fade, John seeks out a doctor, Sarah, played by Sarandon. Later, feeling guilty that she couldn't help him, Sarah goes to their elegant house and meets Miriam. Big mistake. In one of the most famously erotic seductions in the movies, the cool, kinky Miriam soon has Sarah eating out of her hand—actually, her arm. It's all downhill from there. But even as the movie unravels into ghoulish nonsense, it's still fascinating to see Deneuve, that bastion of taste and grooming, with her hair all mussed and blood dribbling down her chin. Does that make me a bad person? **GC**

AR Not a bad person, just one with odd taste—in movies. I *adore* your cold avocado soup.

CT What more could we ask? We could ask for something the least bit entertaining. Somehow, even the sex scenes between Deneuve and Sarandon are dull, which is mind-boggling.

THE PIANO
1993. 121 min. Holly Hunter, Harvey Keitel, Sam Neill, Anna Paquin. Dir. Jane Campion. Australian/French

This movie is so intense, so fierce, and so beautiful that it leaves me speechless. Almost. Set in nineteenth-century New Zealand, it's the story of Ada, a small, tense Scottish woman who has come here with her illegitimate daughter, Flora, to marry a man she has never met. At the age of six, Ada stopped speaking. Why, no one knows, "not even me," her inner voice tells us. But, that voice continues, "I don't think of myself as silent. I have my piano."

Her new husband, Stewart, a dour, introverted farmer, has no time for such luxuries as a piano, and refuses to transport it over the rough, muddy terrain to his farm. A neighbor, Blaine, who has adopted some of the native Maori ways, including their facial markings, takes the piano and strikes a bargain with Ada: He will trade piano lessons for its return. But Blaine, played with a lovely, humble touch by Keitel, wants more than lessons. He wants Ada, is mad for her, and sets about wooing her in one of the most erotic yet discreet courtships I've ever seen on-screen.

Flora, a bright, precocious child, betrays the couple and precipitates a terrible vengeance. Paquin is nothing short of awesome in this major, complex role, for which she won the Best Supporting Actress Oscar. Way to go, Chicklet! Hunter won a Best Actress Oscar for her portrayal of Ada—a stiff-necked, spirited woman whose huge dark eyes blaze with anger and passion. Neill, as Stewart, also speaks volumes without talking much, expressing a torrent of emotions. A third Oscar went to Campion for screenwriting, and nominations were earned in directing, cinematography, costume design, and film editing.

Visually, *The Piano* is enthralling. Outdoor shots are mystical and strange, contrasting with the comfortable Britishness of the interiors.

An outdoor scene in moody gray-green is followed by an inside close-up of a brilliantly painted china cup and saucer. And the climactic scene is smashing. Okay, *now* I'm speechless. **GC**

CT Ditto. And it's even better the second time.

AR Finally, a Campion movie I really appreciated, mostly because of Neill and Keitel, who act the skirts off Hunter.

PICNIC

1955. 113 min. Kim Novak, William Holden, Rosalind Russell, Arthur O'Connell. Dir. Joshua Logan

Ooh, this movie sizzles. Ripe-as-a-peach Novak and studly Holden burn hot as a prairie fire in this hugely popular adaptation of William Inge's Pulitzer Prize-winning play. She's a teenage pageant queen, and he's a charming drifter, and the setting is the Labor Day picnic in small-town Kansas. It's middle America distilled into sunset and fireflies to the tune of "Moonglow."

You've never seen Holden so in-your-face sexual—literally so in one humid scene where his crotch hovers just inches away from Russell's hungry eyes. And the subplot with Russell and O'Connell and their on-again, off-again romance merits a movie of its own.

There's a terrific supporting cast, the sound track is dreamy, and *Picnic* won a slew of awards, including six Oscar nominations and two winners, for Best Art Direction/Set Decoration and Best Film Editing. It's lost none of its heat in 40-odd years. And I thought the '50s were bland. Jeez, Louise, not in Kansas. **GC**

AR The director took a chance on Novak as Madge, and the movie made her a star. She's so often discounted as an actress, maybe because she was so unbelievably blond, but here and in *Vertigo* (page 139) she really struts her stuff. And Holden takes his shirt off a lot.

CT The message? All a woman needs is a brawny, studly man around—so what if he's a flitty, no-good loser. Holden doesn't work for me as a sex symbol, either, although the rooster in the henhouse stuff is hysterical shtick.

WILLIAM SHAKESPEARE'S ROMEO & JULIET

1996. 120 min. Leonardo DiCaprio, Clare Danes. Dir. Baz Luhrmann

This ingenious '90s updating of Will's tale of star-crossed lovers inspires either love or hate. If you think the idea of having the prologue read by a TV newswoman in newscasterese is brilliant, then you'll probably love the rest of the film, too. It's evident from the start—as a helicopter swoops over Mexico City and skyscrapers topped with the corporate monikers of Montague and Capulet—that the filmmakers are having fun with the context while being faithful to the text. Contemporary gangs of Montagues and Capulets fight with guns rather than swords. This makes the action more violent than we're used to, but it is also probably closer in tone to the violence of the sixteenth century, when swords were deadly rather than quaint and theatrical.

This is the kind of flick you want to see at least twice to make sure you catch the extravagant, sly, and witty details, like the boarded-up storefront that says GLOBE THEATER, and the Rosenkrantskys snack stand. Danes and DiCaprio, who have gotten where they have in Hollywood on sheer talent, also happen to have movie-star looks. (See DiCaprio as the retarded brother in *What's Eating Gilbert Grape?*, page 36, and Danes as the dying sister in *Little Women*, page 183.) Good looks alone wouldn't mean much if the puppy love didn't sizzle between Danes and DiCaprio, and it does. Shakespeare's words have not been altered, and somehow it works. My advice: See the Franco Zeffirelli version, with the unbelievably dreamy Leonard Whiting, first. Then watch this one. **CT**

AR   It took me a while to get into the swing of this thing. I closed my eyes and listened to Shakespeare's words for a stretch, and then it pulled me in.

GC   I thought this movie was dynamite, especially Danes. I've never seen a Juliet who looked and sounded so like a crazy-in-love teenager. Shakespeare for the masses, as I bet he intended it to be.

SEA OF LOVE

1989. 113 min. Ellen Barkin, Al Pacino, John Goodman.
Dir. Harold Becker

The New York City cops keep getting called to check out guys found in their beds wearing only a bullet in their heads. The cops have a hunch it could be a female serial killer, one of those lonely New York women who finally found something more interesting to do on a Saturday night than buy a pint of Häagen-Dazs and a Sunday *Times* at the corner deli. So the cops set up this undercover operation, placing an ad in a personals column and waiting for the chicks to come calling. Pacino, as Detective Frank Keller, meets them at a restaurant as a potential date and buys them a glass of wine. Goodman, as the waiter/undercover cop, takes their wine glass, checks it for fingerprints. Ba-bing. If they get a match, they've got their killer. But one date gets away without leaving her prints behind (Barkin). She does leave Keller's heart going pitter-patter, however. He asks her out on another date. Then another. Meanwhile, none of the other prints match the killer's. Could Barkin's? Her cravings for hot, nasty sex do suggest she could be a dangerous woman (but, then, so could some of my friends). It kept me on the edge of my seat all the way through. **CT**

GC   Edgy, steamy story with beaucoup atmosphere and plenty of bang, not to mention bangs, for your buck.

AR   Yessiree, *this* is a sweaty movie, and not only because Barkin and Pacino leave you fanning yourself. There's good detecting stuff going on, too.

And for the Real Thing . . .

As you know, combustion isn't eternal only *on*-screen. Consider Hepburn and Tracy, or Bogart and Bacall, or Newman and Woodward. And if you forget about the "eternal" part, the list grows longer to embody the likes of Warren Beatty and anyone with whom he's ever made a movie, including Madonna, and Madonna and anyone with whom

she's ever made a movie, including Beatty. See if you can
match the men on the left with the women on the right:

Cruise	Barkin
Quaid	Paltrow
Johnson	Griffith
Coen	Kidman
Pitt	Griffith
Danson	Taylor
Banderas	Ryder
Depp	Goldberg
Fisher	McDormand
Byrne	Ryan

(answers see p. 278)

HE DONE HER WRONG, SHE DID HIM IN

"Well, I guess I've done murder. Oh, I won't think about that now. I'll think about that tomorrow."
—*Vivien Leigh, in* Gone With the Wind

So he cheated/lied/left his socks on the floor/fill in the blank/once too often? Herewith, some suggested videos for seeing that it never happens again. Not that you actually need to follow through. In fact, we recommend that you not do so. Some of these chicks obviously were not thinking of the effects of their actions on perfectly good clothes, carpets, and furnishings—oh, yes, and on the children. It's usually enough, we've found, to just watch the video. In extreme cases, you might suggest that he watch it with you. (There's a very satisfying scene with an angry woman, a rapist, and a pitchfork in *Antonia's Line,* page 168, that will probably get his attention.) If this still doesn't do the trick, my sister knows a woman in Chicago. Four thousand tops, no questions. Call me. **GC**

ARSENIC AND OLD LACE

1944. 118 min. Cary Grant, Priscilla Lane, Raymond Massey, Peter Lorre. Dir. Frank Capra. b&w

"Insanity runs in my family," confides Grant's character, Mortimer, in this rib-tickling black comedy. "It practically gallops." He's right. His elderly aunts, Martha and Abby Brewster, have an endearing habit of inviting aged gentlemen into their stately Brooklyn home for a glass of homemade elderberry wine. Poisoned wine. Why, asks a horrified Mortimer, would they put poison in wine? Because, they explain patiently, when they put it in tea, it has a distinct odor. By now they have eleven—or is it twelve?—bodies buried in the cellar. Oh, yes, and one in the window seat.

There's also a brother who thinks he's Teddy Roosevelt, two bona fide murderers on the lam (the goofily eerie Lorre and Massey), and Mortimer's new bride. But you can sort all that out for yourself. I was too busy laughing to care.

Cynthia and Anne are quibbling that nobody actually done the Brewster sisters wrong before they did them in. Technically that's true, but I don't care about that, either. They're so adorable, I wanted to include them, and they'd be thrilled to know they made it into such wicked company. **GC**

AR　　Quibbling aside, it's jolly, and Grant is *so* young!

CT　　It's just too wacky for its own good. I'm almost embarrassed for Grant—doing bug-eyed double takes like he belonged on *The Carol Burnett Show*.

DIABOLIQUE

1955. 114 min. Simone Signoret, Vera Clouzot, Paul Meurisse. Dir. Henri-Georges Clouzot. b&w. French w/subtitles

"Your salads are rotten," are the first words of this classic thriller, spoken by the maid at a seedy boys' school to the delivery man. That's not all that's rotten in this tale of lust, greed, betrayal, and murder—my favorite movie ingredients.

Michel, the sadistic principal, played by Meurisse, abuses his sickly, religious wife, Christina (Clouzot), while carrying on an affair with Nicole, a cynical, ruthless teacher with a murky past (Signoret). Nicole persuades Christina that they must kill the loathsome Michel, and sets the plan in motion. The suspense builds slowly and thoroughly, so that by the time our hearts are jumping out of our throats, we understand thoroughly the motivations of the two conspirators—or do we?

A milestone in the suspense genre, *Diabolique* set a high standard, and is still without equal after almost half a century. There's a warning after the movie not to spoil your friends' enjoyment by divulging the ending. Here's another one: Don't even *think* of renting the sorry 1996 remake with Sharon Stone and Isabelle Adjani. **GC**

CT   This flick is nothing less than the ultimate black-and-white thriller.

AR   Chilling and intelligent. I bet Hitchcock went to his grave wishing he'd made it.

I LOVE YOU TO DEATH
1990. 96 min. Kevin Kline, Tracey Ullman, Joan Plowright, River Phoenix. Dir. Lawrence Kasdan

This funny, complex movie is based on the true story of a pizzeria owner, Joey, played by Kline, whose doting wife, Rosalie (Ullman), discovers he is cheating on her big time. A devout Catholic, Rosalie doesn't believe in divorce, so murder is her only option. Her mother, Nadja (Plowright), is all for it. "In America," she proclaims in her fractured, middle-European accent, "people kill each other left and right. It's national pastime." So they launch an enthusiastic, if not very effective, campaign to fix Joey's wagon, including drug-laced spaghetti, a car bomb, bludgeoning and bullets.

Obviously in need of professional help—the groggy, bruised, and gunshot Joey thinks he has the flu—they finally recruit two cousins, Harlan and Marlin (William Hurt and Keanu Reeves), to finish him off. I still giggle when I think of these two slo-mo, 'lude-addled dudes. They are priceless, arriving by taxi, in a dense but amiable pharmaceutical fog, to perform their dastardly deed.

There's a wonderful scene when everybody's done their worst, and Joey, still the genial host, crawls out of bed to offer refreshments all around. It's funny, it's poignant, and somehow very real for all its absurdity. It alone is worth the rental. Kline's Joey is maybe too broadly played at times—he does love those accents—but Ullman and Plowright, who look amazingly like mother and daughter, are perfectly tuned. The movie drags a little finally, as it ties up all its loose ends, but that's a small price to pay for meeting Harlan and Marlin. **GC**

AR   How on earth could you not appreciate *French Kiss,* in which Kline's French accent is almost as stupid as his Italian accent here? He's great.

CT   This movie always felt like it was missing something, and I was never sure what it was. Plus, there's only so many times you can watch Keanu staring vacantly into space. Watching this flick is like getting a pizza delivered, opening the box, and finding nothing there.

JAGGED EDGE
1985. 108 min. Glenn Close, Jeff Bridges. Dir. Richard Marquand

Close is a lawyer whose skirts are too tight, and Bridges is her possibly slimy but very good-looking client, who may or may not have killed his extremely rich wife in a sensational murder consummated with a jagged-edged knife that has all of Los Angeles in its O.J.-like clutches. From the start you're suspicious of the fellow played by Bridges, an accomplished actor who here is purposely and smartly hard to figure out, though you do understand his lawyer falling in love with him.

Close performs with her emotions much closer to the surface, sometimes right over the surface, which is essential to keeping things moving, and to you guessing whether the lawyer is right to trust her client and to doubt the sleazy and quite possibly downright dishonest district attorney (Peter Coyote, in one of his great supporting roles) for whom she once worked on a nasty case with an unhappy ending. Phew! Robert Loggia is a hard-drinking investigator, and he and the defense attorney get along as well as she and the D.A. don't, almost as well as she and her client do. At the end you'll applaud the lady's retort to a man who didn't treat her right: Make sure the heel won't be able to ever come around for breakfast again. **AR**

GC   Excuse me. Did I miss something? This movie is a confusing mess, a complete waste of time and talent. The only bright spot is Loggia, and that's not enough. Skip it.

CT   Sometimes I so detest the main character, I lose interest in the rest of the movie; that's what happened here for me.

THE LAST SEDUCTION

1994. 110 min. Linda Fiorentino, Bill Pullman, Peter Berg. Dir. John Dahl

Fiorentino looks like she could kill a man with just her wardrobe—slice him open with a crease of her crisp white shirt, strangle him with her tight skirt, and inflict unspeakable horrors with her heels. But that would mean getting her hands dirty, and who needs that? She and her doctor fiancé (Pullman) sell some pharmaceutical cocaine that nets them nearly a million dollars. Then she decides she wants it all for herself. So she heads for the boonies, finds a naive enough guy, and lures him with bawdy sex in a variety of locales. Then she gets him to do her dirty work, aka getting rid of the tiresome spouse. I don't like the fact that *Seduction* fuels the stereotype that highly sexed women are all manipulative masterminds, but it is nice to see a woman kick some butt every now and then. Guys who ever thought about slaps across the face to keep their little ladies in line should rent this immediately. **CT**

GC Kick some butt, and then some! Fiorentino is evil incarnate, a loathsome sexual predator, devoid of the tiniest spark of decency. I like her a lot.

AR Manipulative lady, isn't she? And aren't the guys all stupidly, gloriously taken in by her?

MORTAL THOUGHTS

1991. 104 min. Demi Moore, Glenne Headly, Bruce Willis. Harvey Keitel. Dir. Alan Rudolph

This little jewel of a movie has not received the attention it deserves. It has an unusual premise for Hollywood: the friendship between two ordinary, working-class women. (Come to think of it, it's hard to find a movie outside of *Thelma and Louise* that explores the friendship between *any* kind of women.) Moore and Headley, bosom buddies from childhood in blue-collar Bayonne, New Jersey, prove their relationship is thicker than blood—Willis's blood, that is. He plays Headley's violent, drug-wasted husband, who comes to a bad end at the hands of one of the friends. But which one?

The mystery is sustained throughout, as a detective, played by Keitel, interrogates Moore about the night Willis was killed. Keitel, as usual, makes a minor role memorable and sympathetic. The frequent flashbacks flow seamlessly, the editing is sharp, and the settings ring true. So do all the performances. This was the movie that aroused my suspicions—confirmed later by *Pulp Fiction* and *Twelve Monkeys*—that Willis could act. And if you've only seen Moore in her tiresome Chick-as-Supreme-Avenger roles, you're in for a pleasant surprise. She's great, and so is Headly. So go rent this movie. With a girlfriend. **GC**

CT "Jewel," are you kidding? It has as much worth as a Cracker Jack toy, only it's less interesting.

AR Don't waste your time. The only thing you'll know at the end is that the reason Moore and not Headly became a Big Star is that Headly hired the wrong agent *and* the wrong personal trainer.

ONE DEADLY SUMMER

1983. 133 min. Isabelle Adjani, Alain Souchon. Dir. Jean Becker. French w/subtitles

Here's a very young-looking Adjani, giving a startling performance in a movie I stumbled on by accident. I can't believe I'd never heard of it before, it's so good. It's a story of revenge and regret, played out in a very small, very ordinary French town. Eliane, or "That Girl," as the townspeople call her, moved here a year ago with her German mother and reclusive, not-quite-all-there father. She shocks and titillates both young and old with her wild promiscuity and gutter mouth.

She meets Pin-Pon (Souchon), a nice, uncomplicated young guy with two brothers, a grumpy mother, and a stone-deaf aunt. Eliane soon tricks Pin-Pon into marrying her. Then we begin to find out why. Becker does a fine job of melding scenes of ordinary lives—dances, bars, soccer, and bike races—with Eliane's growing obsession, as she fixates on finding and punishing the three men who raped her mother almost twenty years ago, and left her pregnant with Eliane.

The story, which seemed to start out almost casually, builds in intensity and drama, as Pin-Pon begins to realize he's married more than a hot little hussy, and as Eliane reveals more and more of her troubled soul. By the inevitable, heart-stopping climax, we realize how far we have come in a couple of hours. It's an unusual movie with a powerful impact. **GC**

CT   What is this obsession Gabrielle has with gutter-mouth chick movies? And is there a French movie in history that isn't sexist to the core? I'd pass on this one.

AR   Now, now. It's not as bad as, say, *Wish You Were Here* (page 28), but it ain't no *French Kiss* (page 259).

More Justifiable Homicides

Name the movie

1) Maybe she killed him, maybe she didn't, but she went to the gas chamber, anyway, and won an Oscar for Susan Hayward.

2) In a riveting, unusual movie, Miranda Richardson plays the last woman executed for murder in Britain.

3) When her husband is accidentally killed on their wedding day, Jeanne Moreau tracks down and kills the five men responsible in this French movie directed by François Truffaut.

4) She cheats on her husband, who hires a creepy character to kill her and her boyfriend. He shouldn't have done that. The first movie, and a great one, by our favorite director-writer-producer siblings.

5) Playwright David Mamet's directorial debut stars Joe Mantegna as a slimy but charismatic con man and Lindsay Crouse as a psychiatrist who resorts to unprofessional measures to nail him.

(answers see p. 279)

twelve

A WAIL OF A GOOD TIME

*"Cry? I never knew a woman that size had so much
water in her!"*
—Tony Randall, in Pillow Talk

A chick never forgets the first time she wept at the movies, and
whether she had tissue at the ready or was reduced to blowing her
nose on her date's shirtsleeve. For me, it was as a teenager in a
crowded theater during the last hour of a New Year's Eve viewing
of *Love Story.* Very embarrassing, even though every other female
in the house was boo-hooing, too. Some enjoy cinema-induced
sniveling in groups, but I prefer blubbering in isolation, so these
days, I give the ducts a rest unless I'm alone in front of the VCR
at home. And now and then I search the rental store *specifically* for
sniffle-sure videos—because sometimes the only cure for what ails
me is a good tear squall. Hollywood has produced some bang-up
weepers, the best listed below, including some that might even make
a fella cry. **AR**

FORREST GUMP
*1994. 142 min. Tom Hanks, Robin Wright, Mykelti William-
son, Gary Sinise, Sally Field. Dir. Robert Zemeckis*

Poor *Gump.* This movie about a not-too-bright but truly good man
crazed some critics as being a celebration of anti-intellectualism, as
if the message was that being dumb is a good idea and the pathway
to success. Thankfully, moviegoers knew better. Maybe because in
a culture that worships at the altar of overachievement and superstar-

dom, it's nice to see the validation of a man who's not a master of the universe.

Forrest Gump is a slow child, mentally, but he can run like the wind, and this talent combined with gobs of dumb luck propels him to heroism, fame, and wealth. The movie sweeps us through a cultural history of three decades of American life, through Vietnam, the counterculture '60s, the disco '70s, and then the computer-driven and AIDS-ridden '80s. Using some nifty technology Zemeckis puts Gump, Zelig-like, into a meeting with President Kennedy. Mostly it's a love story, of Gump's friendship with his army buddies (Williamson and Sinise) and his unrequited love for Jenny, his childhood friend and the sweetheart who never leaves his mind. I'm always sobbing by the end. The only clunker is Field as the mother. (Couldn't they have gotten someone more than a decade his senior for the part?) Note: Hanks and Zemeckis also won Oscars in this 1994 Best Picture winner. **CT**

AR Aw, heck. I waited forever to see this because it was so dang popular when it came out. And then, I *liked* it. And teared up, too.

GC Life may be like a box of chocolates, but this movie sure isn't. It's not even like a box of Kleenex. It left me dry-eyed and slightly nauseated.

FUNNY GIRL
1968. 151 min. Barbra Streisand, Omar Sharif. Dir. William Wyler

The best thing about *Funny Girl*—after the songs, Sharif's eyes and accent, Streisand's wonderfully pre-Streisand-like performance, and Kay Medford's perfect turn as a wisecracking Jewish mother—is that it will jerk at least one tear out of even the hardest hard-heart you know. The real-life Fanny Brice was the most celebrated comedian of her day, a kid from the Lower East Side who early in the century became an unlikely star of Florenz Ziegfeld's famous Follies. She not only had fame, but love, too, for a while, with charming gambler Nicky Arnstein.

Streisand and Sharif are truly believable in their roles here, which they're so often not elsewhere, and their characters' tragic romance is backed up with a wow 'em musical production that mixes dancing with slapstick with songs written to be absolutely belted out. Which Streisand does. This movie launched her into the superstardom she occupies today—she won the Oscar for Best Actress—but you may not recognize in *Funny Girl* the self-conscious control freak she is alleged to have become in recent years. Her Fanny is fresh and funny and ill-fated. She grows up, sadder but wiser, before our eyes. You'll probably already be snuffling into the seat cushions by the time she sings "My Man," which will do you in for sure. **AR**

GC   A must-see, but in spite of, not because of, the no-sparks relationship. (He's awful cute, but an awful actor, too.) Streisand is magnificent, and the music is great. But a weepie? Nah.

CT   And the movies don't get any more romantic than this. Can you pass me another hankie? I'll take Gabrielle's.

SOUNDER
1972. 105 min. Paul Winfield, Cicely Tyson, Kevin Hooks. Dir. Martin Ritt

This is a haunting, lovely movie, one that appeals, on different levels, to all ages, and one that is guaranteed to tug at the heartstrings. It's the story of an African-American sharecropper family in Louisiana during the Great Depression.

Nathan and Rebecca (Winfield and Tyson) are struggling to make a living for themselves and their three children when Nathan runs afoul of the law and is sent away to a work farm. David Lee (Hooks), the oldest child, becomes the man of the house. By the time Nathan returns, Rebecca, the children, and their dog, Sounder, have all been put to the test.

Sounder could have been pretty sanctimonious and clichéd. It's not; it's touching and tender, thanks to strong, earthy performances from Tyson and Winfield. They also generate a definite sexual heat, which adds to the realism, and young Hooks is impressive in his screen debut as David Lee. Taj Mahal, who also appears in the movie, composed the beautiful, spiritual-inspired music, which **alone** always makes me blubber. **GC**

AR   Even though you absolutely know that Ritt is working over-time to turn on your taps, it doesn't matter. Actually, you'll appreciate it.

CT   It's like watching a short story—literature comes to the big screen, and I mean that in the best way possible. A truly memorable film.

STAGE DOOR
1937. 92 min. Katharine Hepburn, Ginger Rogers, Ann Miller, Lucille Ball, Eve Arden, Adolphe Menjou. Dir. Gregory La Cava

The dialogue sounds like what we're used to hearing around the Conner dinner table on *Roseanne:* blue-collar, irreverent, sarcastic, and fast and sharp as they come. The setting is the Footlights Club, where starving actresses can get cheap lodgings and a dinner every night, even if it is a glutinous lamb stew. Jobs are hard to come by—sugar daddies not much easier—so the girls have a lot of time to hone their barbs at one another. They don't have great theatrical ambitions; they just want to be in a show and maybe have a guy take them to dinner now and then. Then Terry Russell (Hepburn) shows up, a hoity-toity debutante with high-brow ideas about *the theater,* and trunks of fancy clothes. The girls are repulsed by and envious of her wealth, and find her discussions on Shakespeare as fascinating as the has-been actress who wheezes on about the old days. No-nonsense Terry is determined to make it on her own using just her smarts. She finds out too late that smarts alone aren't enough in the acting business, which leads to a tear-jerking climax. Seeing the likes of Ball, Rogers, et al., in one funny, smart, emotional movie is a gas. High ratings for this chick classic! **CT**

AR   As a chick, I should love this. And I agree that many of the lines are dynamite. (After all, it's where Hepburn made the "calla lilies" speech that followed her around for decades.)

But there's so much going on and so much yakkity-yak that I need to nap halfway through.

GC   Entertaining ensemble piece, but on the whole more cheery than weepy.

SUNRISE
1927. 110 min. George O'Brien, Janet Gaynor, Margaret Livingston. Dir. F. W. Murnau. b&w. silent

This is one of the most beautiful, unusual movies I have ever seen. It's a silent film, in black and white—two strikes against it for many viewers—but it is so full of emotion and so visually gorgeous that it is unforgettable.

Subtitled *A Song of Two Humans,* the movie has a simple plot. The main characters are called the man, the woman, and the woman from the city, played respectively by O'Brien, Gaynor, and Livingston. Infatuated with the woman from the city, the man, a poor farmer, is persuaded by her that he must kill his wife and come with her to the city. He will take his wife on a boating trip and drown her, making it look like an accident.

The couple sets off, he starts to carry out his plan, then cannot. What follows—his shame, her horror, their gradual reconciliation over a day's outing, and the final wrenching drama—is remarkable. The lack of sound is actually a powerful asset as we become voyeurs, following the couple through scenes of pathos, sweetness, and humor.

Director Murnau, who came to Hollywood from Germany after the success of his atmospheric vampire classic *Nosferatu* (1922), took elaborate pains to achieve the Impressionistic, painterly look of *Sunrise.* He used midgets and children dressed as adults to suggest distance, and employed the techniques of Renaissance artists to achieve perspective. He made the screen a canvas. His efforts were rewarded with a special Oscar for a "Unique and Artistic Picture." It is that, and more. It's a gem. **GC**

AR   Once again, I recommend the exercise-while-watching method. But it's good, so watch out—if you become engrossed, you might sprain something.

CT   Don't pay any attention to Anne; the music is part of the experience. Sit down and relax. It would be a shame to miss any of this one.

TO KILL A MOCKINGBIRD
1962. 129 min. Gregory Peck, Mary Badham, Phillip Alford. Dir. Robert Mulligan

If you're about to be attacked by a swarm of racists in small-town Alabama, it sure doesn't hurt when your kids jump in front of you to avert the mob. Not if you're a white man, at least, which is what happens when the townsfolk have their collective heart set on lynching black defendant Tom Robinson and find his white lawyer, Atticus Finch, blocking the way. One thing that's so appealing about this movie, shot in black and white, is how quietly it's played. This face-off and an emotional courtroom scene are not filled with pomp and histrionics or swelling violins but are some of the most moving, weep-inducing scenes I've ever seen.

Peck won the Oscar for his portrayal of Finch, a noble, principled man. It's also one of the most evocative movies of childhood, just as the novel by Harper Lee was. Scrappy Scout (Badham) and her brother, Jem (Alford), have the usual childhood fears of things that go bump in the night, but they also become targets of hatred when their father takes the Robinson case. This would definitely go on my top 10 list. **CT**

AR   I can't count the number of times I've rented this and stayed up late to watch it on TV. Every time, I want to marry Peck and adopt his children.

GC   I agree, it's a lovely movie. And look for Robert Duvall in his screen debut in a small but pivotal role.

A TREE GROWS IN BROOKLYN
1945. 128 min. Peggy Ann Garner, James Dunn, Dorothy McGuire, Joan Blondell. Dir. Elia Kazan

Just when you think the sad parts are all over with and we're headed toward the denouement, there's a sob-inducing scene that strikes again. Keep several hankies ready for this flick about a little girl trying to hold on to her dreams when the world's conspiring to crush them. Garner won a special children's Oscar for her performance as Francie in this drama about a turn-of-the-century family living in a New York City tenement. This is a movie to show to a kid who's complaining about not having the latest video game or computer (although these ploys never really work, do they?). Francie's beautiful but haggard mother, Katie (McGuire), mops the floors of the tenement to help makes ends meet. Her beloved father, Johnny Nolan (Dunn), is a good-hearted alcoholic and big-time dreamer who makes everyone around him feel special. As he goes on about how he's gonna make it big someday after returning home from one of his infrequent waitering gigs, Katie frets over how to feed Francie and her brother. All this is livened by Francie's childhood joys and by Blondell as Aunt Sissy, the serial-marrier. **CT**

AR   The great Blondell again! The movie is timeless, better for me just because she's in it. (Alice Faye was initially considered for the Aunt Sissy role, can you imagine?)

GC   As a child, Betty Smith's book made me into a reader. I loved this story. So I was relieved to find that the movie is just as wonderful, and just as sob-inducing.

TRULY MADLY DEEPLY
1991. 107 min. Juliet Stevenson, Alan Rickman. Dir. Anthony Minghella

Nina and Jamie (Stevenson and Rickman) are lovers. When Jamie dies suddenly, Nina is devastated and withdraws into her rat-infested apartment, grieving, playing the piano over and over, imagining that he is accompanying her on the cello, as he did in life.

Suddenly, there he is, and I like what happens next. Nina goes almost mad with joy, cries, screams, pinches him, asks him what it feels like to be dead. Where did he go? Is there a heaven? Will he stay? It's a normal person's reaction, which is the strength of this unusual and affecting movie. Director and writer Minghella (who made it big soon after with *The English Patient*) wrote the screenplay specifically for Stevenson, and I can see why. She's completely believable. And Rickman, who stole the show as the evil, campy Sheriff of Nottingham in Kevin Costner's *Robin Hood: Prince of Thieves,* gives a tender, moving performance.

The charm of this movie lies in its realistic treatment of an overwhelming grief and how life gradually elbows its way back in. When Jamie's dead friends start dropping over to watch videos and rearrange the furniture, Nina draws the line. The ache of losing a lover and acknowledging that loss is expressed in a scene where Jamie quotes a Pablo Neruda poem. It begins: "Forgive me if you are not living, if you, beloved, my love, have died." It's a beautiful poem. It's a beautiful movie. **GC**

AR Truly, madly, deeply do I wish Rickman (also grand in *Sense and Sensibility,* page 182) would knock on my door one night, even with a bad Spanish accent and cold lips. He tugs at my heart. So does the movie.

CT Touching little movie—I'm a sucker for a cello. I'd love to see more of Stevenson, too.

WUTHERING HEIGHTS
1939. 104 min. Merle Oberon, Laurence Olivier, David Niven. Dir. William Wyler

Good books don't always make for good movies, but this time we got lucky—real lucky. This novel by Emily Brontë, one of the most passionate love stories in literature, also rates as one of the best movies of all time. (Eight Oscar nominations, a winner for photography—which is *really* impressive, since all those barren Yorkshire moors were shot in sunny California.) Olivier and Oberon, both at their most drop-dead beautiful, play the star-crossed lovers, the darkly brooding gypsy Heathcliff and the refined, spoiled Cathy. Growing up together, the two pledge eternal love, but Cathy's essentially a material girl and marries a milksop neighbor for security, whereupon the wounded Heathcliff charges off to make his fortune, comes back, marries the milksop's sister in revenge, makes everybody miserable, and the lovers realize too late that they were fated to be together, that their love transcends all boundaries, even life itself.

I've seen this movie a gazillion times, and it never fails to melt my heart and reduce me to tears. (And I'm no pushover. Bambi's just another deer to me.) The fierce intensity of the emotions, the jealousy, the despair, the longing . . . the howling wind and the racing clouds. And such words! On her wedding day, Cathy feels "a cold wind across my heart." Later, Heathcliff, mad with remorse and grief, pleads with his departed love: ". . . do not leave me in this dark alone where I cannot find you. I cannot live without my life. I cannot die without my soul." And when the housekeeper speaks the last words of the movie, I always join in, through my choking sobs: "Good-bye, Heathcliff. Good-bye, my wild, sweet Cathy." **GC**

AR   I never burst into tears, not even feel a sniffle coming on. But that's not to say it isn't very, very good.

CT   I think Yorkshire-bred Gabrielle just misses the moors. I've not so much as gotten misty-eyed, either, but I would like to sit down and watch it in front of a fire on a dark and stormy night

And if Those Don't Jerk Your Tears, CT, Chief Chick Cryer, Has a Few More for You

In junior high school my girlfriends and I observed an annual ritual of plopping down in front of the TV together and heaving and sobbing through the last hour of *Brian's Song,* a, need I say, made-for-TV movie. Anyhow, maybe it was that bawling bonding experience that makes me wish they would sell hankies with the popcorn and Milk Duds. Even when I know I'm being shamelessly manipulated, I'm a pushover for Hollywood types whose jobs are to extract tears from moviegoers. Here are some movies that suck the saline out of my eyeballs despite my better judgment:

Terms of Endearment (1983): A classic weeper, sure, but Debra Winger just keeps dying and dying and dying till I'm really sick of her . . . but I keep on crying nonetheless.

Mr. Holland's Opus (1995): *Hated* the movie with Richard Drey-fuss as the proto-inspirational music teacher who ignores his own son . . . but did that matter to the ol' tear ducts? Not a bit.

E.T. (1982): Yes, I began dripping when the life started draining out of the adorable, bulbous-headed, beer-drinking creature, even though I kept telling myself, he's just an alien.

Bambi, Old Yeller, or any other movie where animals get their paws or their feelings hurt are almost unbearable. To this day I can't watch *Lassie Come Home.*

thirteen

HUNKS

"Did you see his butt?" —*Geena Davis,*
in Thelma & Louise

What do *we* chicks like in a guy? Let's see, we, too, may comment on a nice butt, but we mean that metaphorically of course. You won't find steroid-bulging tough guys in this chapter—no Arnold, no Sly, no Jean-Claude Van Damme, who are, after all, guys' guys. Who wants to look at monosyllabic greased-up muscle men with big guns? (Okay, Anne does, but that's her problem.) We're more concerned with what a guy has going on in his head—whether he be an angel, a carpet cleaner, or a political hack—than in his abs. Bods aren't everything. Jimmy Stewart, not your stereotypical sexy guy but sexy nonetheless, once blanched at the idea of showing up on the set of *The Philadelphia Story* without his shirt. "If I appear in a bathing suit, I know it's the end of me. I know that and I'm prepared to end my career, but it will also be the end of the motion picture industry." And note: The ever dignified Denzel Washington—who *does* just happen to look mighty good *déshabillé*—kept on popping up here, so we had to farm out his movies to other chapters and give some other guys a chance. **CT**

DEVIL IN A BLUE DRESS
1995. 102 min. Denzel Washington, Tom Sizemore, Jennifer Beals, Don Cheadle. Dir. Carl Franklin

Move over, powdered rhinoceros horn. I've found the perfect aphrodisiac: a plain, white, cotton singlet, as worn by Washington on several occasions (thank you, God) in this movie. It's the perfect frame for his perfect frame—those smooth-as-satin, packed-just-right shoulders, that sculptured neck . . . oh, my. In our first glimpse of him, in That Singlet, it's 1948 in Los Angeles, and Easy Rawlins has just been fired and is considering taking on a suspiciously simple assignment: Just find a woman, a white woman who's hiding out in a black area of town. He needs to pay the mortgage on his beloved, tidy little house (don't you adore a hunk who actually loves and takes care of a house and yard?) and he's been around the block a few times, so he signs on.

Based on Walter Mosley's novel, *Devil in a Blue Dress* is of the film noir persuasion. But with a difference. It's seen from a predominately black point of view, a rarity in that genre. And it works beautifully, delving into the music, fashions, and lifestyles of L.A.'s black community, as Easy gets sucked into a quagmire of race, politics, and brutish behavior from all ethnic quarters. And speaking of brutish, there's a terrific, scary turn here by someone I'd never seen before. Don Cheadle plays Mouse, a hair-trigger, psychopathic buddy of Easy's who just about steals the show. The woman Easy is looking for, Daphne, is played by Beals, who couldn't steal so much as a glance. Not from me, anyway, not when Easy's wearing That Singlet. Hell, I'd probably go for him even without it. **GC**

AR Bill Clinton thinks he made Mosley's novels famous by telling reporters Mosley is his favorite mystery writer. Wrong. It's Washington who made Mosley famous—you'll rush out to buy the Easy books after you eject the video, so you can read a few chapters in bed and then dream about Denzel.

CT Yes, it's true, Denzel's probably one of five men in America who looks good in a sleeveless T-shirt, which is what Gabrielle means when she says singlet. (If only the 3 million men who wear them would realize they're not among the other four.) The movie, though, failed to press any buttons with me.

FOUR WEDDINGS AND A FUNERAL

1994. 118 min. Hugh Grant, Andie MacDowell, Kristin Scott Thomas, Simon Callow, Corin Redgrave. Dir. Mike Newell

Guys think that blinking, bumbling, and stuttering are not exactly the suave traits a woman looks for in a guy. But shyness and fear

combined with the right amount of dimply charm and carefully tou-
sled locks can do a lot for the ol' heart rate. Look at Hugh Grant.
Isn't he adorable! You just want to pinch his cheeks, all of them.
As the English upper crust Charlie, he's a perpetual bachelor who
spends all his time going to weddings. At one of them he happens
upon Carrie (MacDowell, in a hat as wide as a Hula Hoop). They
keep bumping into each other at weddings, hers among them, until,
well, something happens, and I won't say whether the funeral has
anything to do with it. I will say this movie is as much fun as trying
on a big white meringue wedding dress with all the lace and ruffles.
The supporting roles are superb, from the steely ice woman (Thomas)
to the aging Giliff (Callow), who just about spins off the screen in
a kilt.

A warning: *Four Weddings* could also go in the weepies chapter
because of the funeral scene, where the reading of the W. H. Auden
poem choked so many moviegoers with sadness that the dead poet
became a best-seller. And in the interest of fairness, I will say I
could have done without seeing Grant's pasty-white legs in shorts.
(P.S. Who cares about Divine Brown? This is a *movie*.) **CT**

GC   I, on the other hand, just want to pinch his snotty, irritating
little head off. The movie's quite pleasant otherwise, and the
poem's a killer.

AR   Thank goodness Cynthia recognizes at least *one* part of his
person as unattractive. There is hope! But not for the movie.
It drags, and MacDowell is irritating.

F / X

*1986. 107 min. Bryan Brown, Brian Dennehy. Dir. Robert
Mandel*

Gunmen strafe a crowded restaurant and make a mess: spurting
blood, exploding fish tanks, screeching patrons, airborne utensils. A
blonde begs to be spared, only to be thrown off her feet by the force
of the bullets. Then she stands up and asks the special effects man
how she did. "You were great," purrs Brown's character in that
beguiling Australian accent put to such seductive use in television's
The Thorn Birds. "Nobody dies like you." Nobody does special

effects—f/x, in Hollywood shorthand—like Rolie, which is why greasy government agents hire him to fake the assassination of Mafioso Jerry Orbach. He goes through with the job reluctantly, and if you're thinking you know what happens next, you're right, sort of. But director Mandel (who has a wry sense of humor) gets the predictable stuff out of the way in short order. Even Dennehy's smart New York cop, assigned to figure out why the bodies are piling up, has trouble determining who's doing what to whom and why. Special effects, of course, are cleverly used. And Brown—seen several times not wearing a shirt and once *just* in his underwear!—is dandy as the confused, frightened, and determined knockout who has, fortunately, set up a mobile special effects studio in his van. *F/X* is intelligent, suspenseful, and witty and should be watched with all the lights off. **AR**

GC   Yes, it's kinda clever, kinda fun, but not very. And no way is he a hunk. Anybody so unconcerned at what happened to his girlfriend automatically forfeits his hunk status in my book.

CT   Knockout? I didn't even notice he'd taken off his shirt.

THE LAST OF THE MOHICANS
1992. 122 min. Daniel Day-Lewis, Madeleine Stowe. Dir. Michael Mann

Goodness! When Day-Lewis comes thrashing out of the forest, musket in hand, hair flying, pectoral muscles screaming for attention—well, if you've never had the vapors before, slip this into the VCR. Day-Lewis is Hawkeye, the adopted son of Chingachgook, who with Chingachgook's son Uncas escorts a party of English soldiers and two pretty girls to an outpost where the British and French are battling it out over rights to North American in 1757. There's a lot of scalping and hacking of bodies and other savagery throughout, and it's very exciting. And the romance between Hawkeye and Cora (a glorious Stowe) is dreamy.

But nothing holds a candle to Day-Lewis (before filming started, he is alleged to have learned to load a flintlock rifle at full run) and his steely-eyed, come-hither, watch-out-I've-got-a-hatchet look. Your blood will rush when he tells Cora, "You be strong, you survive. You stay alive, no matter what occurs. I will find you. No matter how long it takes, no matter how far. I will find you—I will find you!" Yes! Please! Find me! After you get hold of yourself, you'll note that the scenery is luscious and the music is quadruple-stereo tremendous. A must-see for chicks who appreciate brawn on the run. **AR**

GC   I even lusted after him in *My Left Foot,* so don't expect me to be coherent about him in this movie, with his bare, smooth chest and rippling muscles and flowing flintlocks or whatever . . . oh, hell, just pass the smelling salts.

CT   Yes, girls, he's a beauty, but so is the scenery, Stowe, and the rest of the movie to boot—and I *thought* I was going to be bored.

ROMEO AND JULIET
1968. 138 min. Olivia Hussey, Leonard Whiting. Dir. Franco Zeffirelli

One of the most, maybe *the* most stunningly beautiful people I've ever seen on screen is Whiting as Romeo. (I can't resist adding that we get to see *all* of him, if you catch my drift.) It's the kind of beauty boys inevitably outgrow by the time they turn twenty, which Whiting was three years shy of when this movie was made. Okay, so I'm preoccupied by his looks, but then so is Juliet, and that's what this play is all about anyway. Just as beautiful as Whiting is the production itself, shot by Zeffirelli in Italy with meticulous and lush period detail, and Hussey as Juliet ain't nothin to sneeze at, either. This is no highfalutin mothballed classic. With its zesty sword fights, opulent party scenes, and bawdy banter, it has all the energy but not quite as much noise as the 1996 production by Baz Luhrmann (page 90). Hussey was fifteen when this was made, and it's hard to imagine the lovers' honeymoon bed scene getting made in these politically correct times, which is a shame. Sometimes you just wish people would lighten up. **CT**

AR I had a crush on Whiting in grade school. I think I *still* have a crush on him. Oh, and the film: radiant.

GC It's a gorgeous movie, so beautiful that Shakespeare takes a backseat to the visuals and the music, not to mention the dreamy Whiting.

TAP

1989. 111 min. Gregory Hines, Sammy Davis, Jr. Dir. Nick Castle

You might think of Hines as just an actor, not a dancer, and of Davis only as that gold-bechained '70s dude who made himself sadly infamous by hugging Richard Nixon on prime-time television. But both are dazzling tap masters, putting Gene Kelly and Fred Astaire to big-time shame, and both also share a sweet sincerity the camera loves. Beyond all that, Hines is just darn handsome, tapping or standing still, but particularly when he's in motion. (Why else would you have watched *White Nights*?)

Davis is Little Mo, the manager of a timeworn New York dance club. Hines is an ex-con trying to go straight by virtue of his gifted feet. The plot, predictable but heartwarming, shuffles itself out on three floors of a building on Times Square: the dance club on one; the tap school run by Little Mo's daughter on two; and the apartment on three, where Little Mo lives with a gang of aging tapsters played by some of the real-life best, including Sandman Sims, Bunny Briggs, and Jimmy Slyde. When they kick aside their canes to show their stuff, you'll marvel that tap-dancing went out of favor with Hollywood and Broadway. Maybe you'll wonder, too, about Davis, whose vaudevillian versatility (he started performing at age three) made him one of the best-loved entertainers of the '50s and '60s. No, I'm not suggesting you run out and rent *Robin and the Seven Hoods* to catch his chemistry with Frank Sinatra and Joey Bishop. But Davis, who died a year after *Tap* was filmed, shouldn't be remembered only as the shortest member of the Rat Pack or as the first well-known African-American Jew. (See? he was very interesting.) This movie reminds us of his great talent.

If you're rich and have one of those groovy VCRs with many bells and whistles, use the slo-mo feature on his dance scenes and

see if you can figure out how he does it. While you're at it, freeze
Hines at almost any moment for a loooong look. **AR**

GC   Just a glance is enough for me. All his sex appeal's in his
feet. But by all means FF past the nothing plot to the challenge dance, where all the tapsters strut their stuff. It's awesome. Question: How come it's always little white girls who
take tap lessons and only old black guys who get it right?

CT   All those great dancers together—the past, present, and future of tap—is reason enough to watch this movie. Plus,
Savion Glover—the tap genius responsible for the *return* of
tap to Broadway in the '90s (the star and creator of *Bring
in 'da Noise Bring in 'da Funk*)—makes his movie debut as
a savvy little kid here.

THREE DAYS OF THE CONDOR
*1975. 117 min. Robert Redford, Faye Dunaway. Dir. Syd-
ney Pollack*

A hit back in the Watergate era, *Three Days of the Condor* still
unnerves. Good-looking back in the Watergate era, Redford's '70s
physiognomy still inspires drools. His chin, his eyes, the way those
blond locks caress his forehead, his ever-so-slightly off-center nose—
oh, excuse me.
The movie covers seventy-two fewer tension-filled hours than
James Grady's book *Six Days of the Condor,* and thank goodness.
Another few minutes of it and I'd be eating the popcorn bag. Redford
is the sort of nerdy (okay, he's *supposed* to be sort of nerdy) reader
for the Literary Historical Society, a CIA front in New York. He's
worked there for years and the most excitement he's had at the office,
other than watching the coffee percolate and perhaps gazing at his
impressive visage in the mirror, is hitting on a particularly nicely
phrased bit of propaganda in a Soviet novel. Then, on the rainy day
that it's his turn to fetch sandwiches for lunch, his coworkers are
murdered while he's placing orders at the corner deli. Omigosh, this
reminds him of who his bosses are and that there's a Cold War going
on. He hasn't really been trained for this sort of thing, of course, and
his evolution into a cloak-and-dagger type—code name: Condor—is

fun. To save his hide and uncover the dastards behind the massacre, he kidnaps a photographer (Dunaway) and coerces her into helping him. Once she gets over being scared to the roots of her finely shaped eyebrows, does she find the spook rather attractive? You have to ask? **AR**

GC A classy movie with a terrific cast, a fast-moving plot, and Redford at the peak of his hunkness. And I like the glasses, too. I'd definitely make passes.

CT Yes, Redford's blondsomeness is knee-weakening, but I liked him even better with Paul Newman in *The Sting*.

THE WAR ROOM
1993. 93 min. James Carville, George Stephanopoulos. Dirs. Chris Hegedus, D. A. Pennebaker

Carville and Stephanopoulos have the charisma and sex appeal of Paul Newman and Robert Redford in this documentary about the 1992 presidential campaign of Governor Bill Clinton. In the Little Rock, Arkansas, war room they led a group of young political pre-hacks with college-style idealism as they reshaped political campaigns in jeans and T-shirts. Watch them brainstorm as they deal with each new crisis, tossing around ideas like they're playing a game of pickup basketball. Even if you're cynical about what happened after the election, it's hard not to be batting for this exuberant team, sincere in their goals even when they were cynical about their means. Most fictional movies don't come close to having the narrative buildup of this flick. You couldn't have written better dialogue than what spews out of the power mouths of Carville and George Bush aide Mary Matalin when they're spinning at centrifugal force. What more could you ask for than a great plot, dramatic tension, rat-a-tat dialogue and humor, all led by two dynamic stars who nearly burst off the screen? Because it follows the life span of a campaign, the movie has a defined beginning, middle, and end. It even builds into a weepie, melodramatic moment when crass Cajun Carville chokes up and all but cries like a baby. Cute, funny, smart, powerful, and, of course, sensitive; what more could you ask for in a guy? This is one of my favorites. **CT**

GC   Charisma, you say? This is a guy, Carville, whose own wife calls him "Serpent-head," and pint-size Stephanopoulos looks about 12—make that eight when he's blowing bubble-gum. But, to each her own. Luckily, the movie, and the course of history, don't hinge on their sex appeal. It's fascinating drama, but I would think only for Democrats. I doubt that many Republicans would want to revisit the pain.

AR   Weepie, my eye. When Carville chokes up, I want to knee him. Stephanopoulos uses too much hair spray. Sure, Clinton won, but *then* look what happened.

WINGS OF DESIRE

1988. 130 min. Bruno Ganz, Otto Sander, Peter Falk. Dir. Wim Wenders. German w/subtitles

In this lovely, poignant fantasy, two angels (Ganz and Sander) observe the people of West Berlin, eavesdropping on their thoughts and their lives, longing to escape their eternal isolation and to experience what it is to be human. "It would be quite something," muses Ganz's character, "to come home after a long day and feed the cat . . . to have a fever, to be excited by a meal, the curve of a neck . . ."

Their wistful fascination with all things human is beautifully expressed by director Wenders, both visually and verbally. The camera plays lovingly on faces, on everyday scenes, and the dialogue is infused by the vibrant, yearning poetry of Rainer Maria Rilke. (Are you getting the sense that I am madly in love with this movie?) Falk, playing himself, adds a nice dash of uncomplicated American warmth and practicality to a place and a people still frozen in the desolate aftermath of war.

This is the kind of movie that you just let wash over you, like a cooling breeze or a delicate scent. It's a remarkable experience. (I treat myself to random scenes from it occasionally, especially when the world's not as perfect as I would like.) And Bruno Ganz is my kind of angel: no robes, no wings, just a soft-spoken, sympathetic guy with warm eyes, a ponytail, and a good overcoat. Check him out. Often. **GC**

CT   Gabrielle's right. If I used the word *masterpiece,* I would use it here. Stronger connection to other arts—painting, poetry, photography—than most movies. But, hunks?

AR   Falk can be viewed through certain glasses as rather
hunklike, actually. He's but one of many fine ingredients
in a lyrical experience. At times I felt I was floating
myself.

THE YEAR OF LIVING DANGEROUSLY

*1983. 114 min. Mel Gibson, Sigourney Weaver. Dir. Peter
Weir*

An extraordinary sound track and the very best wet-from-the-rain-
smooch-in-a-stairwell ever filmed hooked me when I first saw this
in my impressionable moviegoing days. And I'm still smitten, with
the movie and with Mel. True, Weir's history is imprecise, to put it
kindly, but don't worry—he displays the politics of Indonesia in
1965 in such a jumble that you'll be too confused to be misled.
What's gripping is his ability to absolutely make you drip in the hot,
humid, strained atmosphere of Jakarta just before President Sukarno's
CIA-engineered undoing.

Gibson, as a ravishing Australian reporter on his inaugural over-
seas assignment, is led into the seedy shadows of Jakarta and the
breathtaking countryside by photographer Billy Kwan, the reporter's
tour guide and conscience. Billy was played so convincingly by
the brilliant Linda Hunt that American audiences had no idea that
she's a she and were surprised to learn she's not half Chinese;
Hunt won an Oscar for Best Supporting Actress, which alerted
folks to her gender, at least. Weaver is an embassy attaché who
loves the two physically mismatched but somehow spiritually con-
nected men.

The marriage of romance, deception, revolution, death, escape, and
ugly politics is impressive. And for those of you who insist on sus-
pecting that Gibson can't act, pay attention: Not only is he darn
good-looking, he roams so persuasively through a bundle of emotions
that you almost forget how fetching he is. Almost. **AR**

CT   And Mel looks so young! What a pup! Weaver looks exactly
the same today as she did when this flick came out fifteen
years ago. How nice to see the guy age faster for once.

GC   Yes, it's a good movie, and the setting is wonderfully captured. But will someone explain to me why Weaver, fresh
from kicking butt in *Alien,* took on this lightweight, Stick
Chick role?

> "I Never Could Wear Another Fella's
> Clothes. I'm Kinda Beefy Through the
> Shoulders." —William Holden, in *Picnic*

Actresses aren't the only ones to use a remarkable chest as a career
asset. Name the actor and movie in the following famous chest
scenes. (Hint: All of the flicks are in this book.)

- He wears a nervous-sweat-drenched, grimy T-shirt
  throughout the flick.

- When he took his shirt off, he changed the history of
  underwear in America.

- He took a break from more complicated characters to take
  off his shirt and run through the woods a lot in this flick.

- Rosalind Russell, one of the many small-town females who
  experienced a hormonal rush when he showed up, tore off
  his shirt in an embarrassing moment.

- He combined full-frontal chestal nudity with full-frontal
  nudity below in this film that gets pooh-poohed "a woman's movie."

- The first and ultimate roll-around-in-the-surf scene.

(answers see p. 279)

fourteen

BECAUSE I'M YOUR MOTHER, DAMMIT!

"Tonight, I want her to call me mother!"
—Bette Davis, in The Old Maid

It's the most elemental of relationships, the one between mother and daughter. Sure, the mother-son bond is strong, too. As that paragon of filial piety, Anthony Perkins, says in *Psycho* (1960): "A boy's best friend is his mother." And James Cagney, in *White Heat* (1949), goes up in flames with the words, "Made it, Ma! Top of the world!" Yes, we know their mums were the driving force in their careers, but it's not quite the same as having a daughter.

Not that it's always sweetness and light, but it's guaranteed to be intense. See Sophia Loren, a tigress trying to protect her cub, in the harrowing *Two Women* (1961); Joan Crawford battling her daughter for the same man in *Mildred Pierce* (1945); or Traccy Ullman going *mano-a-mano* with God for her religion-obsessed daughter in *Household Saints* (1993). And don't forget to call your mother. **GC**

ALIENS

1986. 137 min. Sigourney Weaver, Carrie Henn. Dir. James Cameron

Weaver is back and better than ever as Ripley, the sole survivor of a space voyage rudely interrupted by a burrowing alien. She's rescued after fifty-seven years in a sleep chamber, and awakens to find that everyone she knew is dead. The nightmares are so bad, she fears falling asleep, but not so much as she fears going back Out There. But she takes on the challenge, accompanied by an interesting gang of marine-type space cadets (the chicks as macho as the guys), and they run into some weirdos that have got to have Ripley longing for the comparative serenity of her old nightmares.

Why fight? Because the only human to have lived through the alien invasion of the space colony being visited by Ripley and the troops is a sweet little girl, played by Henn, who is clearly the answer to Ripley's suppressed maternal instincts and the reason for her to go on living, thankful she snoozed away those fifty-seven years. She'll save the kid, by golly, no matter how many ugly, oozing creepoids she has to blow away. It's rather intense and bloody—I mean slimy—but also extremely entertaining. One of the aliens is a mother protecting her brood, too, adding a nice psychological angle. *Aliens* is even better than the original. **AR**

GC   No it's not. The original was an original, a new idea. This is pretty good, but no way better.

CT   One was enough for me. Actually too much for me.

DOLORES CLAIBORNE
1994. 132 min. Jennifer Jason Leigh, Kathy Bates. Dir. Taylor Hackford

A taciturn, whiskey-slugging, Halcion-popping magazine writer returns home after her mother (Bates) is accused of murder. Oh, no, she's at it again, figures daughter Selena (Leigh), who's convinced that Mom offed her beloved pop some fifteen years ago. (A crime Selena never forgave her mother for, though it was never proved that she did it.) As Selena, Leigh plays a rather one-dimensional character as the consummate New York cold fish. 'Course with hackneyed lines like "I *need* this story" (puff puff, stamp out cigarette), who can blame her? But Bates's Dolores is harder to figure out. Many actresses do old by painting some lines on their faces and adding a few wisps of gray, but as the frumpy maid Bates looks worn out to the bones. Is she a seriously disturbed murderer, or just a selfless mother who's been tragically misunderstood? And what really happened to her husband fifteen years ago on the small island off the coast of Maine?

This movie's not only a gripping and moodily filmed whodunit, but an exploration of the weird and profound dynamics of the mother-daughter relationship. Memorable line: "Sometimes, Selena, being a bitch is all a woman has to hold on to." **CT**

GC   Bates acts rings around Leigh, and the relationship between Dolores and her old employer, played beautifully by Judith Parfitt, is also extraordinary. Let's face it, Bates is a powerful talent, and this movie is a great vehicle for her.

AR   No, Bates is *too* talented for this excuse for a thriller. I didn't believe Leigh for a minute—she's so obviously *acting*.

HIGH TIDE
1987. 101 min. Judy Davis, Jan Adele, Claudia Karvan. Dir. Gillian Armstrong. Australian

This movie has a great opening scene: Davis, in a blond wig and skimpy costume, playing backup to a really bad Elvis impersonator in a small Australian town. You have to love her for it. The rest of the movie is a class act, too. It's refreshing, realistic, and pulls no punches.

Lilli, Davis's character, is not doing much with her life. Soon fired from the Elvis gig, she's stranded in this small seaside town, and her car's cratered. She drinks too much, feels sorry for herself, and strikes up a casual friendship with a young teenager, Ally. When Lilli meets Bess, the grandmother who is raising Ally, the two women's faces tell the whole story. They look at each other, recognition dawns and, speechless, they turn and look at Ally. She is Lilli's daughter, born of Bess's son, who died shortly after Ally was born. Lilli, devastated by his death and unsure of her own potential as a mother, had given her baby to Bess to raise and had disappeared from their lives.

Thus begins a simple but searing tale, a drama rich with the details of small, messy lives, as Lilli finally stops running long enough to consider her actions and her options. It's painfully honest and unsentimental, thanks in large part to the brilliant performances of

Davis and Adele, who plays the gruff, resentful, but ultimately generous Bess. You can see why Armstrong likes working with Davis,
who starred in the director's earlier, well-received *My Brilliant Career*. They make a great team. **GC**

AR   An atmospheric original, with lots going on beneath the
surface.

CT   I'm a huge Davis fan—I like anyone with circles under their
eyes—and she's just as intriguing as ever in this good but
sloooooow flick.

MARNIE
*1964. 120 min. Tippi Hedren, Sean Connery, Diane Baker.
Dir. Alfred Hitchcock*

You'll suspect the character played by Connery is several flapjacks
short of a stack, but it's Louise Latham as a superbly loose-screwed
single mother who makes Marnie such a creepy success. Not often
on-screen, she's often on the mind of the viewer, who after a while
shudders at the thought of a childhood with her apron strings involved. Ish!
    Latham's Bernice is dear old mom to Hedren's Marnie, a compul-
sive thief inexplicably driven to hysteria by thunderstorms, the color
red, and men keen on kissing her. Connery is Mark Rutland, a book
publisher who knows all about Marnie's habit of filching from em-
ployers, hires her, anyway, and—this is when you really wonder
about his mental state—appears to fall in love with her. Not, however, she with him, which makes the honeymoon a bit of a bummer.
    The mystery of it all is unraveled by a return to Marnie's youth,
in a quite nicely done series of flashbacks. Watch closely: Hedren's
good, and you'll definitely see her real-life daughter Melanie Griffith
in her. **AR**

GC   Not one of my favorites. I don't think much of Hedren as
an actor, and the romance just doesn't work for me.

CT   I found her frigid, klepto character titillating enough to keep
me watching all the way through.

MERMAIDS

1990. 111 min. Cher, Winona Ryder, Bob Hoskins, Christina Ricci. Dir. Richard Benjamin

Cher plays Mrs. Flax, a trampy but lovable mother of two girls who packs up the family and leaves town whenever her latest love affair (usually with her boss) fizzles out. Ryder, as teenage Charlotte, rebels against her wanton mother by planning to become a nun and trying to live like a saint. The little kid, Ricci, adapts easily to the constant chaos, only concerning herself with her next swim meet. The movie starts with the arrival of the Flax family in a small New England town around the time Kennedy is shot. (*Mermaids* is loaded with cheesy sixties touches, from the goofy songs like "Mambo Italiano" to Cher's skintight pedal pants and teetering pumps.) The entire family falls for a pudgy shoe salesman played by Bob Hoskins, who's both charmed and bemused by the eccentric family that doesn't do normal things like eat dinner together. (Imagine, a time when eating together was normal!) In many ways Mrs. Flax is the mother we all want, loving and fun-loving and a great improvisor of dinners made with marshmallows and jelly beans, but she has this problem with intimacy and security. Just when the two girls are starting to feel at home, Mrs. Flax wants to head out of town. Finally, they rebel. This quirky movie's filled with characters that seem borrowed from an Anne Tyler novel—believably off-kilter and only slightly cinematic. **CT**

GC I admire all the actors, so I was disposed to like it, but they either tried too hard or not enough. It left me cold.

AR Don't know why, but I enjoyed this much more at home than when I saw it in the theater. Cher doesn't scare me so much on the small screen? Anyway, Hoskins is in it, so *of course* you must rent it.

POSTCARDS FROM THE EDGE

1990. 101 min. Meryl Streep, Shirley MacLaine, Dennis Quaid, Gene Hackman. Dir. Mike Nichols

Carrie Fisher never did much for me as an actress. I'm one of the few people in America who *hates Star Wars,* and in her other roles she always seemed sort of mopey and resentful. After watching *Post-cards* we know it's because she *was* mopey and resentful. Thankfully, as a writer she's a *lot* more fun. Based on her largely autobiographical novel, *Postcards* follows a not-so-young starlet (essentially Fisher, played by Streep) who battles a drug problem and her mother simultaneously. In Fisher's real life, mother Debbie Reynolds was dumped by husband Eddie Fisher for Elizabeth Taylor and never really got over it. *Postcards*'s theatrical mother MacLaine (in one of her zippiest roles ever) deals with the same thing. It's a gas watching the emotional hardball played by mother and daughter in this show-biz family, even though Streep is, well, mopey and resentful. One problem: The ending seems tacked on from some other movie, *Coal Miner's Daughter,* maybe. Memorable line: "I don't mind getting old. What I do mind is *looking* old." **CT**

GC I'd forgotten how much I enjoyed this movie. It's got a terrific cast, snappy one-liners, smart digs at Hollywood, and a great ending.

AR What was that other comedy Streep tried her hand at, the one with Roseanne? Fuggedaboudit. Here, she's funny, and MacLaine is a scream.

SECRETS & LIES
1996. 142 min. Brenda Blethyn, Marianne Jean-Baptiste. Dir. Mike Leigh

Here is one of those "sleeper" hits that wows prize-givers at places like Cannes, runs in most U.S. cities for just a few weeks at smallish, artsy theaters, then wins big attention for securing three Oscar nominations—Best Picture, Best Actress for Blethyn, and Best Supporting Actress for Jean-Baptiste—only to be released on video within a month. Go figure. But don't complain, because at least it's available, and in multiple copies, at mainstream rental stores. And it is a gem.

Jean-Baptiste is a black optometrist who, after her adoptive parents die, seeks out her biological mother, the incredible Blethyn, a white factory worker with a drinking problem, cigarette habit, unsociable daughter, angry sister-in-law, and sensitive but unhappy brother. The whole lot of them are vulnerable to the edge of shattering, with the two mother-daughter relationships sure to be either the glue or the hammer. Leigh slips the building blocks onto the screen one by one, constructing a story with as many planks as a seven-layer torte—actually, the credit goes to a cast of cooks, as much of the script was improvised. In fact, Blethyn and Jean-Baptiste didn't meet until the scene in which they meet in the film. Delicious! Definitely to be rented on Mother's Day, and watched with sisters. **AR**

GC   Amen to all that. It's a stunning movie, and Blethyn is unforgettable. I found myself laughing and crying all at the same time.

CT   In a word: *overrated*. I found myself wondering, is Blethyn's creaky accent for real?

SMOKE
1995. 112 min. Harvey Keitel, Ashley Judd. Dir. Wayne Wang

The exquisite mélange of stories that is *Smoke* does at first seem to coalesce into a supreme buddy movie, heavy on the tobacco. Consider the leading characters: Keitel as Auggie, the sweet-hearted manager of a Brooklyn smoke shop; William Hurt as a cheroot-loving, widowed novelist deep into writer's block; and Harold Perrineau as a teenager who, while searching for his father—played by the great Forest Whitaker—saves the novelist's life.

But then comes along Stockard Channing as Ruby, an old girlfriend of Auggie's and the mother of a drug-addicted daughter who may be Auggie's only child. Judd is the daughter, seen briefly but in a scene so powerfully acted and sensationally filmed that it's the most potent in the film. Where did Ruby go wrong? What can Auggie do to help?

From mother and daughter to street-corner chums, *Smoke*, unconventional as far as moviemaking goes, tells that most traditional of tales: Everybody needs somebody (apologies to Dean Martin). Note of trivia: "Auggie Wren's Christmas Story" originally appeared in the op-ed section of *The New York Times*. Written by Paul Auster, it was the inspiration for the movie. **AR**

GC Auster's screenplay celebrates the dying art of storytelling. It's a pure joy to sit back and let this talented ensemble work their magic.

CT I loved the movie and particularly newcomer Perrineau, who stood out among the veteran actors.

THE TURNING POINT

1977. 119 min. Shirley MacLaine, Anne Bancroft, Mikhail Baryshnikov, Leslie Browne. Dir. Herbert Ross

When I watched this again after not having seen it for a long time, I found the gag reflex working on overdrive, but I *so* loved this movie as a teenager that I figured I'd throw it in, anyway. It's great melodrama for any kid who wants to *be somebody*. Plus, even if you can't stand the unctuous Browne or the obvious story—two ballerinas, one becomes a mother (MacLaine), the other a star (Bancroft), and each one envies the other—it's worth watching just to see Baryshnikov in his prime performing several of his signature virtuoso numbers. Then there's the equally entertaining hair-pulling, purse-slugging slap fight between Bancroft and MacLaine (in evening gowns and high heels, no less). Some other good scenes worth fast-forwarding to are any of the performance pieces, including the one where Browne appears as a drunk *Giselle* waif that's pretty funny. It's the only movie I've seen that gives any real hint of what the inner workings of the ballet world are all about—there's blood in them thar toe shoes! **CT**

GC If this is the inner workings of the ballet world, I'd rather not know about it. Your gag reflex was right, Cynthia.

AR No gagging on my couch. *Baryshnikov,* girls!

fifteen

"I GOT GOOSE PIMPLES . . .

. . . even my goose pimples got goose pimples."
—*Bob Hope, in* The Cat and the Canary

The disadvantage to watching a suspense video as opposed to a suspense movie is that it's tough to create at home the theater's it's-very-dark, I'm-very-vulnerable atmosphere. But you can make do: Switch off all the lights and turn off the ringer on the phone. If possible, arrange for it to be a stormy night. (It is not advised to attempt to be ridden with anxiety in daylight hours.) Then settle back—but don't relax—for a few hours of trepidation. It's fun to be terrorized! As Anjelica Huston said in *The Addams Family,* "You frightened me. Do it again." **AR**

CHARADE
1963. 113 min. Cary Grant, Audrey Hepburn, Walter Matthau. Dir. Stanley Donen

This is a suave thriller. It's farce, black comedy, romance, suspense, and a weirdly mustachioed Matthau blended together in a film so sophisticated that critics of the sixties didn't know what to make of it. You, modern viewer, will not be mired in moral doubt just because you find yourself smiling one minute and blanching at a corpse the next. But, anyway, all that is the highbrow stuff: Rent *Charade* if only to whistle along to the Oscar-nominated Henry Mancini theme song (which will be familiar if you ride in elevators), to see Grant sing in the shower with his clothes on, and to see him and Hepburn fall in love as the bodies pile up. He was absolutely old enough to be her father, and you will never see May and December look so fine together in the City of Lights. The *bateau mouche* ride down the Seine is in contention for the *most* romantic scene in the history of Hollywood.

But, hey, the Hitchcockian plot looks good, too. When one-armed George Kennedy shows up at the Paris funeral for the Hepburn character's never-on-screen husband (he's not paying his respects; he wants to make sure the fellow is dead), you know you're in for a gambol. Which of the four fellows after her are good guys and which are bad? Is charming mystery man Grant her rescuer or something more sinister? Was her late husband really a villain? Would you be more attractive if *your* neck were that long? Hepburn is luminous, Grant is dreamy, and their romance is cleverly delivered. *Charade* is matchless. **AR**

CT   The May-December combo kinda kills the whole movie for me. Pushing sixty, he looks like a dirty old man with a young faun.

GC   You have a point, Cynthia, but the funny parts are *really* funny.

DEAD CALM
1989. 96 min. Nicole Kidman, Sam Neill, Billy Zane. Dir. Phillip Noyce

John and Rae Ingram (Neill and Kidman) have just lost their infant son in a car wreck. Devastated, they decide to get away and spend some healing time sailing on their yacht, just the two of them and the dog. "Quiet time on quiet seas," says John. (I love it when they say stuff like that. You know it's going to be anything but.)

Sure enough, they soon spot a man in a dinghy, rowing toward them from a becalmed sailboat. They pick him up and learn that he is the sole survivor, Hughie (Zane). All his shipmates are dead of food poisoning, he says, and the sailboat is sinking. John, a naval officer for twenty-five years, smells something fishy, locks the supposedly sleeping Hughie in the cabin, and rows off to the crippled boat to investigate. Hughie soon turns out to be a raging psychopath, and the battle of wits begins, with John on a fast-sinking boat where nothing as pleasant as food poisoning took place, and Rae alone with a madman and the dog, who has no aggressive instincts whatsoever.

It's a simple premise, with no distractions, no tricky plot. Everything hinges on the credibility of the characters, and it works. They're all terrific. Neill and Kidman are convincing as a nice, ordinary couple hurled into a nightmarish situation. As for Zane—wow. What a creepy, goose-bump-raising villain. Good job, y'all. A big, scary bang for your buck with this one. **GC**

CT   Watching a husband and wife (and a dog) get tortured for an hour and a half is not my idea of fun, on land or at sea.

AR   Predictable, and with plot holes big enough to sink a boat. But, hey—that doesn't mean it's not fun.

DIAL M FOR MURDER
1954. 105 min. Grace Kelly, Ray Milland. Dir. Alfred Hitchcock

The murder occurs rather early on, and there's never doubt about who's behind it, but this is still a great suspense movie. There are lots of reasons, all framed by one question: Will the cad get away with it? Milland is at his calm-cruel best, Kelly is beautifully vulnerable, and the gifted John Williams is masterful as the Scotland Yard inspector who seeks to solve the case with a satisfying flourish. This was adapted from a stage play, and most of the action takes place in the flat where a suave tennis bum (Milland) and his rich and understandably unfaithful wife (Kelly) live in London. Without his wife, the husband would be broke, and he's worried that she might leave him for her American mystery writer friend, played by Robert Cummings. But the fellow doesn't want to dispatch the lady himself, as that would require physical effort and would probably make a mess of his suit. Instead, he blackmails and tricks an old acquaintance into doing the job—but his plan is foiled. And then begins the real skulduggery.

It's all presented engagingly with nice little twists about hidden door keys and planted fingerprints that will give the first-time viewer the willies: Could this happen to *me*? Note of trivia: *Dial M for Murder* was filmed with 3D cameras, which apparently explains why the movie has the look of a stage play—the cameras were big and hard to move and prevented Hitchcock from experimenting with the angles and views for which he's famous. But the straight-on camera work lends the movie a directness that makes what's happening on-screen powerful. **AR**

GC   My least favorite Hitchcock movie. I like it better when he takes me on location and scares the hell out of me: Mount Rushmore, old Spanish missions, creepy motels . . .

CT   The guy's pushing fifty and he's supposed to be a tennis bum? That starts the whole thing off on a bad premise, but Grace looks smashing in that red dress.

DIVA
1982. 123 min. Wilhelmenia Wiggins Fernandez, Frederic Andrei. Dir. Jean-Jacques Beineix. French w/subtitles

The creepy avant-garde look that was so titillating when this picture came out is a little dated now, but the music—from the haunting arias of the diva to the chilling techno tracks—is worth the price of a rental video, not to mention the sound track CD. A cute but slightly weird mailman and opera fan (Andrei) makes an illegal recording of the diva's performance to satisfy his own obsession. He ends up getting some face time with the soprano, but unintentionally embroils her in a sleazy international plot involving hookers from the Third World and bad guys in wraparound sunglasses. The diva's French is a little stilted, to say the least, and her acting lacks the emotion of her singing, but hey, she's a diva. It's the one clunky note in an otherwise sleek flick. *Diva*'s filled with suspense, weird interiors (the mailman lives in a garage), and an interesting Asian Lolita played by Thuy An Luu. It also has a great chase scene, which I would usually think of as an oxymoron, through the Paris subway. Your average chase scene has to be the most overused, unsuspenseful, booooring technique in the movies. A final thought: Put *Diva* on the see-before-going-to-Paris list. **CT**

GC   It's all a bit too self-consciously smart to be white-knuckle suspenseful, but I'd recommend it for the great Metro chase and the diva's glorious singing.

AR Hey, it's not dated at all! (By which declaration I'm sure I'm dating myself.) And yes, absolutely, the chase scene will knock your helmet off.

DRESSED TO KILL

1980. 105 min. Michael Caine, Angie Dickinson, Nancy Allen, Dennis Franz. Dir. Brian De Palma

This movie doesn't make a whole lot of sense, but it *does* make a whole lot of suspense. It's a cheap thrill, nasty—in the De Palma tradition—and concerned with hookers, transsexuals, slashings, and other amusements. Caine plays a psychiatrist whose patient, played by Dickinson, is brutally murdered. Her son teams up with another almost-victim (Allen), and they set out to find the killer. Along the way, we learn quite a bit about sex-change operations, psychiatry, and picking up people in museums—and we also get a preview, from a much skinnier Franz, of his future *NYPD Blue* character.

The music is wonderful, sucks you right in to the dark, evil world of stalkers and slashers and other kinky denizens of the night, and De Palma succeeds, yet again, in placing us squarely in the action, playing with our senses, making us question every movement, unable to separate nightmare from reality. Good stuff. **GC**

CT This is just a highfalutin version of your average "stalk woman, kill woman" genre, which I don't find entertaining.

AR Me, either. And too bad, because Dickinson reminds us how talented she is.

THE LADY FROM SHANGHAI

1948. 87 min. Rita Hayworth, Orson Welles, Everett Sloane. Dir. Orson Welles

"Personally, I don't like a girlfriend to have a husband," says Michael O'Hara (Welles), setting the stage for a violent love triangle between working-class Irishman O'Hara, ice princess Elsa Bannister (Hayworth), and her smarmy husband Arthur (Sloane). The characters, with one exception, have calculating minds and hearts of stone.

Even as they sail on a yacht stopping at balmy ports like Acapulco, they're so cold they're chill-inducing, particularly Mr. Bannister. When he calls his wife "lover"—almost always with a sneer—it's enough to make your skin crawl. There are plenty of twists and turns as romances and alliances are sorted out, and it ends up in a climactic shoot-out in a fun house that's worth the price of admission (and I'm sure must be studied in film classes). The black-and-white photography and camera work are sophisticated and over the top—every now and then the camera cuts to stormy seawaters and equally stormy music. Anyone who would try to colorize this film would have to be shot on the spot, because what's most intriguing about this flick isn't so much the story or the characters per se so much as the way they're filmed. Memorable quote: "When I start out to make a fool of myself, there's very little can stop me." **CT**

GC   A hard-to-follow, depressing mess. Hayworth's trademark, her lush sexuality, is kept tightly under wraps. Wish I could say the same for Welles's bogus Irish brogue. But true, the fun-house finale is a must-see.

AR   I agree with both Gabrielle and Cynthia. I like all the shifting images and Elsa's femme fataleness, but it greatly confuses me.

LAURA
1944. 88 min. Gene Tierney, Clifton Webb, Vincent Price, Dana Andrews. Dir. Otto Preminger. b&w

This is noir at its best, with the mystery surrounding who offed Laura, a bold and beautiful advertising exec with shiny hair and bad taste in men. A smarmy suitor, played by Price, Webb's Walter Winchell-type priss, and the "dick" on the case (Andrews) stalk Laura's apartment trying to figure out who killed her. Somehow—with all the nifty black-and-white shadows, the seductive cigarette smoke, the tumblers of whiskey—when Andrews says, "When a dame gets killed, she doesn't worry about how she looks," well, it just seems like the right thing to say. One little problem: The Waldo Leydecker character has loads of great Oscar Wildey lines ("In my case, self-absorption is completely justified."). But how we're actually supposed to believe he's straight enough to have fallen in love with Laura is beyond me. I guess since homosexuals didn't exist in movies in the '40s, you could have a character like this fall in love with a skirt on the screen and no one would be the wiser. The new generation of martini sluggers playing Sinatra CDs should rent *Laura* to learn from the masters of the essence of cool. **CT**

GC Right, Cynthia. This is a class act, and the haunting theme song is icing on a very satisfying cake.

AR And so *many* fantastic lines, including two more from Waldo: "I don't use a pen. I write with a goose quill dipped in venom." "I'm not kind, I'm vicious. It's the secret of my charm."

THE MORNING AFTER
1986. 103 min. Jane Fonda, Jeff Bridges, Raul Julia. Dir. Sidney Lumet

Put yourself in Fonda's shoes: A washed-up actress who drinks to forget, and often succeeds, you wake up with a titanic hangover and crawl out of a bed you don't remember having gotten into. You slosh a little gin to clear your head, which hurts so badly, it's hard to keep upright on your neck. You wonder foggily where you are and who the guy still under the sheets might be and why he has a knife sticking out of his chest. Yikes! Did *you* put it there? Stumbling out into the painfully bright daylight, you happen upon Bridges, an ex-cop who lives in a Quonset hut, and the two of you go about falling in love and solving the mystery.

The small problem with *The Morning After* is that the plot has a couple of holes as big as a sumo wrestling team after dinner. So why do I like it? Fonda is great, Bridges is wonderful, the late Julia is fantastic as Fonda's estranged husband, and director Sidney Lumet plays the three of them beautifully against the backdrop of his version of Los Angeles. There's scary stuff and suspense, too. Actually, the plot is quite clever. You just have to do the suppress-disbelief thing a few times. It's worth the small effort to enjoy Fonda and Bridges together. And to once again see Julia, who is sorely missed. **AR**

GC   Even the beloved Julia couldn't help this ill-conceived mess.
No wonder she had a hangover. I did, too, and I hadn't even
been drinking.

CT   Even though I'm not a Fonda fan, I enjoyed the twists and
turns, almost despite myself.

NOTORIOUS

*1946. 101 min. Ingrid Bergman, Cary Grant. Dir. Alfred
Hitchcock. b&w*

Forget *Indiscreet* if you're hankering to see Bergman and Grant
together. Released 12 years after *Notorious,* it made audiences happy
by teaming them up again, but it's a clunker, with Bergman looking
darn close to dowdy and playing a chick with marriage on her mind.
(*Indiscreet* does contain two priceless lines, which I'll share with
you so you can avoid renting it: "I don't know what you expect
from men. You know there's a limit to how entertaining they can
be." And: "Come on. You'll feel better in a girdle.")
   In Hitchcock's offering, Bergman's a tormented beauty with a
past—"a woman of that sort" is how it's so delicately put—not to
mention a father convicted as a Nazi spy. For a slew of complicated
reasons, she agrees to become a spy herself, but for the Americans,
and heads down to Rio to let a friend of her father's make love to
her. Claude Rains, nominated for a Best Supporting Actor Oscar, is
the mama's-boy friend. Mama is a cigar-smoking Leopoldine Kon-
stantin, one of the scariest parental units ever filmed. And Grant?
He's Bergman's American contact, and surely the very best kisser
in all of spydom. The twisted love affair between these two sizzles
with just as much heat as the blowtorch that fires every time Bergman
and Bogie are together in *Casablanca.* There's romance and suspense
enough to make you wish Hitchcock hadn't been so efficient—the
movie's about thirty minutes too short. **AR**

CT   I don't think any movie can ever be 30 minutes too short,
but I agree this one is worth every second, particularly with
Bergman in the unusual role of the ever so slightly slutty
babe.

GC   Isn't this a smashing movie? Aren't they the most divine couple on the planet? And is it hot in here or is it just me?

SHADOW OF A DOUBT

1943. 108 min. Joseph Cotten, Teresa Wright. Dir. Alfred Hitchcock. b&w

Of all the movies he made, this is said to be Hitchcock's favorite. He convinced playwright Thornton Wilder to write the screenplay, and Wilder and co-writers Alma Reville and Sally Benson cleverly twisted the true story of the Merry Widow Murderer, a notorious strangler of the '20s, into the tale of Uncle Charlie, a lady-killer who comes to live with his sister and her family in a small California town. The wonderful Cotten is Uncle Charlie, and Wright is his niece, Little Charlie, who just before he arrives is complaining about the monotony of life in sleepy Santa Rosa. "Guess we'll just have to wait for a miracle or something," she sighs, and the miracle turns out to be her beloved uncle.

We know that Uncle Charlie has just murdered a woman for her money back East, and that the cops are after him, but Little Charlie is determined to believe her mother's little brother is the generous, witty, well-traveled businessman she has always adored—and, more importantly, that her mother has always adored. Her gradual realization that she might be wrong and Uncle Charlie's increasingly ominous responses make for outstanding creepiness. Harry Travers as Little Charlie's father, and Hume Cronyn as his best friend, provide comic relief: They relax after work by arguing about how they would murder one another without getting caught. Note of trivia: Wilder finished the script while aboard a train from Hollywood to Florida, where he was headed to join the army's psychological warfare unit, and Hitchcock was on the train with him. That no doubt explains the movie's alarming ending. **AR**

CT   What I like is that you get the idea something fishy's going on at the beginning but you have no idea how heinous it actually is.

GC   Not as flamboyant as many Hitchcock movies, but very creepy in its understated, small-town way.

THE THIRD MAN

1949. 104 min. Joseph Cotten, Orson Welles. Dir. Carol Reed

Have you ever heard a zither? An evening with *The Third Man* will leave you zithering forever. Anton Karas's incredible score, performed on the stringed instrument, is one of the haunting sensations in a movie full of them. Suspense master Graham Greene wrote the script, legendary Robert Krasken was behind the camera, and Welles penned and delivers the famous Ferris wheel monologue. The debonair Cotten is Holly Martins, who arrives in postwar Vienna to find his friend Harry Lime, who has promised him a job. Holly is informed that Harry is dead, struck by a car, and that before his demise he was a black-market scoundrel, to boot. Holly can't believe this of Harry and sets out to clear his buddy's name, and to determine whether his death really was an accident. A witness says there were three men at the scene, but Holly meets only two.

Who was the third man? Holly's sleuthing leads him into the heart of dark and beautiful war-battered Vienna, and introduces him to Harry's lover, the beautiful Alida Valli (wonderful in *A Month by the Lake,* page 145), who doesn't want to believe the worst about Harry, either. The excellent Trevor Howard is the British officer who tries to convince the two that Harry wasn't the sort of fellow they thought he was. From the camera work to the dialogue to the music, *The Third Man* is chillingly good. Welles appears only briefly, but grandly. Here he is in the Ferris wheel high above Vienna's Prader: "Look down there. Would you really feel pity if one of those dots stopped moving forever? If I offered you twenty thousand pounds for every dot that stopped, would you really, old man, tell me to keep my money? Or would you calculate how many dots you could afford to spare? Free of income tax, old man, free of income tax. It's the only way to save money nowadays." Classic stuff. **AR**

GC And try getting that theme out of your head afterward! In fact, try getting any of this atmospheric thriller out of your head afterward. Can't be done. It's too good.

CT Harry Lime is dead and I don't care—nor did I care for any of Graham Greene's novels. I liked the zither, though. Nothing like a tinge of hula music in postwar Vienna.

VERTIGO

1958. 128 min. James Stewart, Kim Novak. Dir. Alfred Hitchcock

If you've just been kissed awake by a handsome prince after 40-odd years in a rose-decked glass coffin, you may not be familiar with the plot of *Vertigo,* to my mind Hitchcock's most beautiful and fascinating movie. Stewart plays Scottie, an ex-cop who had to leave the force because he suffers from acrophobia, a fear of heights, which gives him vertigo, the sensation of moving, or falling, through space.

He falls in love with Madeleine, a mysterious woman whose husband hires Scottie to follow her, and he eventually watches, paralyzed by his fear and powerless to help her, as she falls to her death. Then he meets her double, Judy, becomes obsessed by her, and is drawn into a strange, upside-down world where reality and nightmare converge. So are we.

Scottie's pain and longing is beautifully conveyed by Stewart, surely the screen's most sympathetic Everyman. Novak, in a dual role as the cool, tailored Madeleine and the common, unpolished Judy, is awesome, and a perfect clotheshorse for the Edith Head costumes that are pivotal to the story. San Francisco, a city Hitchcock adored, is lovingly showcased, and the music is superbly effective, all the more so since *Vertigo* was restored and the sound digitized in 1996. It's a stunning movie. See it and be glad that Alfred Hitchcock lived. **GC**

CT   I watched this with great expectations but found it sluggish and leaden. Now it's considered a "masterpiece," but I agree with the moviegoers of 1958, who didn't exactly flock to see this flick.

AR   It *is* a masterpiece, with nary a hair out of place. Hitchcock invented the blend of zoom-forward, reverse-track to convey vertigo, and spent something like twenty thousand dollars on the few seconds' view of the mission's stairwell. His efforts pay off.

VILLAGE OF THE DAMNED

1960. 78 min. George Sanders, Barbara Shelley. Dir. Wolf Rilla

Have you ever wanted to trade in your scruffy, loutish little morons for perfect children? Superbright, superpolite, supergood-looking, and perfectly outfitted in their little school uniforms? Well, see this movie and you'll probably decide to cut them some slack. I know I did. And a video's a lot less expensive than psychotherapy.

It all starts when everybody in this charming little English village suddenly falls over unconscious. A few months later, they find that all the women of childbearing age are pregnant. Their babies turn out to be even more above-average than Lake Wobegon kids. But they're strangely cold and emotionless, and before long the villagers realize they're no match for these beautiful, blond little creatures.

The fun, and the creepiness, of this movie lies in the fact that the villagers react like regular, decent people when faced with an unbelievable situation. There are no lurid effects, no *Species*-style gore and goop. Everybody is very reasonable and British-stiff-upper-lip. And if George Sanders can't save civilization as we know it from these polite little monsters, by God he'll jolly well die trying. Way to go, George.

One small thing: The title of the novel this movie is based on is *The Midwich Cuckoos*—cuckoos being the bully birds that kick eggs out of a nest and lay their own there. I like that a lot better. And one big thing: Don't get confused and rent the 1995 remake with Christopher Reeve and Kirstie Alley. You'll be sorry. But it will be too late. **GC**

AR   Why didn't you warn me earlier? I did rent the later video, and you're right. But the original's good and weird enough that knowing the plot wasn't at all a problem.

CT   A scary movie that I liked? Maybe it was just such a relief there were no vampires involved, I could actually enjoy myself.

THE WAGES OF FEAR
1952. 156 min. Yves Montand, Charles Vanel. Dir. Henri-Georges Clouzot. b&w French w/subtitles

Clouzot's famous black-and-white suspense drama is short of perfect mostly because it's too long. The video viewer might fall asleep on the sofa during the first half and then miss the second half, which is the nasty, nail-biting part that's the reason for the fame. So it's worth sitting through some off Clouzot's introduction to the hot, dusty, corrupted South American village of Las Piedras. Simply fast-forward when you start yawning. I experimented and discovered it's possible to keep up with most of the subtitles even at top speed, though this might accelerate your accumulation of crow's-feet.

In Las Piedras, a pathetic collection of European men (there is but one minor chick role, best ignored) is stranded, penniless and desperate. Their savior might be the big U.S. oil company exploiting the local resources. When one of the company's wells blows out and catches fire three hundred miles away, four of the Europeans are hired at two thousand dollars each to drive two trucks carrying nitro-glycerin through an obstacle course of ravines, swamps, and rocky switchbacks to the well site. It's a dangerous and volatile business, physically and emotionally, and the movie's title becomes horrifyingly unambiguous with each mile. Forty years on, Clouzot shocks and terrorizes us as artfully as he did movie house audiences in the '50s. *The Wages of Fear* is thrilling. (Also, it's a chance for a look at a baby-faced Montand. Oooh la la!) **AR**

GC   Stick Chick alert! But to be fair, Clouzot redeemed himself with the divine *Diabolique* (p. 94), even more suspenseful than this one. And that's saying a lot.

CT   The tension here is similar to being in tooth-grinding traffic for two hours, yet somehow it's entertaining.

The Trouble with Alfred

He's the undisputed master of suspense, and his movies are among the best of any era, but Alfred Hitchcock obviously had a problem seeing women as adult persons. He called all actors cattle, but he cast his women as victims, decorations, or loonies, only to be redeemed, if they weren't dead first, by the love of a hero. He was fixated on his blond, ice-princess stars, and especially on their hair. Maybe his mother didn't breast-feed him, or maybe she was frightened by a curling iron while she was pregnant. Consider the following:

Kim Novak: crazy and conniving, and beautifully dressed and coifed, in *Vertigo*

Tippi Hedren: crazy, a thief, and beautifully dressed and coifed, in *Marnie,* and terrorized by feathered, frenzied predators in *The Birds*

Janet Leigh: paid the ultimate penalty for being blond and pretty in *Psycho*

Joan Fontaine: a timid, bullied mouse in *Rebecca*

Ingrid Bergman: a sickly drunk in *Under Capricorn;* self-destructive in *Notorious;* and frigid, then schoolgirl-swooning in *Spellbound*

Grace Kelly: always decorative, beautifully d. & c., always cool, always rich; an heiress in *To Catch a Thief,* a rich wife who is targeted for murder in *Dial M for Murder,* and a society model-fashion consultant in *Rear Window*

Eva Marie Saint: beautifully d., etc., a love interest and a pawn in *North by Northwest.* And did I mention they are all blondes?**GC**

sixteen

LOOK AT IT THIS WAY:
AT LEAST YOU CAN DRINK THE WATER

"I need a vacation."
—*Arnold Schwarzenegger,*
in Terminator 2: Judgment Day

Yes, Arnold, but *you* can afford one, and any time you like. Our pockets aren't nearly as deep, so we must sometimes make do with discount holidays via the VCR. When the powder's fresh but my credit card is over the limit, I schuss with *Downhill Racer*. If I have a hankering for schnitzel but not a schilling to spare, I take *The Third Man* (page 138) out for a Viennese waltz. But be warned: The globe-trotting videos recommended below contain such alluring footage that you might well be tempted *into* taking a trip. Bon voyage! **AR**

INDOCHINE
1992. 155 min. Catherine Deneuve, Vincent Perez, Linh Dan Pham. Dir. Régis Wargnier. French w/subtitles

I know, it's two and a half hours, but you'll be glad you did. Honest. It's a beautiful, moody picture. Deneuve is her usual drop-dead poised and gorgeous self, but this time she has competition: the jewel-green, achingly lovely landscape of prewar Vietnam. I can't recall another movie that so powerfully captures a sense of place, of light, of humid, languorous beauty.

In the 1930s, the last gasp of French colonial rule in Indochina, Eliane (Deneuve) is a wealthy French rubber plantation owner raising her adopted daughter, Camille (Linh). Her privileged life seems indestructible, but revolution is stirring. Eliane begins an affair with Jean-Baptiste, a young French naval officer played by the handsome Perez, especially yummy in that crisp white uniform. But Camille loves him, too, runs away with him, bears his child, and commits to the revolution.

Eliane can only watch in despair as her safe world crumbles. One image that stays with me is of the halcyon days when all was still right with her world. At a Christmas party, as Eliane dances an elegant tango with Camille, a servant is instructed to keep fanning the record player because "It wasn't made for this climate." Neither were the French, it seems. Or those who came after. **GC**

CT   Two and a half hours? I didn't notice. Sex, beauty, lust, passion, love, exotic locales, national uprisings, and Deneuve. What more do you need in a movie?

AR   Yes, Cynthia, it *was* two and a half hours. I felt every minute of it. The splendors of Southeast Asia are indeed splendid, but what goes on against the pretty backdrop moves too slowly over too much time.

IT STARTED IN NAPLES
1960. 100 min. Sophia Loren, Clark Gable. Dir. Melville Shavelson

Gable (a little long in the tooth at this point) is the worst kind of ugly American—prejudiced, cold, demanding, and, a lawyer. He goes to the Italian isle of Capri to settle the estate of his formerly wandering and now deceased brother and discovers, much to his surprise, that the brother has a son named Nano. This eight-year-old street hustler has been watched over by his sexy aunt, Loren, who loves the boy but figures he can pretty much take care of himself. The über-American Clark is infuriated that his nephew is being brought up with *la dolce vita* attitude of nightclub singer Loren, not to mention of Italian society in general. He vows to take this cute little urchin back to America and get him a real education, so he can make something out of himself. A culture-clashing custody struggle ensues amid the beautiful scenery of Capri. You feel like you're on a patio overlooking the Technicolor-blue Bay of Naples and you can almost smell the tomato sauce cooking. (The voluptuous Loren once said, "Everything you see, I owe to spaghetti.") Unlike, say, *Rome Adventure,* where the city was cleared of Italians and the Americans skipped around empty piazzas, this flick is filled with Italians engaged in the exuberant conversations we often mistake for verbal warfare. **CT**

GC Yes, the scenery's lovely, but there's no heart in this movie. Gable falls embarrassingly flat, Loren hams it up, and the kid has no charisma at all. Skip it and go out for a nice pasta Siciliana and a glass of Chianti.

AR Awww, come on. At one hundred minutes, it's a breezy little thing. Loren is having *fun.* And Gable, even long in the tooth, is still my kinda guy.

A MONTH BY THE LAKE

1995. 94 min. Vanessa Redgrave, Uma Thurman, Edward Fox. Dir. John Irvin

Filmed around Italy's lush Lake Como—a onetime honeymoon capital of Europe—this is one movie I'd recommend for the scenery alone. Another reason to see it is for Redgrave, who gets to play a really rare kind of role for a woman, a romantic lead pushing sixty. While on vacation at the lake resort shortly before the start of World War II, the Englishwoman falls for a buttoned-up fellow English major who has his eyes on the seductive young tease played by Thurman. Redgrave needn't feel a total loss of self-esteem, though. Despite being overlooked by the major, she's pursued by a droolingly handsome Italian villager young enough to be her grandson. (Lest anyone find the age difference preposterous, the actress has been known to dally with men considerably younger than herself.) Watch the romantic entanglements sort themselves out as the vacationers skip around the gorgeous Italian lake, breakfast *al fresco,* and dance in the swanky hotel dining room. **CT**

GC   I, too, would recommend it for the scenery. But the rest of it is pretty bad fare, with terrific actors who just coast. Disappointing.

AR   The plot's inane, but I'm a sucker for silly romances in exotic settings.

NIAGARA

1953. 89 min. Marilyn Monroe, Joseph Cotten, Jean Peters, Max Showalter. Dir. Henry Hathaway

When this movie was made, Niagara Falls was still the number one honeymoon destination in the United States, with a romantic, even sugary, image. So it makes the perfect, ironic setting for this bleak, suspenseful story of adultery and murder. It's also an awesome force of nature, wild and elemental, and since it figures heavily in the plot, we get to know it and its surroundings probably more intimately than most visitors.

At the picturesque little motel, George and Rose Loomis (Cotten and Monroe) are obviously not on their honeymoon. He's a jittery Korean War veteran who's already lost his ranch, his self-respect, and most of his sanity trying to satisfy his rapacious wife. She's plotting his murder with her latest boyfriend and teases and taunts him cruelly. This was Monroe's first top billing, and it's refreshing to see her as a hard, controlling woman, not just a dumb, compliant cupcake. Cotten, too, is impressive as the tortured, lovesick George.

And the falls are equally impressive, a constant, pounding presence—a metaphor in the movie for love, or at least lust. As George says, looking mournfully out at the thundering torrent: "It's okay up top, where it's all calm and peaceful . . ." But as the water rushes down, it picks up such momentum and power that "not even God himself can stop it." **GC**

CT   I also liked Jean Peters as the pretty but far from bodacious wife. Too bad we never got to see much more of her.

AR   Quite a satisfying thriller, with perhaps Monroe's best acting.

OUT OF AFRICA

1985. 150 min. Meryl Streep, Robert Redford. Dir. Sydney Pollack

There is a well-attended school of criticism that contends that Streep's Danish accent is akin to the sound that would emit from a toothless person gumming marbles. Oh, yeah? How do they know Danes don't *really* sound like that? Such petty faultfinding has wounded *Out of Africa*'s reputation, and phooey on you if it stops you from bringing this marvelous, magical, romantic, feminist (no kidding) movie home. Right, the irrefutably American Redford as a hunter named Denys Finch Hatton might be hard to swallow, like the marbles, but if you don't know the story on which the film is based, you can wholeheartedly believe that Denys is spelled "Dennis" and get on with enjoying a sweeping, beautiful look at Kenya after the turn of the century.

Pollack interprets with an appropriately slow pace the memories of Danish baroness Karen Blixen, who brought to Africa her fine china and crystal and designer gowns as well as her skill with a rifle and willingness to thumb her nose at the white imperialist class that ran the country. There is an awful lot to recommend *Out of Africa.*— humor, drama, war, suspense, love, hate, disaster—all the great stuff. But what I most appreciate is its sense of place. As you watch, you feel you re really *there*. Toward the end, as the camera pans the sky, a chorus of children sing a cappella a native song that moves with the clouds and then, suddenly, in midverse, stops, no echo. At that moment, you really feel death in the air. Pollack's brilliant at this, and Streep and Redford are just as good. **AR**

GC   Yes, it's good-looking and has a great sense of place, but it moves at an elephant's pace. I'm not usually a fan of Redford's acting, and, since his skin in this movie resembles a dry riverbed, I much preferred Klaus Maria Brandauer, the husband of convenience. What a cad!

CT   This is like *Wild Kingdom* meets *The Way We Were*, and I'd rather watch either one of those than this.

A PASSAGE TO INDIA

1984. 163 min. Judy Davis, Victor Banerjee. Dir. David Lean

The first question that pops into your head on watching this is, "Those repressed Brits! How did they ever produce the likes of GC?" The second is, "Did Lean invent epic, or what?" In this case, he takes E. M. Forster's novel and makes it bigger than life-size (perhaps a bit too big for some—FF to the rescue!) to wow us with a sweeping clash of cultures and a dizzying, mystical visit to India under British rule. It's hugely entertaining, and more than a little creepy, too (and I'm not referring to the strange casting of Alec Guinness as Professor Godbole, whose lips make him look as though he's just lost a fight with a bowl of grape Jell-O).

The scenes around which all others flow take place in the eerie Marabar Caves, to which the solicitous Dr. Aziz (Banerjee) escorts the massively messed up Miss Quested (Davis). Davis is so white, she's almost translucent, and it's clear that Miss Quested lusts after Dr. Aziz's chestnut skin and dreamy dark eyes. What precisely occurs in the caves has been a mystery since the novel was published in 1924, but we know it's right for Dr. Aziz to be bewildered when he is accused of rape. Lean handles it with dreamlike, discomfitting polish, giving new parameters to passion. You will not believe this is the same Davis who plays the evil White House chief of staff in *Absolute Power* (if any of you saw that stinker). In the courtroom scenes, you'll absolutely want to slap her! And those silly British imperialists, too. **AR**

GC   It's Lean's last film, the Indians are uppity, the Brits are hysterical, and the Empire's crumbling all around. But not to worry, stiff upper lip and all that. The scenery's spectacular, and so is Dame Peggy Ashcroft as the gallant Mrs. Moore.

CT   It's beautiful to watch once, but too emotionally upsetting to sit through a second time.

ROME ADVENTURE

1962. 119 min. Troy Donahue, Suzanne Pleshette, Angie Dickinson, Rossano Brazzi. Dir. Delmer Daves

Pleshette is an American virgin in Rome for, well, an adventure. She finds it in Troy Donahue, who is supposed to be a dream boat, but to me has all the appeal of a soggy doughnut. The story here is of the goofy, '60s, virgin-meets-competing-hunky-seducers-in-a-sexy-city vein, but the movie's worth it, anyway, for its cinematic tour of Italy. Better Donahue than that PBS travel guy Rick Steves. I was going to say the only reason to watch this adventure is for the sightseeing tour, but then I changed my mind. There is something charming about this flick, à la *If It's Tuesday, This Must Be Belgium* (which Pleshette also appeared in; she may not have ended up a big movie star, but she sure worked her way across Europe). Italophiles will love the jaunts the lovers take to Verona, Arezzo, and Orvieto (although it's funny how they supposedly toured half the country in one day—just so the plot didn't have to deal with Pleshette and Donahue NOT sleeping together in town after town). Another thing that puzzles me: The filmmakers must have cleared out the entire city of Rome, because the two lovers have entire piazzas all to themselves. **CT**

GC   I know why they had entire piazzas to themselves. It's because Italians have class and wouldn't be seen dead anywhere near this dreadful soap opera with its third-rate stars. The scenery is indeed dreamy. So rent a travelogue.

AR   Get outta here: a movie starring Troy Donahue! Even nuttier, I *liked* it. (It was originally titled *Lovers Must Learn*. Hah!)

A ROOM WITH A VIEW
1986. 115 min. Maggie Smith, Helena Bonham Carter. Dir. James Ivory

If you don't know it, I shouldn't tell you, but I can't resist: Daniel Day-Lewis is Bonham Carter's insufferable fiancé Cecil in this gorgeously filmed, flawlessly acted romantic-comedy-travelogue (a neoteric cinematic genre, and you heard it here first). He is so dexterous a performer that I was stunned when, after drooling over his brawny manly-manness in *The Last of the Mohicans,* I made one of my frequent revisitings to this flick and spied his name in the credits. Wow! As Cecil, he's a fastidious, skinny prig in a *pince-nez,* for goodness' sake, as far a cry as any from the muscle-flexing, female-saving, bad-guy-bashing frontiersman Hawkeye. But I digress from what is supposed to be the point. Which is this: *A Room with a View* so agreeably plunges you into the splendor of Florence and the charm of English village life in the latter nineteenth century that just sitting back and watching the scenery canter by is a calming joy. More than that, I think it's the best movie director Ivory and producer Ismail Merchant have made yet. (Author E. M. Forster did lend a hand by writing the novel first.)

They lovingly tell the story of the budding feminist-who-doesn't-know-it Lucy Honeychurch, who, in Italy on the grand tour with Maggie Smith as her dotty lady companion, meets and then, standing on a sunny hillside outside Florence, is shockingly kissed by Julian Sands, who is as unlike the straitlaced Cecil as Cecil is different from Hawkeye. With Denholm Elliott as Sands's Thoreau-loving father, and Simon Callow as the amusing Reverend Beebe, and Smith as the eventual and unlikely saver of the day, the landscape in the background might well be missed on the first viewing. Don't miss it on the second, and I'm sure there will be a second and a third and more. Then explain why I always cry at the end. **AR**

CT   I can't believe Anne failed to mention *Room* has something rare in movies: full-frontal male nudity—full-frontal frolicking male nudity at that! Who says Merchant-Ivory productions are nothing but stuffy Victoriana?

GC   And even more unbelievable: the full-frontal guy wasn't Harvey Keitel!

THE SECRET OF ROAN INISH
1994. 102 min. Jeni Courtney, Mick Lally, Eileen Colgan, John Lynch. Dir. John Sayles

My family came from Ireland, so maybe I'm a wee bit biased, but this movie is one of the most beautiful I've ever seen. The actors are wonderful, and the story is fondly crafted by director-screenwriter-editor Sayles, but it's the scenery, the wild and lovely coast of western Ireland, that is the star. Photographer Haskell Wexler handles it like a lover, caressing its tawny sands and blue-green waters, its wind-stroked hills and milk-white clouds. It's a magical place, the perfect setting for this mystical tale of seals that take on women's shapes and the men of Roan Inish who loved them, only to lose them again to the jealous sea.

When Fiona (Courtney) comes to live with her grandparents after her mother's death, they have left their old home, the island of Roan Inish, and settled on the mainland. But the island, a small green jewel within sight of their new lodgings, still casts a powerful spell, and moves the old couple to bitter tears. On the day they left, three years ago, Fiona's baby brother, Jamie, was washed out to sea in his cradle. Fiona hears about strange happenings, about "the dark ones," and sets out to discover the secret of Roan Inish.

To watch this movie is to become a child again, enthralled by a favorite bedtime story told by a loving grandma or uncle, since several characters tell parts of the tale. "His eyes, dark they were and with a great soul behind them . . ." "Wee Jamie, sleeping in his cradle . . ." Just curl up with your softest blanket and let these lilting voices carry you to one of the loveliest, most magical settings ever to grace your VCR. **GC**

AR   No blarney, this film has soul. I've not visited Ireland, and the cinematography—all those bleak seascapes—made me sorry.

CT   Give me a movie with cute animals and I'm happy. I like the take-charge Fiona, too.

THE RUSSIA HOUSE

1990. 123 min. Sean Connery, Michelle Pfeiffer. Dir. Fred Schepisi

Complicated? Yes. Romantic? Absolutely. Old-fashioned? No question. And the bonus? *The Russia House* was the first U.S.-produced film to be shot for the most part in what was then the Soviet Union, and the cinematographer, Ian Baker, makes Leningrad and even parts of Moscow look as stunning as they are (though a heck of a lot cleaner).

Since it's based on the novel by John le Carré, you know the story line is going to pack a punch. But it's not your regular old spy tale, for the Cold War is over, the main characters weren't trained for espionage, the real operatives aren't sure who their enemies are, and a subversive love story gets all tangled up in the goings-on. With Connery as Barley Blair, a boozy book publisher from London, and Pfeiffer as Katya, a Russian who passes him a top-secret manuscript penned by a dissident physicist (Klaus Maria Brandauer in a grand turn), amour is at the story's heart. After all, what else is going to save the world but true love? Barley and Katya, like Russia, are emancipated as the plot unfolds: He discovers ardor, she discovers trust, they discover each other, to heck with the CIA and the KGB. Sigh. My cockles are warm just thinking about it. **AR**

GC   Not mine. Connery and Pfeiffer generate no heat. Come to think of it, Connery's a lot sexier in guy movies like *The Rock, The Man Who Would Be King,* and *The Untouchables* than he is when he's the romantic lead. *Marnie* doesn't work for me, either. Watch this one for the scenery, and if you yearn for a good, tense spy thriller from the le Carré stable, watch Richard Burton as the tortured *Spy Who Came in from the Cold* (1965).

CT   Connery, Pfeiffer, Moscow, spies, Lisbon, lust, booze, intrigue . . . works for me.

SUMMERTIME
1955. 99 min. Katharine Hepburn, Rossano Brazzi. Dir. David Lean

Hepburn—a spinster rapidly approaching the age when people stop asking when she's going to get married—alights on Venice for a solo vacation. Despite her all-American cheeriness, we get some glimpses of the desperate loneliness beneath all that outward sunshine, and they're brief but harrowing. The scene where we first see Brazzi, her lover-to-be, in the Piazza San Marco has to be one of the all-time great first shots. It's also nifty to watch what cool guys could look like, when they could be cool without being ridiculous. Of course, the Italians could always get away with it better than Americans. The drama is played out against a photo album of sun-dappled Venice, and its beautiful decaying pastel *palazzi.* I don't think I'll ever go to Venice without thinking of the lonely Hepburn and all of those who for over a thousand years have gone to the most beautiful city in the world looking for romance. (I know this last part is going to make the other chicks gag.) **CT**

GC   Gag? *Moi?* Not on this one. (But don't worry, I'm saving that for some of your other picks.) Hepburn is superb, and the scenery is magical. Let's hear it for cinematographer Jack Hildyard.

AR   Yes, but I'm always a tad depressed, or maybe a bit lonely, while watching. Don't rent it before a vacation in Venice unless you're going with lots of companions.

More Vicarious VCR Trips

To be transported back to a place we've visited or would like to go to one day, great scenery is enough. It doesn't have to be a great movie. Sometimes you don't want too much plot, dialogue, or drama obstructing the view. A quick rundown of some other cinematic travelogues.

Bad movies, great locales

Stealing Beauty (1996): Liv Tyler stares vacantly into the beautiful Tuscan scenery for two hours while supposedly exuding sexual scents stronger than the olive trees.
Summer Lovers (1982): Peter Gallagher, Daryl Hannah, and other beautiful people have sex in Greece.
Gidget Goes to Rome (1963): Gidget goes to Rome.

So-so movies, great locales

Shirley Valentine (1989): One frustrated middle-aged English housewife goes on solo vacation in Greece.
Enchanted April (1991): Four repressed English women share a villa in Tuscany.
Three Coins in the Fountain (1954): Three single preliberation chicks look for love in Rome.

Great movies, great locales

La Dolce Vita (1960): Marcello Mastroianni romps with scandalous, moral-free Roman aristocrats.

Roman Holiday (1953): Audrey Hepburn, princess incognito, and Gregory Peck, reporter, dally in Rome.

To Catch a Thief (1955): Grace Kelly on the equally beautiful Riviera falls for cat burglar Cary Grant.

seventeen

NUN BUT THE BRAVE

"I'm not from the Inquisition,"
protests psychiatrist Jane Fonda, in Agnes of God.
"And I'm not from the Middle Ages,"
snaps Mother Superior Anne Bancroft.

Now here's a subject I'm familiar with, and I have the scars on my knuckles to prove it (oh, I'm just kidding). I was taught by nuns from the time I was three until the age of nineteen. I figure I saw *The Song of Bernadette* (1943) at least three hundred times, and it's a long movie: 156 min. Actually, it's pretty good. It won four Oscars, including Best Actress for Jennifer Jones as Bernadette. Linda Darnell played the Virgin Mary, if you can call it playing. She just stood in a grotto in a long white dress. And why don't we see more of her—Mary—in movies? She's a great subject. I guess her son would still get top billing, though.

My nuns were a mix of *The Bells of St. Mary's* (1945)—saintly and sweet—and *Sister Act* (1992)—smart, worldly, and funny. I used to fantasize that a couple of them came straight out of *The Devils* (1971), an outrageous, sacrilegious English movie where nuns do unspeakable things, but I could never prove it. Oh well, now that I'm mature I can see that nuns are just chicks with a mission, neither better nor worse that the rest of us, just different. God, I hate being mature. **GC**

AGNES OF GOD
1985. 98 min. Anne Bancroft, Jane Fonda, Meg Tilly. Dir. Norman Jewison

This is a strange, absorbing movie. I must admit I'm not a big fan of Fonda's, but Bancroft and Tilly more than compensate.

Sister Agnes (Tilly), a young novice in a cloistered convent in Montreal, has given birth and apparently killed her baby, which was discovered in a bloody trash can in her room. Martha Livingston (Fonda) is a state psychiatrist assigned to the case, and Bancroft plays Mother Miriam, the convent's tough, worldly-wise mother superior.

The problem is that the childlike, saintly Agnes refuses to admit, or doesn't remember, either giving birth or killing the child. What follows is an absorbing battle of wills and intellect between the mother superior and the psychiatrist. Is Agnes touched by God, as Mother Miriam insists, or just touched, as Martha suspects? One wants to protect Agnes's unquestioning faith, the other wants to make her aware of reality and responsibility.

It's refreshing, and rare, for a movie to wrestle with matters of conscience, especially with women as its major protagonists. Not that this is a talking-heads movie. Far from it. It's also a detective story, as Martha delves into a society within a society, with its own laws and allegiances. The photography, by the gifted Sven Nykvist, is glorious, and left some indelible images with me, especially of the shining Agnes, a fragile innocent caught between two equally complex and powerful worlds. **GC**

AR   I greatly enjoy Fonda and Bancroft together, and the mystery is keen. But Tilly always gives me the willies.

CT   But in this odd, intriguing movie she's *supposed* to give you the willies.

AMATEUR
1994. 105 min. Martin Donovan, Isabelle Huppert, Elina Lowensohn. Dir. Hal Hartley

Okay, she's not really a nun. But she used to be. Now she writes porno novels and calls herself a nymphomaniac, but she's still a virgin, so I think we can keep her in this chapter. (One of the best lines in this full-of-great-lines movie is, "How can you be a nymphomaniac and never have sex?" "I'm choosy.")

You've probably guessed by now that *Amateur* could only have sprung from the slightly bent brain of Hal Hartley, the master of coolly perverse black comedy, aided and abetted by his droll company of players.

Isabelle, the ex-nun-virgin-nympho-pornographer, is played by Huppert, who carries it off so jauntily, you'd swear she plays those roles all the time. She falls in love with Thomas (Donovan, Hartley's leading man of choice), who has unfortunately lost his memory as a result of a nasty fall from a window, from which he was pushed by Sofia (Lowensohn, another Hartley fave). We discover later that Sofia had excellent grounds for the defenestration.

They're a sorry, sordid bunch, but Hartley is an indulgent sort, and they all get the chance to pull themselves together, or what passes for together, in his movies. But not before they've led us on a merry, deadpan chase, dropping great one-liners all the way. **GC**

AR   What is it with you and Hartley, GC? His movies are almost always way too cool for me. I don't mind watching them, but I'm glad when they're over.

CT   Oh dear, not another defenestration flick! I agree with Anne. I like a little more life in my films.

DEAD MAN WALKING
1996. 122 min. Susan Sarandon, Sean Penn, Dir. Tim Robbins

Written and directed by Robbins, this is one of the great movies of the decade. It's based on the real-life story of Sister Helen Prejean, a Louisiana nun (Sarandon), who becomes the spiritual advisor to a death row inmate (Penn), who like all killers on death row, insists he's innocent. Penn's performance is so good, he completely obliterates Sean Penn. He *is* Matthew Poncelet, a scumbag no doubt, and probably a vicious murderer of two young lovers as well. At times he seems composed of nothing but pure evil, at others there's something that suggests a human core. Sister Prejean tries to help him find the humanity she sees in him and make peace with God before he dies. While the movie focuses on their relationship, it never lets us forget the horrifying murder or the relentless pain that haunts the victims' parents. This is not an anti-death penalty movie by any means. Nor is it likely to change any opinions on the subject. What

it will do is make you think about things like the nature of Christian-
ity, of goodness, of evil, of justice. When was the last time a movie
made you do that? **CT**

GC   Amen, Cynthia. I was moved, not just by the great perfor-
         mances, but by the generous spirit of the director. He makes
         a powerful statement that the big issues are never black and
         white, and that we need to bring compassion to our
         differences.

AR   You are so right about Penn, CT. Incredibly, he outshines
         Sarandon.

THE NUN'S STORY
*1959. 149 min. Audrey Hepburn, Peter Finch. Dir. Fred
Zinnemann*

When I was growing up, "nun" wasn't among the professions to
which I aspired, and not just because I'm not Catholic. Sometime
during my formative years I saw *The Nun's Story,* and that did it.
Poor, beautiful Sister Luke (Hepburn) is an awfully obedient girl,
but still has one heck of a time with the subservience necessary to
make a success of nunhood in Belgium in the years before World
War II. Her father is a surgeon, and her dream is to become a nursing
nun in the Congo. First she must survive the convent, schooling in
tropical medicines, and a stint in a Belgium mental hospital, where
a homicidal inmate played very, very convincingly by Colleen Dew-
hurst almost does her in. And then, when she finally makes it to
Africa, she's assigned to a hospital for Europeans, not natives. But
at least she gets to work alongside an irascible doctor, played by
Finch, who can hardly suffer women, let alone nuns. All of these
experiences help her make a vital decision about her future when the
war and personal tragedy conspire to force her to reevaluate what is
important to her, and to society.

The story of Sister Luke, based on a book by Kathryn Hulme, is
beautifully told in a straightforward, no-hankie way, and the quiet,
stunning ending will stay with you for a long time. Note of trivia:
Hepburn was a young girl in Belgium during the war and had so little
to eat, she was malnourished by the time of the Allies' victory. **AR**

GC   Hepburn strikes just the right note in this honest, sympathetic story. And is there anything, including a frumpy black habit, that she doesn't make look like haute couture?

CT   My God, the first forty-five minutes of this film is like watching a slow, ritual slaughter.

THE SOUND OF MUSIC

1965. 174 min. Julie Andrews, Christopher Plummer. Dir. Robert Wise

My friend Lisa Hoffman so loathes the saccharine overload in *The Sound of Music* that whenever it's on television, I ring her answering machine and hold the receiver up to the set and let 'er rip. I get a kick out of imagining her reaction to the treacle of "I Am Sixteen, Going on Seventeen" or "My Favorite Things." When I told her I was going to recommend it to lucky readers of this tome, she asked, "Is your *real* name going to be on the book?" Yessir, and I'm proud of it. The story of a nun turned governess turned wife of an anti-Nazi is a *chef d'oeuvre* of its genre, beautifully filmed with memorable songs and the greatest cast of nuns this side of *Lilies of the Field.*

Forget that none of the children can act, that Salzburg is on Austria's border with Germany, not Switzerland, and that the real Von Trapp family escaped Nazi-controlled Austria not by decamping during a concert and fleeing through the mountains, but by simply taking a hiking vacation to Italy and not coming back. Who cares? This is a musical, boys and girls, a frolic through the Alps in play clothes made from curtains, a fantasy where the mother superior belts out tunes in the abbey, a love story with only a couple of smooches, an anti-Nazi diatribe with not one mention of the Jewish religion. It was the first movie I saw in a theater and I've loved it ever since. I know the words to every song and get teary-eyed when the captain chokes up during "Edelweiss." Yes, Leisl is an idiot, and her brothers and sisters all need a good spanking. I watch for Andrews and Plummer, and a great turn by Eleanor Parker as the bleached-blond fiancée from Hades. Makes me feel like a kid again. **AR**

GC   I don't know Lisa, but I like her—a lot. I also like Christopher Plummer, who dubbed this sugary songfest *The Sound of Mucus.*

CT　A thoroughly indulgent guilty pleasure, like those pink Hostess snowballs I love so much.

Other Nun Stuff

Movie	Featured habit matter
Nuns on the Run	Two guy crooks who hide out in a cloistered Catholic girls school, disguised as Sister Euphemia and Sister Inviolata
Two Mules for Sister Sara	Shirley MacLaine as a cigar-chomping Wild West nun who really isn't, and Clint Eastwood, who doesn't know it
Sister Act	Whoopi Goldberg as a Vegas vocalist who dons a wimple after witnessing a murder
Girlfriend from Hell	Nuns who wield rocket launchers and semiautomatic weapons

eighteen

WHORES D'OEUVRES

Why Do Prostitutes Get All

the Tasty Roles?

*"If I'da been a ranch, they'da named me the Bar
Nothing."*
—Rita Hayworth, in Gilda

It was ever thus: The first Oscar for Best Actress went to Janet Gaynor in 1928 for her *Street Angel* role. She beat out Gloria Swanson, who played—you got it!—in *Sadie Thompson*. Things had hardly improved by the 1996 Oscars, when three of the ten nominations for Best Actress and Best Supporting Actress went to prostitutes: Sharon Stone, in *Casino;* Mira Sorvino, in *Mighty Aphrodite;* and Elisabeth Shue, in *Leaving Las Vegas.* (The Best Actress winner played a nun—Susan Sarandon, in *Dead Man Walking*—and Sorvino won the Best Supporting Actress award. The other six were housewives or spinsters. Such choices for chicks.)

So what is it with Hollywood? Molly Haskell, who wrote a great book called *From Reverence to Rape: The Treatment of Women in the Movies,* calls it "hooker chic." It's where male and female fantasies collide, she says, where men get the woman they think they want, and women get to be bad, rebellious, sexy. Fine, but imagine the roles reversed. What if the best parts for guys were prostitutes and pimps? Would they be the men women want? The ones we would lust after? Would male actors appreciate the chance to stretch, to try new avenues of expression as a whore? I don't think so.

So wake up, Hollywood. Give us more variety. Not that you can't still make movies about whores. Just include a few other occupations, kinda like you do with the guys. Meanwhile, we pounded the pavement and found some movies we liked in spite of all the odds. **GC**

BUTTERFIELD 8

1960. 109 min. Elizabeth Taylor, Laurence Harvey. Dir. Daniel Mann

This gem is perpetually trashed by slumming movie critics. That's because it *is* trash. It was *designed* to be trash. And it is *magnificent* trash. It's the kind of movie that just screams *out* for italics. Liz had recently filched Eddie Fisher from Debbie Reynolds and had not yet dumped him for Richard Burton when *Butterfield 8* was filmed, so you can imagine how nutty people were to get into the theater to watch. They were well rewarded for their zeal.

Liz is a New York girl with rocket-launcher breasts who spends most of her evening hours with lascivious men who are not her husband and never will be. Her mother (Mildred Dunnock; you'll recognize the face but not be able to place it) wills herself to believe that her daughter scores all those swell and figure-flattering clothes from her work as a model and that when she doesn't come home nights it's because she gets a great rate at the downtown YWCA. Laurence Harvey is the married creep who lives on Fifth Avenue with his extremely blond (or is that bland?) wife, Dina Merrill, but who likes to take Liz to a cheap suburban motel managed by the wise but ignored-until-too-late Kay Medford. The aforementioned Fisher is Liz's platonic friend from childhood, whose girlfriend doesn't believe the platonic part.

Are these the fixings for a great plot or *what?* There is actually some zippy dialogue and several scenes worthy of loud hoots, including one that starts with Liz grinding her spike heel into Harvey's shoe and ends with an extremely passionate kiss. Did I mention that Liz won the Oscar for Best Actress for her efforts here? And it had nothing to do with her almost dying of pneumonia shortly before Academy members cast their votes. She *deserved* it. *Aieeeee!* **AR**

GC   And all this time I thought it was a chicken bone that nearly killed her, or was that Mama Cass? I always get those two confused. Oh, the movie? Trash.

CT   Worth a go for Liz as the slutty tramp to end all slutty tramps and particularly Dunnock as the see-no-evil mother.

KLUTE
1971. 114 min. Jane Fonda, Donald Sutherland. Dir. Alan J. Pakula

Okay: If you refuse to rent the video, at least buy the sound track. In fact, without the music, *Klute* just might not work its wonders for me. The spooky, beautiful sounds in the background highlight and enliven the world of high-class call girl Bree Daniels (Fonda, with a *fantastic* haircut) and the puzzling state of affairs that endangers it.

Bree has constructed a life that allows her to sell her body while retaining some dignity, but when small-town detective John Klute (Sutherland) blackmails her into helping him find his best friend, who has disappeared in New York City, the secure walls crack, one by one. Fonda is simply tremendous as a frightened, defensive, capable, fragile woman. Her work here is as excellent as in *They Shoot Horses, Don't They?* The plot provides a fair share of thrills, and Sutherland is rock solid, a sort of titan of morality against which Bree can rail without too much fear. They're fantastic together. Throw in the music, and you've got a sensation. **AR**

GC   Great, and rare, psychological profile of a prostitute: "For an hour, I'm the best actress in the world . . . You control it, you call the shots, and I always feel just great afterwards." And Fonda—not usually one of my faves—is superb.

CT   Waaaay too much of this film is spent on Fonda's close-ups and way too much time with her yakking to her therapist. Plus, every time I heard her name, I couldn't help thinking her cohookers must be called Chevre, Gruyère, and Camembert.

LEAVING LAS VEGAS

1995. 111 min. Elisabeth Shue, Nicolas Cage. Dir. Mike Figgis

Of all the drinking movies I've seen, this induced the biggest hangover. And I mean that as a compliment: It's unforgettable, more powerful than *Days of Wine and Roses* or *The Lost Weekend,* though they're excused because they were filmed in such cautious times.

Leaving Las Vegas is anything but cautious. Figgis doesn't flinch. His movie is grain alcohol, not sippin' bourbon, and you'll be glad. Cage is Ben, committed to drinking himself to death, and Shue is Sera, a Las Vegas hooker with an honest-to-goodness heart of gold. She falls for him, against all good sense and his own advice, but you can almost see why: He's sweetly sick, self-deprecatingly funny, sadly lovable, though you gotta figure he doesn't smell so good most of the time.

Only a prostitute—one who's seeing a shrink, of course—would take the chance of letting such a fellow move in with her. Shue makes it all seem quite reasonable. And Cage, well, he is simply brilliant. He moved on after his wild success here to make a lot of bang 'em up action flicks, which is too bad. Yes, he was fun to watch in *The Rock,* and handsomely pumped-up in *Con Air.* But rent this one to see that he can *act.* **AR**

GC And don't be put off by the theme. Yes, it's grim, but these two are so terrific, and bring such humanity to their roles, that the movie transcends its subject matter.

CT This movie is so sickly and wonderfully redolent of alcohol that in the pool scene, I thought I could actually smell it.

MONA LISA

1986. 104 min. Bob Hoskins, Cathy Tyson, Michael Caine. Dir. Neil Jordan

This movie is one of my all-time favorites. If you've never seen it, you might wonder why anyone who's not a blood relative of the Marquis de Sade would recommend a movie about whores, pimps, and unspeakable acts. Just trust me.

George, Hoskins's character, is a small-potatoes ex-con who lands a job as chauffeur to an expensive prostitute, played by Tyson. Simone may be a "tall, thin, black tart," as he calls her, but in his spaniel-brown eyes she's a lady, and he's the closest thing she's ever seen to a knight in slightly rusty armor. He falls in love with her and is drawn deeper and deeper into London's sleazy, kinky underworld of vice and violence, and into the exquisitely slimy clutches of Caine's pimp/businessman. It's an unremarkable plot—a walk on the vile side—but Hoskins makes this an unforgettable movie. With his portly little bod and balding pate, he's an unlikely romantic lead, but he burns with such ardor and sweetness that none of that matters.

The elegant, swan-necked Tyson, a stage actor in her first movie role, brings shades of sadness and humanity to her world-weary character, and Caine performs his usual spot-on magic as the cold-fish degenerate who calls the shots. Minor characters are painted vividly, and the story unrolls smoothly.

For such depraved subject matter, the movie is quite restrained. But it packs a staggering punch. Like Hitchcock, Jordan can suggest a world of horror with a few well-chosen hints—a whip here, a rubber glove there. But it's not a downer. Hoskins's luminous performance and Tyson's grace lift *Mona Lisa* to the level of art. **GC**

AR If not for Hoskins, one of the best in the business, the movie wouldn't work for me. But you're right, he makes it sweet and beautiful and believable. The sadness and dirt fall away, for a moment or two.

CT Given her taste in movies, I'm inclined to believe that if Gabrielle went far back enough in the family tree she'd run into the marquis, but she's right about this flick. If it reminds you in spirit of *The Crying Game,* it's for a good reason: Both were written and directed by Neil Jordan.

"I don't take whores in taxis."

That's what Dirk Bogarde said in *Darling,* but men in Hollywood clearly weren't paying attention. While female actors spend a lot of time reading for roles as prostitutes, their male counterparts are out there chatting it up with the real thing. And—big surprise—even before the tabloids become bored with their antics, their careers move right back on track.

Consider Charlie Sheen, the star of *Platoon* and *Wall Street* who testified during Heidi Fleiss's trial that he hired hookers from the notorious madam at least 27 times, shelling out more than $50,000. Yes, most of his movies since have flopped, but the point is that he still finds work, and as of this writing is shooting in Canada with no less than Marlon Brando and Donald Sutherland.

Or take Eddie Murphy: After police stopped him in the middle of the night and discovered a transsexual prostitute sitting in the passenger seat, he was hired to pretend to be Rex Harrison in the remake of *Doctor Dolittle.* Or Cynthia's beloved, Hugh Grant: He was arrested along with working girl Divine Brown for engaging in "lewd conduct" just before the release of *Nine Months,* which was (though we can't imagine why) a hit. Then he went on to star in *Sense and Sensibility.* Not only that, but his girlfriend didn't even dump him.

There is a lesson buried in all this, and we shudder to imagine what it is.

nineteen

THEY DID IT THEIR WAY

"Never underestimate a man's ability to underestimate a woman,"
—*Kathleen Turner, in* V. I. Warshawski

A good amount of time over the course of world history has been dedicated to keeping little ladies in their place. They must work hard, but only at certain things, primarily keeping their men and their children happy, clean, and supplied with an ample amount of ironed shirts. Some of our most popular (and despised) stars today are ones who buck the whole idea of what *a woman* should be, from Madonna to Roseanne. Too often in the movies the actresses are mere accessories to the action, but sometimes they get to strike out on their own, whether it be a young woman who takes on a whole German village by exposing its Nazi past (*The Nasty Girl*), the pitchers and outfielders of the first women's baseball league (*A League of their Own*), or those who aren't afraid to use sex to get what they want (*Red-Headed Woman*), which sometimes is just sex (*She's Gotta Have It*). **CT**

ANN VICKERS

1933. 72 min. Irene Dunne, Walter Huston. Dir. John Cromwell. b&w

Imagine a movie about a good-hearted social reformer who rises to the top of her profession, thanks to her guts, smarts, and determination. Sounds preposterous, right? For Whoopi Goldberg to be convincingly powerful in 1996 in *The Associate,* she had to make herself over as a man. But this ambitious-woman's movie somehow squeaked through the Hollywood system. Our heroine does have one little problem: She keeps getting pregnant, and she's not married. So what, big deal, right? No big deal in the 1990s. Huge deal in 1933! Dunne is the trailblazing social worker in this Depression era—and pre–Hays Code flick. She's not even a hell-on-wheels heroine with vicious eyebrows and killer lipstick. She's more like Donna Reed as a social pioneer. Vickers's first baby was by a swain who promised to marry her, then dumped her for someone else. Her second child was the product of an affair with a married man. I'm not sure what the moral of this story is at the end. It could go a couple of ways, particularly given the mores of the day—although the movie seems to say those mores don't matter much, anyway. It's a good movie worth puzzling over, or to watch and then read the novel by Sinclair Lewis, on which it was based. **CT**

GC   Melodramatic stereotypes run amok. And there was no mistaking the moral when I saw it. By the end of the movie she's resigned her job, learned how to cook, and says that her unethical lover and their child have released her from "the prison of ambitions." Bummer.

AR   Oh, it's not *that* bad. Suspend your '90s sensibilities, put yourself in your mother's or grandmother's day, and you'll enjoy it.

ANTONIA'S LINE
1995. 105 min. Willeke van Ammelrooy, Els Dottermans. Dir. Marleen Gorris. Dutch, w/subtitles

Some critics were wearing their half-witted *Thelma & Louise* glasses when they saw Gorris's chronicle of four generations in a Dutch village. The *Washington Post*'s Desson Howe described it as focusing on "a big cast of women who live mostly for themselves, while husbands, boyfriends and other male necessities (including a sperm donor) pass incidentally through." Well, sure, that *can* be read as an endorsement, but Mr. Howe did not mean it to be, and he has it wrong, anyway. Men do happen to matter in *Antonia's Line*. In fact, their characters have substance, as opposed to the likes of, say, the Bridget Fonda chick in *City Hall,* who was tossed into the script because the writer figured it needed someone in pantyhose. Did anyone complain about *her?* Come to think of it, did anyone else see that movie? Anyway, *Antonia's Line* happens to be *about women,* so, golly gee, it focuses on women. Cripes! What whiny thin-skins some guys are. All right, I'm done ranting. The upshot: This movie is a joy—funny, moving, bizarre, tense. And the chicks do it their way. **AR**

GC   Oh, don't stop, Anne. I love it when you rant, especially about such a terrific, life-affirming movie.

CT   Anytime a chick points a weapon at a guy in a movie, male critics go ballistic. Hee hee hee. This is a great movie. Who cares if it makes guys cover their crotches and run out of the room?

CHILDREN OF PARADISE
1945. 195 min. Arletty, Jean-Louis Barrault, Pierre Brasseur. Dir. Marcel Carné. French w/subtitles. b&w

This is a must-see movie, for many reasons. First, because it's great entertainment, funny and captivating, with an awesome cast, but also because it's a milestone in moviemaking and revered by the French as a symbol of their resilience and spirit as they emerged from the ruins of World War II. (Many of the actors were also Resistance fighters.)

The action takes place in nineteenth-century Paris, on the Boulevard of Crime, teeming with pickpockets, prostitutes, sideshows, and pantomime—and, shades of the real world, collaborators and traitors. Garance (Arletty) strolls through it all completely at home, amused and detached, inspiring love, or at least lust, in almost every man who sees her, including Baptiste, a mime, and Frederick, an actor. Garance finally falls, hard, for Baptiste (Barrault), but never compromises her independence. When a rich suitor offers to change her life, she responds: "You mean my life is nothing? *You* will decide what I do with my life?"

Baptiste eventually achieves fame and fortune—and a wife. Frederick (Brasseur) also becomes a famous actor. These two characters bring us some of the funniest, most enchanting moments of the movie; Baptiste as he wordlessly reenacts a street crime for the police, thereby proving Garance's innocence, and Frederick as he improvises outrageous, crowd-pleasing scenes in his plays. The "Paradise" in the title also refers to the highest balcony in a theater, the cheapest seats, where the poorest people sit. The camera lingers often on these children of paradise, capturing them in the streets, in the theaters. As Frederick says, "Their lives are small, but they have big dreams." It's movies like this that nurture those dreams. **GC**

CT   I never thought I'd say this about a mime, but Barrault is so lyrical and balletic, he's beautiful to watch. The rest of the movie is, too, although I'm not as breathless about it as Gabrielle.

AR   This is not a short movie, though it's not as long as some of the movies I like best. The thing is, there's something almost lazy about it. So what you do is settle in, put a pillow in the small of your back, surround yourself with snacks from the fridge, and, *voilà!* You'll end up satisfied.

CITIZEN RUTH
1996. 105 min. Laura Dern, Swoosie Kurtz, Mary Kay Place, Kurtwood Smith. Dir. Alexander Payne

Ruth is, in a word, gross. She gets high, passes out, and then throws up on the officer arresting her yet again for inhaling drugs on the sidewalk. She's one of the most unsympathetic characters around—a drug addict, a liar, a manipulator. She's stubbornly ignorant and cares nothing about anything but her next high, not even her four kids. When she's arrested for the zillionth time and finds out she's knocked up again, the judge says she'll be charged with endangerment of her fetus unless, well, she makes the problem go away. So lanky, stoned Ruth becomes the epicenter of a tug-of-war between hymn-singing Christian Baby Savers (led by Place) and lesbian, moon-goddess-worshipping pro-choicers (led by Kurtz). Anyone who thinks this is parody hasn't spent much time watching what goes on outside clinics. It's not at all a polemic for either side, although the pro-choicers come out slightly less smarmy. And there's only one person who comes through with any dignity. If an abortion comedy strikes you as unseemly, try to overcome the squeamishness and give *Ruth* a shot. She's worth it. **CT**

GC The battleground may be abortion rights, but *Citizen Ruth* is a wickedly funny black comedy, drawing a bead on hypocrisy and radicalism on both sides. Dern is terrific.

AR It's like *Dead Man Walking* in the way it points the finger at both sides of the debate. Forget Dern in *Jurassic Park;* she's really got it here.

MARRIED TO THE MOB
1988. 103 min. Michelle Pfeiffer, Dean Stockwell, Matthew Modine. Dir. Jonathan Demme

This movie has style—it's bright and cheesy, and loaded with gum-cracking, Brooklyn-tawkin' housewives. Pfeiffer and her pals are married to guys with names like Vinnie, whose chances of an on-the-job fatality rank pretty high. They live in high-suburban-mobster-style homes where "everything we have fell off the back of a truck." When Pfeiffer's husband gets knocked off by Tony the Tiger, she escapes to a crummy apartment in Manhattan to start a clean, mobless life for her and her little boy. But Tony has a thing for her and won't leave her alone. And because of that she's tailed by a cute FBI agent, Modine, who she thinks is a plumber. Everything's a little over the top in this flick—not *completely* over the top—the colors, the costumes, the Brooklyn accents. You get the sense director Demme and his cast were having a blast when they went to work each day. It's so quirky, I'm not even really bothered by the damsel-in-distress plot. **CT**

GC I love this movie, the whole feel of it. Pfeiffer is fine (pfine?), but I'm crazy about Stockwell's slimy but lovable Tony the Tiger and his hysterically fearsome wife, played by Mercedes Ruehl.

AR   One of my favorite, favorite movies. Modine, who so often fades into the wallpaper, is given a chance to make something of himself, and he does.

THE NASTY GIRL

1990. 92 min. Lena Stolze, Monika Baumgartner, Michael Gahr. Dir. Michael Verhoeven. German w/subtitles

This is a terrific, inspiring chick movie, based on the true story of a young girl who cares passionately for the truth and who defies her family and her community in her search to uncover it. Although the subject is deadly serious, the movie has a jaunty, good-humored feel, thanks to its mock-documentary style and the exuberant personality of its intrepid heroine.

When Bavarian schoolgirl Sonja (Stolze) wins a trip to Paris in an essay competition, she decides to enter another one, and to write about "My Hometown During the Third Reich." It's around 1980, and her town prides itself on its resistance to the Nazis in the '30s and '40s. A funny thing happens, though, as she starts to dig for information on the fate of the town's Jews. Instead of heroism, she begins to uncover evidence of collaboration and worse. Doors are closed, information is refused, and she is threatened and reviled. She's a "nasty girl" to be stirring up all this trouble for her friends and neighbors.

But the more she is thwarted, the stronger she gets. It's exhilarating to watch Sonja grow up, get married, have children, and never waver in her mission. This is a crusader who doesn't need a cape. She's awesome. **GC**

CT   And it would still be a good movie even if she wasn't a chick.

AR   I knew Sonja's story well from newspaper accounts and that didn't at all ruin the film. Verhoeven gambled by applying a comedic touch, and the bet paid off.

THE PRIME OF MISS JEAN BRODIE

1969. 116 min. Maggie Smith, Robert Stephens. Dir. Ronald Neame

The amazing Smith scored an Oscar for her portrayal of an inspirational teacher, and something of a ding-a-ling, in a private girls' school in Edinburgh in the 1930s. Smith is as able at drama as she is at comedy, and puts all her formidable skills to use in a film marred only by a dash too much melodrama and a really stupid theme song.

But Smith and the cast are so good that plot and music hardly matter, anyway. There's Celia Johnson as the headmistress and teacher's antagonist, and Diane Grayson and Jane Carr as two of the gaggle of girls besotted with their instructor, never mind that her sentiments encourage her to find the Fascists in Italy rather romantic. Speaking of romance, there's that, too, and with a married man, no less. Here is a teacher all chicks would have cherished in school, and the very one our parents feared would pop up in front of the blackboard. Bravo! **AR**

GC   Isn't she fantastic? And I liked the politically incorrect Fascist fetish. It gives the movie an unsettling edge.

CT   What an intriguing, unusual role for Smith—a proper, inspirational, art- and beauty-loving, misguided lusty Fascist! Those kind of parts don't come along every day.

REBEL WITHOUT A CAUSE
1955. 111 min. Natalie Wood, James Dean, Sal Mineo. Dir. Nicholas Ray

Actually, young Jim *does* have a cause—and he's not the only rebel. In fact, Judy is the bolder renegade, a teen who defies her parents and, ultimately, "the kids" in her clique at Dawson High to take up with new-to-town Jim, instead of staying with Buzz, the black-leather-jacketed leader of her gang. Both Judy and Jim befriend a disturbed rich kid shunned by everyone else. The powerful trio of Wood as Judy, Dean as Jim, and Sal Mineo as Plato—three actors who died young and tragically—is riveting.

So is the movie, even today. It broke new ground in the '50s, advertised in collector's-item posters that screamed, TEENAGE TERROR TORN FROM TODAY'S HEADLINES. The terror, really, is emotional, the kind inflicted on kids by inattentive parents and by their own peers. And in the end, the teens' response is uplifting. Notes of trivia: Mineo was so sure he would win the Oscar for Best Supporting

Actor that he threw a party the night before the Academy Awards, only to be greatly disappointed the next day. Mineo was murdered in 1976, Dean died at twenty-four in a car crash, and Wood drowned off Catalina Island while her husband, Robert Wagner, apparently slept inside their boat. **AR**

GC　　Great portraits of alienated teens, and still as powerful as it was then.

CT　　The cinematic classic reminder of how mean, petty, violent, and psychotic teenagers can be. It's a wonder any of us live through it. It's thrilling to watch the man who inspired the phrase "He's the next James Dean."

RED-HEADED WOMAN
1932. 79 min. Jean Harlow, Chester Morris. Dir. Jack Conway

The main reason to watch this is to see a chick getting away with something guys have been getting away with forever: outrageously manipulating people so they can get exactly what they want. In this case, redheaded good-time girl Lil (Harlow) lures a society guy into marriage. But the townsfolk shun her nonetheless, even to the point of inviting her husband to dinner but not her, that hussy. So she splits, tells her guy she needs a break from the small-town small-mindedness, goes to New York, and promptly shacks up with one of the richest men around, and then . . . well, I don't want to give it all away. This flick is short, funny, and apparently one of the reasons the censoring Hollywood Production Code was no longer voluntary after 1932. Women's groups and the Catholic Church complained about the overtly sexual nature of the film. (A shameless hussy who remains a shameless hussy? No more!) It's written by Anita Loos (who took over after F. Scott Fitzgerald was fired), who wrote the screenplay for *The Women,* and might be one reason it's so snappy and fresh. **CT**

GC　　"I'm the happiest girl in the world," she confides. "I'm in love and I'm gonna be married!" She's talking about two different guys, of course. Don't you love it? And check out the young, hot chauffeur—it's Charles Boyer.

AR Lil *does* carry on just like a man, which isn't exactly praise. And then, when a fellow slaps her, she says, "Do it again. I like it." Yuk. But that said, the movie is moderately entertaining, especially from a wow-this-was-made-in-'32 perspective.

SHE'S GOTTA HAVE IT
1986. 84 min. Tracy Camilla Johns, Tommy Redmond Hicks, John Canada Terrell, Spike Lee. Dir. Spike Lee

This is Lee's first major movie, and it already has his distinctive signature all over it; a chatty Greek chorus of interested parties, his dad, his sister, a musical number, and—best of all—a window on the lives of ordinary African-Americans with the same foibles and concerns as the rest of society: namely sex.

It's the story of Nola Darling (Johns) and her love life. She has three lovers, all jealous of each other and all of them desperate to convince us, the audience, why they should be the one, the only one. Jamie (Hicks) is the straight-arrow buppie, romantic and thoughtful. Lee plays Mars—smart, edgy, and not a good bet for a young career woman, Terrell plays Greer, a hilariously narcissistic hunk whose idea of foreplay is folding his pants just so before he honors Nola with his attentions.

It's great fun to hear Nola, and the guys, and everybody else in their lives, throw in their two cents' worth about Nola and her relationships. As she finally points out: "It's about control. My body, my mind. Who's gonna own it, them or me?" I'll give you three guesses. **GC**

CT Lee's Mars is a classic! "Please baby, please, baby baby baby please, baby please."

AR Not the best Lee ever made, but with good back talk. Worth a rental.

SILVERADO

1985. 135 min. Kevin Kline, Danny Glover, Scott Glenn, Kevin Costner, Rosanna Arquette, Linda Hunt. Dir. Lawrence Kasdan

I know what you're thinking: I delight in this flick just because Kline and Glover and Costner and Glenn do a lot of swaggering in chaps and thundering astride horses. Because John Cleese puts in an appearance as a sheriff. Because Brian Dennehy is a bad guy (who says things like, "We're gonna give you a fair trial, followed by a first-class hanging.") Because Jeff Goldbum is a gambling dandy in ruffled shirts. And because Kasdan, who also wrote the script, directs in the same fun-loving, caution-to-the-wind way that made *Raiders of the Lost Ark* so engaging. What, that's not enough for you?

Fine. You also have a whole bunch of independent chicks. You have your prostitutes (who say things like, "I want to build something. Make things grow. That takes hard work. A lifetime of it. That's not why a man comes to a pretty woman. After a while I won't be so pretty, but this land will be."), your dance-hall girls, your strong pioneer ladies, and, most importantly, your feisty barmaid (the scene-stealing, marvelous, beautiful, outta-my-way Hunt, who says things like, "Some people think because they're stronger or meaner, they can push you around. But it's only true if you let it be. The world is what you make of it."). A dynamic piece of work. Nothing John Wayne did ever left me so out of breath. And the good guys win! **AR**

GC   This movie is great fun. So are most of Kasdan's other directing gigs; *The Big Chill, Body Heat, I Love You to Death, Wyatt Earp* . . . So can I forgive him for the disgusting *French Kiss*? No way.

CT   Boooooring, and I thought I was going to fall off my chair when Arquette gave that pretty-woman speech in a typical stick-chick monotone.

The Following Clues Should Lead You to Some of the Most Spirited Women in the Movies. Name Them and the Films:

a) She begins her list of demands to Warren Beatty in this epic movie with, ''Here's what I want. I want to sign my own name to my own stories . . .''

b) ''Embrace your liberty and see what wonderful things come of it,'' says this nineteenth-century mother to Winona Ryder, one of her daughters.

c) This director explores women's sexuality in a visually gorgeous movie set in sixteenth-century India.

d) In this movie, the woman who set the standard for independence says, about herself, in her inimitable drawl, ''I guess all talented people are a bit peculiar. It's part of their charm, really.''

e) This princess brings a young Harrison Ford down to earth with, ''I don't know who you are or where you came from, but from now on you do as I tell you, okay?''

f) This feisty star of the 1930s opines in this hilarious but finally flawed movie, ''I know for some women men are a household necessity. Myself, I'd rather have a canary.''

g) Oscar Levant swore he knew this icon of '50s career-girl comedies before she became a virgin. In this movie she crosses wires with Rock Hudson.

(answers see p. 279)

twenty

SISTERHOOD

"Do you love Laurie more than you love me?"
asks Amy (Kirsten Dunst) in Little Women
"Don't be silly!" says Jo (Winona Ryder).
"I could never love anyone more than I love my
sisters."

It's not easy being a sister; just ask Jan Brady driven schizo by
Marcia's perfectness, or Sadie in *Georgia*. Even though I found her
and hence the movie irritating as hell, I could almost feel sorry for
the untalented, underachieving Sadie, who pales in her sister's
shadow. There's a lot to deal with: sibling rivalry, the constant
comparing of looks, smarts, and personality, not to mention the
competition for Mom and Dad's affections, for boys, for clothes. No
wonder sisters' relationships are so complicated. Apparently, though,
like children, they are worth the bother—a special bond of family
and friend. **CT**

GEORGIA

1995. 117 min. Mare Winningham, Jennifer Jason Leigh.
Dir. Ulu Grosbard

This is an original, gutsy movie, a tale of two sisters. And don't
ask me why it's not called Sadie, 'cos it's her story. Georgia (Winningham) has it all—stardom as a country rock singer, a family, a
well-ordered life. Drugged-out, alcoholic Sadie, played in her usual
take-no-prisoners style by Leigh, is a grungy, no-talent mess who
worships Georgia and yearns desperately to sing like her.

I like this movie a lot. It's smart enough not to push any big dramatic developments, it just lets us see Sadie wrestling with her demons, usually in public, and her slippery relationship with her sister. One beautifully rendered scene, when Sadie unravels as she sings Van Morrison's "Take Me Back" on-stage, is a microcosm of the movie, as Georgia, perfect Georgia, watches her sister self-destruct and finally steps in to help ease the pain.

I usually have a hard time watching Leigh. Sure, she can act, but I don't want her killing herself over it. But in this movie she delivers the best performance of her career, so give it a shot.

And here's a welcome switch: You know all those movies that have stick chicks? That's chicks who don't advance the story one iota, or serve any discernible function except as decoration, icing on the cake. (See, or better yet, don't see, *City Hall, A Time to Kill,* and a million other movies.) Well, in *Georgia,* it's the two husbands who play the dependable, supportive spouses.

Another bonus is that all the music is live, and it's tasty, performed on location by Seattle artists. **GC**

AR   Puhleeze! *Georgia* is a self-absorbed, time-consuming, mannered, excessive, exhausting spectacle. A lot like Leigh. Who's given great lines (by her mother, the writer, no less) like *this* to utter: "In the dark we're all scared. We're all scared, and there are more of us all the time." She sure scared me.

CT   Really, insufferable and trite.

HOWARDS END
1992. 142 min. Emma Thompson, Helena Bonham Carter, Vanessa Redgrave, Anthony Hopkins. Dir. James Ivory

One of the things that makes E. M. Forster's novels interesting is that, even though he was writing nearly a hundred years ago, his works have interesting women in them, not mere virginal sex symbols. And *Howards End* is no exception. Thompson and Bonham Carter are the progressive, unmarried Schlegel sisters living in London after the turn of the century. As upper-class do-gooders with comfortable incomes, they take on as a charity case one Leonard

Bast (Sam West), a lowly clerk with a low-class hussy of a wife. The hapless Bast, the victim of good intentions, has to rank among the sorriest men in literature. The sisters occupy themselves with finding a new home for themselves, rescuing Mr. Bast, and falling in love. Redgrave is spectacular as a dying and cherished friend who has a country house named Howards End, and Thompson nabbed the Best Actress Oscar for her role. Once again, as in all Ismail Merchant-James Ivory productions with a screenplay by Ruth Prawer Jhabvala, the film is faithful to Forster's novel. The only thing I find irritating, through no fault of the filmmakers, is that so many on-screen women find happiness by marrying boorish, insensitive—but manly, to be sure—men. **CT**

GC   So forget the guys and admire the flowers. They're some of the most beautiful you'll ever see on-screen. The movie is a visual feast, chockablock with spectacular gardens and interiors. Take notes.

AR   *Almost* as good as the book. And much better looking.

A LEAGUE OF THEIR OWN
1992. 128 min. Geena Davis, Lori Petty, Tom Hanks, Jon Lovitz, Madonna, Rosie O'Donnell. Dir. Penny Marshall

While our boys are off fighting World War II, a candy bar magnate decides to profit off of American's passion for baseball by filling the stadiums with women's, or rather, *girls'*, teams. Lovitz, a baseball scout with a Don Rickles sensitivity, is a scream as he sets his sights on catcher Dottie (Davis) and reluctantly agrees to try out her sister Kit (Petty), too. (Poor Kit, not only is Dottie a better player, but she's better-looking to boot, which will eventually be too much for Kit to bear.) Both girls make the team, the Rockport Peaches, managed by alcoholic has-been Jimmy Duggan (Hanks in one of his most memorable performances—you can all but see the acid reflux working in his gut). The irascible and inattentive Duggan's last chance in baseball is to manage the Peaches, who besides pitching, stealing bases, and hitting the ball out of the infield, have to wear short skirts and attend charm and beauty classes. When he finally realizes these girls can *play ball,* he starts sobering up and getting into it. (He hustles half his team out of church one morning, saying, "God knows we have a game.") Davis is smashing as Dottie, who has "the looks of Greta Garbo" and the talent of Lou Gehrig. Madonna, basically plays her randy self as May, "that's more than a name, it's an attitude," and Rosie O'Donnell is, well, Rosie O'Donnell. There are plenty of gags about the anachronism of *girls* and baseball in this consistently funny comedy (although more than one too many homely jokes). But the ending, which shows actual women from the league visiting their exhibit at the Baseball Hall of Fame in Cooperstown, New York, makes me tear up like a girl. **CT**

AR I whipped out the tissue long before the end and, funny, it's Hanks's character who really gets me.

GC I don't believe you two! This is an okay movie, not crazy enough to be a great comedy, not enough depth of emotion to be a satisfying tearjerker. Cynthia, I know you weep when your yogurt hits its expiration date, but Anne, I thought you were tough. Did Arnold and Jean-Claude teach you nothing?

MANNY AND LO
1996. 90 min. Scarlett Johansson, Aleksa Palladino, Mary Kay Place. Dir. Lisa Krueger

This is a lovely little movie that didn't get the exposure it deserved on the big screen. Manny, eleven, and Lo, sixteen, are on the run. Their drug-abusing mother has died, and the sisters have run away from their respective foster homes. They fend for themselves remarkably well, driving around in their mother's old station wagon, which Lo (Palladino) thoughtfully hid when Mom died. They siphon gas, sleep in model homes, shoplift their food and toiletries. They're tough little cookies, but maybe not that tough. Manny (Johansson) always checks the missing kids' pictures on milk cartons while pilfering the supermarket, just in case somebody cares, and she sprays whatever bed she's about to sleep on with Arrid Extra Dry, because her mother smelled of it.

There's just one fly in the ointment, and it's a rather big one. Lo, although she insists she's just getting fat, is pregnant. Ever practical, they kidnap a woman who looks like the right stuff—she dresses like a nurse and works in a baby-gift store—to help them until the baby is born. But Elaine—played by Place, in fine, batty form—is not quite what they had hoped. And to Elaine, these two scruffy, untamed kids are no prize, either.

Eventually, they all come to realize some basic truths about themselves and each other. And it's fun to watch. The characters are nicely shaded: Manny is the smart, observant one, while Lo is bullheaded and impetuous, and Elaine speaks volumes with her prim, deliberate utterances. Although a lesser movie could have drowned in syrupy sentiment, in writer-director Krueger's capable hands *Manny and Lo* is a small triumph of understated humor and eccentricity. **GC**

CT   I just kept thinking these people remind me of Sally Jessy Raphael show guests, and I don't want to spend an hour and a half with them either.

AR   A sly piece of work, and Gabrielle's right: It could easily have succumbed to the sappiness that would no doubt have ensured it more success at the box office. I'm glad Krueger resisted.

SENSE AND SENSIBILITY
1995. 135 min. Emma Thompson, Kate Winslet, Hugh Grant. Dir. Ang Lee

I think about my sister and me when I watch this, and I really, really love to watch this. It was a standout during the mid-nineties Jane Austen craze, and will be a superstar for as many generations to come as passed before the novel was made into a movie. (Right, that would be two hundred years, and there probably won't be any VCRs in the twenty-second century.) Austen knew how to bring characters to life, and Thompson, who wrote the screenplay, does her no injustice. And Lee makes everything—people, landscape, houses—look beautiful. Except for Hugh Grant, who appears as though he's just suffered whiplash in a carriage accident and let a horse kick sand in his eyes, to boot, though CT would have him anyway, poor thing.

But Hugh can't ruin the tale about the daughters left behind when

Henry Dashwood dies and English law forces him to leave his estate to his son from an earlier marriage. The suddenly impoverished Elinor (Thompson) is rational and calm, while her sister Marianne (Winslet) is burning with passion. "Cold-hearted Elinor!" shouts Marianne when her sister allows that she "greatly esteems" one fellow. "Oh! Worse than cold-hearted! Ashamed of being otherwise." They fall in love with quite different men, and fall in love in quite different ways, but for both, marriage and poverty can make an unpleasant mix. It was a silly era, with its excessive civility and nutty class structure, and Austen knew it. Thompson brings it all up to date with a wry humor. The product is an absolute joy, with the sort of ending that will leave you weeping and wanting for more. **AR**

GC   To me, the most delightful of all the Austen adaptations. And that lovely, witty screenplay won Thompson an Oscar.

CT   A winner in every way, plus it'll make you laugh out loud.

Hollywood's Favorite Sisters

Little Women, written by Civil War–era feminist Louisa May Alcott, is not only one of the most enduring children's books of all time but is also a tale filmmakers can't resist. The story about four nineteenth-century sisters—three lively, one dying—has been made into a motion picture five times, starting with a silent British version in 1917. Maybe it's because it's one of the great weepies of all time, or because it's gloriously nostalgic, or maybe because no one's writing good movies with women's characters, so it's just easier to keep redoing an old classic. Anyhow, in the '90s they came up with the best version yet—even better than the one starring Katharine Hepburn—directed by Gillian Armstrong *(My Brilliant Career, High Tide)* and starring Susan Sarandon, Winona Ryder, and Clare Danes. The 1949 June Allyson version is widely regarded as the flimsiest of the bunch, but it does have the funniest scene of any of them: When Allyson, as Jo, sits too close to the fireplace and her dress catches on fire, Peter Lawford shoves her to the floor and starts pounding on her butt with a fireplace implement.

Test your *L.W.* knowledge with this quiz:

1. Which *L.W.* featured Elizabeth Taylor?

2. In which version do they all—daughters and mother— huddle together like a cat and her newborn kittens?

3. Did Italian actor Rossano Brazzi ever appear in *L.W.?*

4. Did American actor Burt Reynolds ever appear in *L.W.?*

5. What year did Hepburn play Jo, and what did she say about the character?

(answers see p. 279)

twenty-one

DRESSED TO THRILL

"It's the first dress in three years that didn't make me look like a Quaker."
—Carole Lombard, in Twentieth Century

Clothes in the movies are always used as shameless sartorial tricks borrowed from Cinderella, and all she had to do was put on a shoe. All a movie chick needs is a prom dress, a new Chanel suit, or a matching top and pants in black leather to signify her transformation. (See *Sabrina, Roxy Carmichael, Muriel's Wedding* . . .) Wardrobe is also a way to decode chick character: Big fussy clothes suggest vanity (Scarlett, in *Gone With the Wind*). Tight and tailored duds means you've got a murderer or outlaw on your hands (*The Last Seduction, Sea of Love, Johnny Guitar*), and the power suit completes the transformation from country bumpkin with a bad perm to city sophisticate with sleek locks (Michelle Pfeiffer, in *Up Close and Personal*). Wives wear mommy smocks and comfortable shoes, while the other woman wouldn't be caught dead without her high heels and black stockings *(Fatal Attraction)*. My favorite dressers are the Hepburns, either one, who always knew what to wear—Katharine always looking rather butch compared with Audrey's ultralithe porcelain teacup femininity. And, thank God, you don't have to be a woman anymore to dress like one *(La Cage aux Folles, Paris Is Burning)*. **CT**

BELLE DE JOUR
1967. 100 min. Catherine Deneuve, Jean Sorel, Michel Piccoli. Dir. Luis Buñuel. French w/subtitles

Out of circulation for many years, *Belle de Jour* is now widely

available again, and not a moment too soon. Legendary for its cool,
elegant look and its daring portrayal of sexual fantasies, this movie
is one of a kind—chilling, poignant, and funny as hell.

The gorgeous Deneuve plays Séverine, a young Parisian woman
who cannot respond sexually to her hunk of a husband, played by
Sorel, although she truly loves him. Brief flashbacks hint at childhood
sexual abuse—or do they? It's hard to tell where reality gives way
to Séverine's overheated imagination. In her adult fantasies, she is
sexually abused and humiliated. Which doesn't sound that hilarious,
but the master surrealist Buñuel stages these scenes with a wicked
mock-seriousness that tickles the funny bone. Deneuve is shockingly
beautiful, perfectly groomed, and oh-so-tasteful, plus she's dressed
by Yves Saint Laurent, and suddenly there she is, this ice queen,
being dragged through the woods, her chic red suit ripped almost
off, being used and abused and loving it. (I particularly admired the
effect of great gobs of barnyard mud on her gossamer white evening
gown in one pastoral sequence.)

Her fantasies lead her to become a high-priced call girl in the
afternoons, hence the title, *Belle de Jour,* Beauty of the Afternoon.
(She arrives at work in a severe black wool coat with matching fur
hat, very professional.) The perverse fun continues with a deadpan
parade of all of the kinky antics of the brothel's patrons—seedy
interludes framed in the most proper, middle-class surroundings.

Inevitably, Séverine's double life begins to unravel, and her self-
indulgent fantasy life collides with brutal reality, with tragic results.
It's a roller-coaster ride all the way to the stunning ending, so just
hang on to your seat and don't worry if you can't tell fact from
fiction. Neither can Belle. Or is that Séverine? **GC**

CT   I've never been as shocked at Gabrielle's opinion as I am
        now. I don't care how beautiful she looks, or how "French"
        or chic this movie is. The idea that Deneuve loves to debase
        herself by having sex with creepy men makes my skin crawl.

AR   *Shock* is a word with too much substance to be associated
        with this movie. It made me yawn.

BREAKFAST AT TIFFANY'S

1961. 115 min. Audrey Hepburn, George Peppard, Patricia Neal, Buddy Ebsen. Dir. Blake Edwards

Talk about your sleazy couples: Holly Golightly is a whore, and not even an honest one—she takes the money and runs out on clients. She's also run out on an older husband and his kids, and her most strenuous pursuit seems to be window-shopping at Tiffany's. Paul calls himself a writer, but is actually a kept man, a boy toy for a wealthy older woman with the ridiculously affected name of 2-E, who has set him up in a handsomely furnished flat.

Put them together, add a maudlin theme song and a silly plot, and what do you have? Just one of my, and I suspect everybody's, favorite movies. And it's all because Hepburn, as Holly, is a divine, irresistible clotheshorse. Early in the movie, when she puts on that big black hat to go visit her pal in Sing Sing and gives Paul (Peppard) that impish grin, I'm lost. She's enchanting. Her clothes are by Hubert de Givenchy, who must have thought he'd died and gone to heaven to have her model them. Neal, the fearsome 2-E, is dressed by Pauline Trigère, whose strong, dramatic designs provide a perfect foil for Givenchy's more romantic creations. And the legendary Edith Head ran herd on every stitch.

The movie is a sanitized version of the novel by Truman Capote, and won Oscars for the score and that dumb, grating song "Moon River." But, hey, with Hepburn—who could make a flour sack look elegant—dressed by Givenchy and looking so incredibly beautiful, I can forgive anything. **GC**

AR   Capote was unhappy with the film translation, but it suits me more than fine. Peppard, before all those horrible television shows he made, is choice. And, ahem, "Moon River" was one of my grandmother's favorite tunes.

CT   Why do I love that woman so much? She's never been a chick in charge—always a waif or a lost princess. She's just so beautiful that I could watch her no matter what part she's playing.

CLUELESS

1995. 97 min. Alicia Silverstone, Paul Rudd, Stacey Dash, Dan Hedaya, Wallace Shawn. Dir. Amy Heckerling

"What did you do at school today?" asks Dad. "Well, I broke in my purple clogs," answers Cher in this exuberant, utterly delightful movie, where clothes, accessories, and hairstyles rule. *Clueless,* based on Jane Austen's *Emma,* is set in contemporary Beverly Hills, and is narrated by the precocious Cher, played dazzlingly by Silverstone, who explains early on that she and her best friend, Dionne—were named for "great singers of the past who now do infomercials."

The fashions are a blast, and provide much of the movie's humor, but Cher, like her inspiration, Emma, is a good-hearted meddler who wants everybody to be happy and to achieve their potential. She counsels a friend that not only should her daily regimen include care of her mind and her body, she should also "take care of the planet for a few hours," too. Even her despair at Dionne's lack of fashion smarts is without malice: "I must give her snaps for her courageous fashion efforts," she allows.

Heckerling, who directed the acclaimed *Fast Times at Ridgemont High* (1982), has another winner here. Silverstone is perfect as Cher, and she's supported by a wonderful array of talent, including Hedaya as her predator-lawyer father with a heart of mush, Shawn as her long-suffering teacher, and Rudd as her love interest. It's funny, smart, goodhearted, and great to look at. Can't beat that. **GC**

AR   Here's how good this movie is: My *parents* liked it!

CT   And yet Anne and Gabrielle didn't like *The Brady Bunch Movie.* Go figure.

DRACULA'S DAUGHTER

1936. 70 min. Otto Kruger, Gloria Holden, Marguerite Churchill. Dir. Lambert Hillyer. b&w

I adore this stylish, tongue-in-cheek movie. The dialogue is vintage vampire flick, and the fashions, by Brymer, are veddy, veddy elegant. Here's the plot: The old bat's daughter, aka the Countess Marya

Zaleska (Holden), comes to London to claim his body. Suffering pangs (no, not fangs) of remorse at following in Daddy's footsteps, she seeks help from smoothie psychiatrist Jeffrey Garth (Kruger)—aren't these great names?—but blood is finally thicker than no blood, and she reverts to type.

Here's a sample of lines and looks: "This is a case for Scotland Yard!" Civilized British upper-class accents, shooting-party tweeds, and white tie affairs. "If we only knew what caused those two sharp puncture wounds above the jugular!" Backless gowns and great posture, one hell of a ring with hypnotic powers. "Sherry, Marya?" "Thank you, I never drink . . . wine." Chignons and flowing chiffon. Words to a forlorn young woman on a bridge: "The river is cold and dark. I know where there is warmth and food . . . and money. You have nothing to fear. Come." And my favorite line, from the debonair, clueless Dr. Garth, in tails, to his black-crepe-with-bugle-beads-clad hostess: "You know, this is the first woman's flat I've ever been in that didn't have at least twenty mirrors in it!" **GC**

CT Of all the vampire movies recommended by Gabrielle, this is the one I'd watch. It's the least self-conscious, not to mention the shortest.

AR And it boasts some of the best eyebrows ever filmed.

MARKED WOMAN
1937. 96 min. Bette Davis, Humphrey Bogart. Dir. Lloyd Bacon

Chicks in the '30s really knew how to deck out. And "clip joint" chicks were the most chic of all. They didn't call themselves chicks, but girls, and Davis and her roommates, who work nights "entertaining" male patrons of the Club Intimate, are as in vogue as they are in danger—and in control. They parade around the plot in plumes, furs, outlandish hats, face veils, sequins, feathers, and shoulder pads, plucked eyebrows arched and silver cigarette cases at the ready.

A cheesy gangster melodrama, *Marked Woman* is based on the real-life story of New York District Attorney Thomas Dewey's prosecution of mobster Lucky Luciano, whose own hookers' testimony brought him down. Bogart has the Dewey role, and sinister Eduardo

Ciannelli is the Luciano character. But it's the women who carry
the show. They're brave, hard-bitten heroines, realistic about their
profession but not so cynical that they don't want to do the right
thing, once the killings get out of hand. Davis is, as usual, huge fun
to watch.

Note of trivia: One of the girls is Mayo Methot, who fell in love
with Bogart during production and when married to Bogart during
the making of *Casablanca* in 1942 threatened to kill him if he left
her; the nervous agents who negotiated Bogie's contract for the
movie took out an insurance policy on his life for one hundred
thousand dollars. **AR**

GC   Yes, the clothes are great, but they might as well be on
        hangers for all the life in this movie. You have to be really
        committed to silver lamé to sit through this one.

CT   Give me a movie with cynical broads, '30s style, and the
        likes of Davis and Bogart, and you've got me hooked.

PARIS IS BURNING
*1991. 71 min. Dorian Corey, Pepper Lebeija, Venus Xtrava-
ganza, Octavia S. Laurent, Willi Ninja. Dir. Jennie
Livingston*

Forget about tired old drag queens wearing gold lamé dresses the
size of Volvos. The new generation aim to be as sleek and understated as a supermodel wearing Chanel. This documentary of the
Harlem scene where voguing was born is an eye-opening, funny, and
sad exploration of the lives of the young men who have three strikes
against them, being black, gay, and poor. In the words of Venus
Xtravaganza: "I never felt comfortable being poor. Even middle class
doesn't suit me . . . I'd like to be a spoiled rich white girl. They get
what they want whenever they want it." These outcasts have created
a rich and elaborate subculture so outside the mainstream that the
ultimate drag is to look like your average nondescript straight person
on the street, whether it be an enlisted man, a schoolgirl, or the
gangsta who's going to put a gun to your head and take your money.
The queens gather at the balls, where they compete in categories
from Butch Queen to Executive Realness to High Fashion Su-

permodel. Corey, who belongs to the look-like-a-Vegas-showgirl generation, is a font of weary wisdom in the drag world, who misses the sequins and boas of the old days. With interviews and clips from the balls, the film follows several queens over several years, enough time to result in good and tragic endings for some of the movie's stars. **CT**

GC   This movie makes me weep. It's almost unbearable that something as modest as wanting to look like an ordinary person with a regular job is so far out of reach for some people that it's a fantasy.

AR   I'm reduced to quoting a professional critic, David Denby of *New York* magazine, who put it perfectly: "It's the opposite of camp and finally heartbreaking in its longing for the power to be oneself, a power that most of us take for granted."

PILLOW TALK
1959. 105 min. Doris Day, Rock Hudson, Tony Randall, Thelma Ritter. Dir. Michael Gordon

Pillow Talk is pure, frothy, retrograde fun. Its premise is flimsy: Interior decorator Jan Morrow (Day) shares a phone line with songwriter Brad Allen (Hudson). They've never met, but she loathes him because he spends all day on the phone—which she needs for business—sweet-talking one gullible bimbo after another. This leads to all manner of farcical goings-on, but it's all an excuse for sharp one-liners and even sharper fashions and interiors. It's a '50s homage to the good things in life.

It's also a giant milestone in movie history. It's the first in a hugely successful string of Day-Hudson collaborations, and its international popularity helped shape a worldview of the United States as a giant, pastel paradise. I remember seeing it as a teenager, growing up in drab, austere England, drinking in its gorgeous color and frivolity—and wondering if American women had breasts of steel or was Day wearing a bra under that diaphanous nightie? (She was.)

Retro as it is, the movie holds up well. In fact, it's even better today in some respects. Jan's fur-trimmed coats and matching hats have a special endangered-species charm, and to see Hudson, a gay man playing a straight romantic lead, pretending to be gay to get himself out of a tight spot, is double the fun, and double the entendre. And the dialogue stays fresh: "That woman has the taste of a water buffalo." "Why do you do business with her?" "She's a rich water buffalo." And, "There are *some* men who don't end every sentence with a proposition." **GC**

AR   My secret is that *anything* with Day, Hudson, and Randall sends me over the moon. And I love her hats.

CT   This is a great Saturday-afternoon-when-you-can't-deal-with-the-world movie.

SOMETHING WILD
1986. 113 min. Melanie Griffith, Jeff Daniels, Ray Liotta. Dir. Jonathan Demme

What an odd movie this is! It starts out as a romantic comedy and then goes in a completely different direction. Griffith is Lulu, a downtown Manhattan girl dressed like a Masai dominatrix with a Cleopatra black haircut and a spare pair of handcuffs in her purse. Daniels plays Charlie, suburban dad dweeb extraordinaire, the epitome of the dorky white boy as just-promoted vice president. Lulu offers Charlie a ride one morning, takes him to a hotel in Jersey, and takes us on a wild ride of a movie. The funky road trip starts turning into a nightmare with the appearance of Ray (Liotta), who's just about the scariest bad guy I've ever seen in the movies. All the more so because he's sexy and charming—in a Freddy Krueger kind of way—and looks damn good in a T-shirt and tight pants. As always, Demme adds a lot of nice small touches, and has a color scheme seemingly inspired by '60s lunch boxes. One thing that bugs me about the flick is Griffith's character. Without giving away the story, I will say that this bright, mod movie does follow a traditional theme when it comes to taming wild women. **CT**

AR   Odd is right. But Liotta's great, and at least Griffith is in a role where her voice (I know, it's not *her* fault she squeaks) and talents aren't all wrong for the scene.

GC   I love the look of this movie, and it's fun being jerked around by the talented Demme, but God save us from these pat endings.

UNZIPPED
1995. 72 min. Isaac Mizrahi. Dir. Douglas Keeve

Watching *Unzipped* is like getting to hang with one of the country's great fashion designers for a couple of weeks and seeing him in all his moods. That intimate feeling might have something to do with the fact that filmmaker Keeve was Mizrahi's lover when they were shooting, although the relationship was kaput by the time the movie came out. The movie follows the designer in the chaos that goes with putting together a fall collection on a tight deadline. Mizrahi riffs continuously on ballet, pop culture, and old movies, sources of inspiration. ("I'm doing Giselle meets Fred Flintstone," he says of one of his ensembles.) He's a hoot of a mimic and remarkably on target. When he's describing his meeting with Eartha Kitt, the movie toggles back and forth between their conversation and Mizrahi describing their interaction later. It's a scream. He loves her yuppie little dogs, finding them the perfect accessories. "You know it's almost impossible to have any style at all without the right dogs," he says in his fey drawl.

Once again, this is an example of fact being more entertaining than fiction. Robert Altman's *Ready to Wear,* which was supposed to be a send-up of the fashion world, was a deserved bomb. With this kind of material, who has to make stuff up? All you have to do is point the camera at someone like Mizrahi and watch him work with the likes of Naomi Campbell, Kate Moss, and Linda Evangelista. **CT**

GC   Mizrahi is a gas, with his loopy, pop-centered sensibility. "Between Mary Tyler Moore and Jackie Kennedy," he declares, "they shaped this country." For a giddy hour or so, you're ready to believe him. There are some flaws, but as

Mizrahi says about fashion designing, "Is it worth it? Oh, yes. Even when it sucks, it's worth it."

AR   I read far, far too much of the hyped-up publicity about this before finally watching, to the point where I wouldn't wear his outfits even if they fit me. But still, I got a bit of a kick out of the glib look inside a world I can't afford.

THE WOMEN
1939. 133 min. Norma Shearer, Joan Crawford, Paulette Goddard, Rosalind Russell. Dir. George Cukor

Can you imagine the kind of reaction there would be to a movie made today that had not one man in it? Not a good guy, not a bad guy, not a waiter, a bellhop, a TV repairman? Men with hurt feelings would be picketing quicker than you can say *First Wives Club*. Somehow *The Women* got away with it nearly sixty years ago. Still, this flick has been sniffed at by some feminists for portraying women at their manicuring, back-stabbing worst. Plus, while no men are in it, it's actually all *about* men—those pitiful scoundrels. I figure you can cut some slack to screenwriter Clare Boothe Luce given that we're talking 1939. The oh-so-perfect Mary's (Shearer's) husband is fooling around with perfume-counter hussy Crystal (Crawford), and everyone knows it because of Russell's quintessential gossipy busybody. The one-liners fly faster than a tennis ball between Martina Hingis and Monica Seles, particularly in the fashion showroom showdown between wifey Mary and other woman Crystal: "May I suggest if you're dressing to please Steven, not that one, he doesn't like such obvious effects," says Mary. And Crystal responds: "Thanks for the tips, but when anything I wear doesn't please Steven, I take it off." Yowza! *The Women* also has spa scenes right out of an *I Love Lucy* episode, a *Wizard of Oz* effect as the black-and-white movie goes Technicolor just for the fashion show, and the most glamorous ladies' room in history. **CT**

GC   Sniff, sniff. So what if it *was* 1939? That was the golden era of strong, smart, independent women in movies, whereas every character in this movie is a cheap-shot stereotype. If you want to see these talented women act, watch them in almost any other movie, starting with Russell, in *His Girl*

Friday (page 58); Crawford, in *Mildred Pierce;* Shearer, in *The Divorcée,* and Goddard, in *The Cat and the Canary.*

AR Much as I loathe Luce and her marry-up pretensions, she knew her women and put great words in their mouths. "I am what nature abhors—an old woman with frozen assets."

Clothes to Our Hearts

AR Since movies are mostly illusion, I can fantasize—make that hallucinate—about having the figure (and the neck) that would allow me to slip into the designer finery donned by Audrey Hepburn in almost every one of her films, from *Sabrina* to *Breakfast at Tiffany's* to *Charade* to *Roman Holiday.* But not *The Nun's Story* or *Robin and Marian,* please.

CT Put me in the other Hepburn's attire, except for *The African Queen,* where she wore a dress. Otherwise, I subscribe to Sally-wear from *When Harry Met Sally,* which must be modeled after that other Manhattan single girl, Annie Hall. There are enough layers—T-shirt, shirt, vest, tie, jacket—to cover imperfections of the bod.

GC My inner self is tall, elegant, and willowy, with exquisite taste, so I'm drawn to the expensive, layered silks worn by Catherine Deneuve in *Indochine,* or the classic pants and flowing scarves favored by Terence Stamp in *The Adventures of Priscilla, Queen of the Desert*—his stylish day clothes, mind you, not those vulgar stage outfits. For casual, I love the long linen skirts and loose cardigans sported by Vanessa Redgrave in *A Month by the Lake.* My outer self, however, is somewhat shorter and wider, and veers wildly between basic black and flash and trash, with a particular emphasis on loud socks.

twenty-two

I GAVE AT THE OFFICE

*"I read about the guts of pioneer women or the women
of the Dust Bowl and the gingham goddess of the
covered wagon. What about the women of the covered
typewriter?" —Ginger Rogers, in* Kitty Foyle

The office hasn't exactly been the movie chick's domain, except for
a great run in the '30s and '40s. Look at what the movies had to
offer in the '80s: the secretaries of *Nine to Five,* and the sexist,
cartoonish characters in *Working Girl.* I'd like to see more movies
with the zest of 1933's *Female,* where the chick is the CEO of a
car company, or *Woman of the Year,* with international columnist
Tess Harper. (The only problem with some of these old flicks is that
you have to ignore the last ten minutes, where the female is tamed
by some man and has to abandon her office for *the home.*) All too
often, even today, there's the notion that working women are making
a great sacrifice by working instead of getting married. I've never
understood this reasoning, because if a person doesn't work—unless
she's independently wealthy—she'll starve. So that's supposed to be a
choice? If you sit around the house all day and do nothing, a husband
will magically appear at the table you'd be eating breakfast at if you
had enough dough to buy a dozen eggs? Gimme a break. **CT**

BROADCAST NEWS
*1987. 132 min. Holly Hunter. William Hurt. Albert Brooks.
Dir. James L. Brooks*

This is like a 1980s version of *Woman of the Year* (page 200),
another movie about a hyperdynamic newswoman that came out fifty

years earlier. What's astounding is how little has changed in those fifty years as far as plots involving smart, ambitious women are concerned. In the old days, women were having too much fun at their jobs to realize they were missing anything, until the right man came along and showed them what being a *woman* was all about and sent them packing to the kitchen. Nowadays, women may be aces at work, but they're always moping about the fact that there's not some guy leaving his dirty underwear around the house on a permanent basis.

Hunter is Jane, a smart, competent, irritatingly ethical network news producer who spends her spare time sobbing uncontrollably, presumably at the lack of a husband. Her best friend, Alan, is everything a woman likes in a guy: brilliant, funny, multilingual. The only thing is, he's sort of a nebbish. ("Wouldn't this be a great world if insecurity and desperation made us attractive?" he says.) Jane, though, falls for Tom (Hurt), the dim, blond news anchor who's succeeded solely on his looks and who stands for everything Jane hates. (This kind of thing is supposed to happen in eighth grade. Unlike men, most women wise up by the time they're thirty and cast their votes with the smart, funny guy). Despite all that, I like it just to watch the fireworks of Jane at her job running the nightly news, and the performances by all three leads are swell. **CT**

GC Well said, Cynthia. And there's an uncredited cameo by Jack Nicholson that's a gem.

AR I laughed, yes, but in the end, Jane annoyed me. I wanted to scream, "Get a life!"

DESK SET
1957. 103 min. Katharine Hepburn, Spencer Tracy. Dir. Walter Lang

A math quiz: What does silly plot plus silly dialogue plus Hepburn plus Tracy equal? Marvelous movie-watching. This, the eighth of the duo's films, has Hepburn, named Bunny, as the director of a broadcasting company's research department, engaging in this sort of conversation with Tracy as Richard, the efficiency expert hired to secretly computerize the office. Richard: "What's the first thing you notice about a person?'' Bunny: ''Whether the person is a man or a woman.''

And oddly enough, it all comes off swimmingly. Hepburn and Tracy are clearly having a grand time, as are Joan Blondell, Dina Merrill, and Gig Young. Their gusto is infectious, and the role played by the massive, often incompetent computer (the sight of it is funnier every time Bill Gates makes another billion) is as important as that of the humans. But what I really, really like about *Desk Set* is that the women are smart. Very smart. A lot smarter than the men. Without them, computer or no, the company would go down the tubes. Well, without Hepburn and Tracy, the movie would, too. But fortunately, they're on screen most every second and as full of life and love as ever. **AR**

GC   Not one of their better efforts. But, hey, any movie with this pair beats a poke in the eye with a sharp stick.

CT   Hepburn is smashing, and that computer is a gas! Remember when we were afraid computers were going to take over the world? Now that they have, we don't seem to mind.

FEMALE

1933. 60 min. Ruth Chatterton, George Brent. Dir. Michael Curtiz. b&w

This is a hoot of a role-reversal movie, with Chatterton as an auto plant CEO who runs through men almost as fast as her assembly line puts together sedans. Decades before the phrase ''sexual harassment'' was uttered, she was as rapacious as any cinematic Don Juan. Dean Martin or James Bond had nothing on her. When a handsome young engineer designs a new car, she'll tell him to show her the plans later . . . during dinner at her place. After dinner comes vodka, after vodka comes, well, you know. The film makes it very clear what's happening as she tosses satin pillows on the floor. There's not a whole lot to this movie the length of a *60 Minutes* episode. The fun is watching Chatterton bagging every man in sight without being treated as a wanton woman, just another sex fiend executive. Some writers about women in the movies have looked at the ending of this flick as a reason to dump on the whole thing. I don't want to give away the ending, but I will say that the way I look at it, the end seems so absurd and tacked on as a mere afterthought that it shouldn't even be taken into account. **CT**

GC   I'm furious! The movie was great—cheeky role-reversal, hilariously elegant settings, smart dialogue—until the god-awful ending. And no, I can't ignore it. The ending is the logical conclusion of everything that happened, and it stinks! Watch the first fifty minutes, then quit while we're still ahead.

AR   Marvelous! A movie about a strong chick just one hour long. The ending is indeed stupid, but it goes by really fast.

SILKWOOD
1983. 131 min. Meryl Streep, Cher, Kurt Russell. Dir. Mike Nichols

This movie is too long, and there's no suspense because it's based on a real person and we know how it's going to turn out. So why see it? Because it has a lot of other things going for it.

It's 1974, and Streep's character, Karen Silkwood, works in a Oklahoma nuclear-parts factory, is contaminated ("cooked," she says) by plutonium, becomes a union activist, and dies in a one-car wreck while on her way to meet with a *New York Times* reporter, supposedly carrying proof of company safety violations and cover-ups. So that's the plot.

Now for the good stuff. It's all in the characters and their relationships, and the nitty-gritty details of their blue-collar lives. Silkwood lives with her boyfriend, Drew, played by Russell, and her lesbian friend, Dolly, played by Cher. And they're all terrific. (Streep and Cher won Academy Aware nominations for their roles.)

I don't think it's coincidence that this movie was written by two chicks—Nora Ephron and Alice Arlen. Sorry, guys, but I think that's the key here, their chickness. They *notice* stuff like moldy bologna sandwiches in the refrigerator, and not being able to visit your kids because you didn't call ahead and now they have other plans. And how being "cooked" and scrubbed raw plays hell with your skin. And how being a lesbian isn't what defines you as a person. (Quick!

Name two other movies where lesbians are also regular people. Neither can I.)

A postscript to the movie: Kerr-McGee, the company where Silkwood worked, claimed there was no truth to her allegations, and that she was drunk and on painkillers when she died. But for some reason they closed the plant within the next year, and ended up paying her family several million dollars in reparations. Makes you wonder. **GC**

CT　　Okay, so I'm an idiot. Silkwood was one of the news stories I was major tuned out of in college, so I watched it to find out what would happen (and I suspect in 1997 I'm not the only one). Although, I admit, I also wondered if Cher and Streep were gonna end up in the sack.

AR　　Great flick, and proof that Russell doesn't have to wear a lot of leather and fake tattoos to make an impression.

WOMAN OF THE YEAR

1942. 112 min. Katharine Hepburn, Spencer Tracy. Dir. George Stevens. b&w

Hepburn's girl reporter Tess Harding is one of the coolest chicks in movie history. She speaks innumerable languages, impacts the course of international affairs, and is elegant, charming, and yes, beautiful to boot. She falls for a scrappy sportswriter played by Tracy, who, of course, isn't half the man she is. She's the one coming home late for dinner while he holds down the home fort. He puts up with it . . . for a while. Then this flick gets extremely painful to watch as he decides he needs a more traditional wife, and she agrees to try. It's depressing that it was viewed as okay to try to shove successful women back in their cookie-baking places. On the other hand, it may be even more depressing that it's hard to think of any women characters in the movies in the past few decades that are as neat as she is. (In *Broadcast News* Holly Hunter is a dynamic, successful newswoman, but she's also a basket case.) It's hard to even think of a cinematic equivalent to Murphy Brown or any of the strong leading ladies of television. Despite the half-time irritation, *Woman of the Year* is a blast to watch and filled with some hysterical, perfectly underplayed slapstick scenes. **CT**

GC   This was Hepburn's and Tracy's first movie together, and what a treat, even with the woman's-place-is-in-the-kitchen horsehockey.

AR   It's worth the rental because of the two of them, but it infuriates me nonetheless, particularly since Tracy, on all but his good days, really held those sorts of opinions.

These Days in Hollywood, Chicks Earn Half the Bucks.

That wasn't always the case, though hardly a surprise since today's Big Chick Stars are the likes of Demi Moore, Sandra Bullock, and Julia Roberts, no match for yesteryear's Ingrid Bergman, Katharine Hepburn, and Bette Davis. Still, the discrepancies are interesting. Consider: Jim Carrey got $20 million for the disaster that was *The Cable Guy,* while Demi Moore earned $12.5 million for the disaster that was *Striptease*; Julia Roberts earned $12 million for both *Mary Reilly*, a bomb, and *My Best Friend's Wedding,* not a bomb, while Arnold Schwarzenegger pulled in $15 million for *Last Action Hero,* so big a bomb, it was practically an atomic weapon. Even a Big Chick Star on the heels of an enormous hit can't compete with the men folk—Whoopi Goldberg made a measly $8 million for *Sister Act II.*

twenty-three

CADS AND BOUNDERS

*"Oh, men! I never met one who didn't have the instincts
of a heel."*
—*Eve Arden, in* Mildred Pierce

You've met him. Without a doubt, you've dated him. Who is he?
The heel who never remembers your birthday, the scapegrace who
tells you he's going away for the weekend with his sister when he's
actually taking another woman to the romantic bed-and-breakfast *you*
told him about, the sod who hauls the television into the dining room
so he can watch the big game while he chows down on the meal
over which you spent four hours slaving, the rascal who makes eyes
at the waitress *and* the coat-check chick when you're telling him
over a fifty-dollar bottle of champagne that will end up on your
credit card how much he means to you. Goodness, you're not *still*
dating him, are you? If so, you've all the more reason to watch one
of these. **AR**

ALFIE
*1966. 113 min. Michael Caine, Shirley Anne Field, Alfie
Bass. Dir. Lewis Gilbert*

Who else but Caine could have played Alfie, the Cockney
cocksman? He's perfect. He's so good, you want to jump into the
screen and throttle him for being such a callous, self-centered pig.
Not only does he treat his "birds" with contempt, he rubs it in by
taking us, the audience, into his confidence, talking directly to us at
regular intervals. "Any bird that knows its place in this world can

be quite content," he says at one point. He always has a "fiddle," a scam, and prides himself on his lack of entanglements. London is littered with his conquests—naive girls, hard-bitten floozies, housewives, aging playmates. They're all the same to Alfie—he loves 'em and leaves 'em.

After a near-tragedy, Alfie begins to realize how barren and cold his life really is, but he blames that on the birds, too. "If they ain't got ya one way, they got ya another. Know what I mean?" Yeah, Alfie, we know what you mean, you sorry little bastard.

Okay, it's a pretty dated movie, and Alfie would be dead meat if he tried to pull that stuff today, but it's still a must-see. And not just because of Caine's immaculate performance. The rest of the cast is terrific, with polished cameos by people like Shelley Winters and Denholm Elliott, and the famous title song is sung by a barely pubescent Cher. Watch for her in the closing titles. **GC**

AR   Coldhearted Caine! It's impossible to imagine any other fellow pulling this off, not in '66 and certainly not now.

CT   Why is this movie in our book? Sure, Alfie's misogyny is so blatant, it's satire, but it still leaves a bad taste in my mouth. Partly because, like Archie Bunker, I suspect he remains a hero to many men.

THE APARTMENT
1960. 125 min. Jack Lemmon, Shirley MacLaine, Fred MacMurray. Dir. Billy Wilder. b&w

Movie-wise, as Lemmon's C. C. Baxter would say, *The Apartment* is terrific. The opening scene with Baxter's voice-over explaining life in a mammoth, faceless New York office hits the perfect note of cynicism. He's a little fish in a very big pond who lends his close-by apartment to his superiors for their assignations so he can creep up the corporate ladder.

His plan works out fine until he falls for MacLaine's Miss Kubelik, the elevator operator, who just happens to be having an affair with the big boss, played to sleazy perfection by MacMurray, and suddenly Baxter doesn't want to fork over his key anymore.

There's a magnificent supporting cast, and the movie won five

Oscars, three of them to director Wilder, for Best Picture, Direction and shared screenwriting honors with I. A. L. Diamond. It's a strange movie, though, hard to categorize. It's part comedy, part drama, and its subject matter is pretty sleazy. The guys wink and leer and cheat on their wives, and the chicks sleep their way out of the secretarial pool, but somehow—pimp and liar and coward that he is—Baxter is a funny, sympathetic figure, and MacLaine, who attempts suicide over the married boss she's screwing, is cute and virginal. Oh, the magic of the movies. **GC**

CT   I find all those sneering, butt-pinching executives depressing. All I can say is I'm glad I wasn't in the working world back in the '60s.

AR   This is so clearly a product of its day, but what the heck. I like it, anyway. Lemmon is a pip, trying to strain spaghetti with a tennis racket, and the dialogue, actually, isn't really dated at all.

FRENCH TWIST
1996. 100 min. Victoria Abril, Josiane Balasko, Alain Chabat. Dir. Josiane Balasko. French w/subtitles

What a better way to get back at a compulsively two-timing cad of a husband than to invite the van driver who broke down in front of your house to move in? Particularly if the driver (Balasko) is a woman who likes the way you look in those short cotton summer dresses. Abril, a Spanish double of Rosanna Arquette who frequently stars in Pedro Almodóvar's movies, is Loli, the feminine, kid-rearing wife who stays home cooking and cleaning while her real estate agent hubby, played by Chabat, takes prospective buyers to fabulous (and empty) country homes in the south of France—using as many of them as he can for as many extramarital liaisons as he can fit into his busy extramarital schedule.

Loli finds out about her energetically philandering husband just when Marijo shows up at the door and offers a sympathetic shoulder to cry on, a cuddly pair of arms to collapse in . . . and a whole lot more. Hubby realizes the only way to fight for his wife is to stay home—even when the other woman moves into his marital bed—

and hope Loli comes to her senses. Which she does. Or does she? This is a breezy *ménage à trois* comedy as only the French can do with some spectacular South of France scenery thrown in as a bonus. **CT**

AR   Aha! So Cynthia *does* appreciate French slapstick. Any chick who gets a kick out of *French Twist*—as I did—should like *The Tall Blond Man With One Black Shoe* (page 240), too.

GC   Breezy? Must be because it's full of holes. A screws B so C gets even by screwing D, so A screws D to spite C, then B screws C . . . oh, screw them all, they're an unpleasant, implausible bunch of stereotypes.

RASHOMON
1950. 88 min. Toshiro Mifune, Machiko Kyo, Masayuki Mori. Dir. Akira Kurosawa. Japanese w/subtitles. b&w

All we know in this famous, unforgettable story of truths, half-truths, and lies is that a bandit, Tajomaru, has raped a woman, Masago, in front of her helpless, bound husband, and that the husband, Takehiro, is dead. In a series of flashbacks, we are given four different accounts by four different witnesses, the bandit, the wife, the dead husband (through a medium), and a passing woodcutter.

Depending on who's telling the story, Masago, played by Kyo, is either a victim, a willing partner, or a heartless opportunist. Innocent or no, she can't win. The guys see to that. If she was raped, her husband (Mori) considers her damaged goods and is more worried about the loss of his horse; and the bandit, played by the electrifying Mifune, can't even be bothered to look for her when she runs away. If she was willing, her husband wants her dead and the bandit is shocked at her wantonness.

The movie is compelling, haunting, and beautifully photographed. It begins and ends in a ruined temple, where three men, one of them a priest, are seeking shelter from a downpour and retelling the episode. "I don't understand," says one, over and over, as they seek to make sense of the terrible thing that has happened. Don't even try, advises the priest. "Men lie, even to themselves." But, despicable as human behavior may be, the movie ends on a hopeful note as the rain finally stops and one small act of kindness is revealed. **GC**

AR Dang it, I tried (*twice*, having fallen asleep during viewing number 1) to appreciate the importance of this important movie, but I just could not get into it.

CT Not too exhilarating to watch, but so important in movie history, you'll feel better if you do and get it over with.

ROOM AT THE TOP

1959. 115 min. Laurence Harvey, Simone Signoret. Dir. Jack Clayton. b&w

Talk about cads! This movie's chock full of them. Harvey is Joe Lampton, a social-climbing fellow unsure of himself around men, but not women. They rather like him, too, with his semidebonairness and long-drink-of-water looks. But beneath the smooth lurks a tormented, confused jerk of the sort Mother warned us all about.

Joe seduces the silly daughter of the richest man in the English factory town, but also carries on a dangerous dalliance with an unhappy older woman (Signoret), married to a bore who's even more contemptible than Joe. He honestly believes he can get away with this duplicity, and keep himself happy with both women, no one being the wiser. But, oh, what a rude shock awaits him—and viewers, too. Stick with this one, through the rather languid, too-much-talk beginning. Things heat up, thanks much to Signoret and her character's uncomfortable attraction to Joe. Harvey is his best slithering self in this role, astonishing because at several points along the way he convinces us to actually feel some pity for him and understanding for his plight. The most dangerous rascals are the ones who tug at our hearts. Don't say you haven't been warned. **AR**

GC This was one of the first, but by no means the best, for my money, of Britain's Angry Young Men movies, which are full of cads and bounders, including my favorite, the gritty, funny *Saturday Night and Sunday Morning* (1960), with Albert Finney. This movie's best feature is, I think, Signoret. She wipes the floor with Harvey.

CT   I know it's because he does such a great job of being despicable, but I *despise* Harvey deep in my gut. He's just too creepy by half. Even Signoret isn't enough to make me want to watch this flick—even though she won the Best Actress Oscar for this role. I'd rather watch her in something French.

SUDDEN FEAR
1952. 111 min. Joan Crawford, Jack Palance. Dir. David Miller

Palance wasn't *always* old and crotchety à la *City Slickers*. Once upon a time, he was a dashing dude with a nearly full head of hair. He looks good in this glossy black-and-white number, a film noir entry with a bang-up ending. Crawford is an immensely wealthy heiress and playwright who fires Palance from the lead in her latest Broadway romance because he just doesn't look like the kind of guy a girl would fall madly in love with. But when she spends time with him on a train bound for San Francisco, by golly, it turns out he *is* that kind of guy. Does he adore her for her money or for her slightly old-maidish self? If it's the former, how will he get his hands on it? Does she adore him only because no man has ever adored her before? Why is so much time devoted to instructing the viewer how the voice-activated dictating machine in Crawford's study works? Did rich people back then really don ball gowns to play bridge? Why didn't they all die of cancer from smoking so many filterless cigarettes? Most of these questions are answered, and entertainingly, too. The mood is ultra '50s, and part of the fun of watching. Crawford plays her best terrified self, with some of the facial expressions used so well later in *What Ever Happened to Baby Jane?* And the pace after the setup is frolicking. Note of trivia: The actor Touch Connors, in a supporting role, later changed his first name to Mike. **AR**

CT   Sure, it's worth a go. Together they're quite the creepy couple.

GC   I should never have watched that Academy Awards night TV show a few years back, when Palance did those one-armed push-ups. It's hard to take him seriously as a love interest after that. And this movie didn't help, either. I think he's just a bad actor.

And Here Are a Few More Worthwhile Degenerates

Dirk Bogarde: A winner in this category for his sinister, sadistic character in *The Servant* (1963), who gradually, and horribly, usurps his master's authority. Written by playwright Harold Pinter.

Burt Lancaster, Tony Curtis: A twofer, a pair of consummate cads in one dynamite movie, *Sweet Smell of Success* (1957). Lancaster plays J. J. Hunsecker, a powerful and feared journalist based on Walter Winchell, and Curtis plays Sidney Falco, the quintessential slimy, bottom-feeding press agent.

Laurence Olivier: In one of my favorite movies, *The Entertainer* (1960), he re-creates his famous stage role of Archie Rice, a seedy, egotistical vaudeville performer who disappoints and betrays everybody who should matter to him.

Kevin Spacey: He's supremely revolting as an abusive studio executive who finally gets a satisfyingly humiliating comeuppance in *Swimming with Sharks* (1994).

Dabney Coleman: The master of sleazy, venal roles slithers through *Nine to Five* (1980) as the sexist boss of three strong women, played with gusto by Lily Tomlin, Jane Fonda, and Dolly Parton, in her first film role. **GC**

twenty-four

MEN IN UNIFORM

"If sailors didn't exist, we would have to invent them."
—*Jeanne Moreau, in* The Sailor from Gibraltar

Cops, soldiers, preachers, prison guards, mail carriers, UPS deliverymen, flight attendants, astronauts, cosmonauts, baseball players, carpet cleaners, security guards, Republicans (don't they all wear the same outfits?), dental hygienists, and surgeons—hubba, hubba. You know what they say about men in uniform, usually during a military court-martial: Their pants are tight, their shoes polished, and their name tags seductively pinned to their manly chests. But more important, they are quite often strong, dedicated, and courageous. And those are the ones we *really* salute. **AR**

APOLLO 13

1995. 149 min. Tom Hanks, Ed Harris, Kevin Bacon, Bill Paxton, Kathleen Quinlan, Gary Sinise. Dir. Ron Howard

Director Howard turned this historical 1970 space flight into one of the most suspenseful movies of all time, even though we know what's going to happen at the end. Jim Lovell (Hanks) and his crew take off on what is supposed to be the second-ever trip to the moon. Not too long after they've settled down into their space trip, everything goes disastrously wrong. This movie feels like a thriller like *Alien,* where you know a monster is lurking out there somewhere but you never know when it's going to come roaring out. One catastrophe after another threatens the astronauts, from loss of oxygen to an excess level of CO_2. The macho astronauts and the hordes of Mission Control nerds in short-sleeve shirts and ties desperately improvise ways to keep the crew alive and get them back to Earth. The movie, with clips from Walter Cronkite and other newscasters, builds into a climactic scene that will propel most viewers out of their seats. *Apollo 13* won Best Picture at the Oscars (yay!), and Quinlan was nominated for Best Actress (huh?). Her part was to look worried for five days . . . what's that say about women's roles in the movies, even today? **CT**

GC   Great job, Opie. I never expected it to be so white-knuckle suspenseful and dramatic.

AR   How'd he do that, anyway? Loved it.

DAS BOOT
1981. 150 min. Jurgen Prochnow, Herbert Gronemeyer. Dir. Wolfgang Petersen. German w/subtitles

Don't take *Das Boot* home if you tend toward claustrophobia. Instead, rent *Voyage to the Bottom of the Sea*, the most famous and most awful submarine movie ever produced. You won't alight from *Das Boot* nearly as gently, though you will have a thought or two in your head, once you stop sweating. Hmmmm. On second contemplation, even if you fear small spaces, go ahead, and drag the VCR and TV into a large room. Set in 1941 on one of the Nazis' famous U-boats, *Das Boot* is a suffocating two and a half hours of authenticity. (Yes, two *and a half* hours. This is why the Japanese invented the fast-forward button right after they invented the VCR.) The way the camera moves focuses your attention on how confined and enclosed a ten-foot-wide submarine is.

Petersen throws tedium next to horror, in a nice cinematic description of what war is about. Prochnow is compelling as the intense, kind captain whose men don't much like war, but are noble Germans who do their duties—reminding you of just the same sorts of fellows you've seen in countless American and British war dramas. I first watched this in a theater, with English subtitles, and then rented the English-dubbed video. If you can find it at your video store, select the original. Subtitles remind you that you're watching a *German*-made film about *Germans* who think Hitler's a drag. **AR**

GC   Hitler a drag? That's a tad mild for a genocidal monster. This poignant movie puts a human face on just one of the tragic statistics of World War II. Of the forty thousand sailors who served on U-boats in that war, thirty thousand were lost.

CT   Call me shallow, but I couldn't get into it.

DEAD POETS SOCIETY
1989. 128 min. Robin Williams, Ethan Hawke. Dir. Peter Weir

Williams is Mr. Keating, the teacher for whom we'd all bring polished apples to school. He is smart, dedicated, and unconventional, willing to go to nearly any extreme to pass on his love for poetry and prose. "Why do we need language?" he asks his students, boys in a conservative prep school in the '50s. Comes the answer, "To communicate?" "No!" says Mr. Keating. "To woo women!" Williams is tremendous, good in the funny bits, of course, better when he's called upon to be serious. *"Carpe, carpe diem!"* he shouts. "Seize the day, boys! Make your lives extraordinary."
    But Williams is not why you should rent *Dead Poets Society*. Instead, do it for the kids: Hawke, Robert Sean Leonard, Gale Hansen, and Josh Charles. They're tremendous individually and together. Each of their stories is believable. They may well break your heart as they are inspired by Mr. Keating's lectures against conformity, and follow advice he may not have meant to give, some with tragic consequences. And then there is the poetry, recited by the young men in the secret hiding place where they make their society. Thoreau sums it up: "I went into the woods because I wanted to live deliberately. I wanted to live deep and suck out all the marrow of life . . . to put to rout all that was not life; and not, when I came to die, discover that I had not lived." **AR**

GC   This is such a tiresome, coy movie. It may be 1959, but it might as well be 1859 for all these sheltered little slugs and their keepers know or care about the world. No beat poetry, no rock-and-roll, no nothing. For two terrific, and Oscar-winning, teacher roles, see Robert Donat, in *Goodbye, Mr. Chips,* (1939) and Maggie Smith, in *The Prime of Miss Jean Brodie* (see p. 172).

CT   "Suck the marrow out of life?" Thoreau belongs in books, not in a Robin Williams flick. Still, I must admit, guiltily, I liked it.

FROM HERE TO ETERNITY
1953. 118 min. Burt Lancaster, Montgomery Clift, Deborah Kerr, Frank Sinatra. Dir. Fred Zinnemann

This is an epic movie about army life on a Hawaiian base at the time of Pearl Harbor. Most famous for the love-in-the-pounding-surf scene between Lancaster and Kerr, it has much more to recommend it. For example, Lancaster in his formfitting khakis. Maybe I've been around Anne too long, but that man has a fine tush. Check it out.

The movie has a mammoth, excellent cast, with some memorable performances. Kerr plays an unusual role for her, a woman of overt, and not too discriminating, sexuality. Lancaster's first words on seeing her are: "I bet she's colder than an iceberg." Sure. Lancaster crackles with energy and animal magnetism as the sergeant who loves an officer's wife but loves the army more. Sinatra is terrific in his Oscar-winning portrayal of the scrappy, bighearted Maggio, and Clift—three years before the dreadful accident that rearranged his face—is especially poignant as the moody, reluctant warrior Truitt. The cast includes Ernest Borgnine, perfect as a malevolent bully, Donna Reed, Jack Warden, Claude Akins, and too many other fine actors to mention.

My favorite scene is when Maggio and Pruitt, dressed in their other uniform, Hawaiian shirts, hit the town together, laughing and clowning. They're so young and goofy and somehow innocent, I was moved almost to tears, both at the fragility of young lives in wartime, and to know that Sinatra would become a coarse, arrogant s.o.b. as he aged and that Clift would hardly have time to age at all. You know it's a good movie when it gives you more to think about than you bargained for. **GC**

CT   Don't forget Donna Reed, who won the Best Supporting Actress award for playing (can you believe it?) a prostitute, a mere five years before she became the nation's number one perfect postwar housewife and baby boomer breeder on TV's *The Donna Reed Show.*

AR   And the wags were worried that, without the four-letter words and sex in James Jones's best-seller, the movie wouldn't work. How wrong they were.

GALLIPOLI

1981. 110 min. Mel Gibson, Mark Lee. Dir. Peter Weir

An antiwar movie of the first order, *Gallipoli* gives the history-challenged a brutal lesson in the suicidal World War I invasion of Gallipoli by the Australian-New Zealand Army Corps. But it's also a touching reading of friendship, and of dreams lost to the harshest reality.

Frank (Gibson) and Archy (Lee) are sprinters, tempted by the vastness of Australia to run, by youth to compete. But patriotism convinces them to abandon track careers for the ANZACs, a decision you absolutely know is foolish as it's being made. You also know, even if you didn't learn about Gallipoli in school, that calamity is ahead as they approach Turkey. And that it will be the young men and their hopefulness that suffer, not the stupid generals or inept communications equipment that gives the Turks and their German allies a deadly upper hand. The battle scenes are beautiful—if such things can be described with such a word—and Gibson and Lee are wonderful together. Fact is, I'd have insisted *Gallipoli* be in the hunks chapter, if all the boys' loveliness weren't, in the end, such a waste. **AR**

GC   And that last frame is a killer. A lovely, sad, atmospheric movie.

CT   Together they were just a little too pretty for me. If they had been lovers it might have been more interesting. They sure gazed into one another's eyes like they were.

GORKY PARK

1983. 128 min. William Hurt, Joanna Pacula. Dir. Michael Apted

One great thing about this flick is that it's set in the Soviet Union *before* Gorbachev and the Berlin Wall smashup and the end of the Cold War. Director Apted pulls you convincingly into bureaucratic, seedy, corrupt, snowy Moscow (actually, it's Helsinki, as the Soviets in the early '80s refused requests for shooting on-site). But Apted, following the plotline in Martin Cruz Smith's best-seller, doesn't take the usual entry ramp. Hurt, as Renko, isn't a KGB agent or Communist leader or dissident, but a hardworking police officer, a guy who—like honest movie cops everywhere—just wants to close the case. His challenge is to figure out who killed three young people whose bodies, the skin removed from their faces and fingertips, are discovered near the skating rink in Gorky Park. Hurt's challenge is to maintain a consistent Russian accent, but his performance, not to mention his very fine looks, is rock-solid enough that you'll only infrequently wonder why he sounds Swedish.

A very good murder mystery, *Gorky Park* also succeeds in offering a harsh look at what life was really like in Soviet Russia. The mystery and the Soviet system can't be separated, really, and the conditions under which Renko is forced to work are many of the reasons he is such a dedicated and ultimately successful police officer. The reminder that there really was an Iron Curtain is all the more powerful when you know that when the movie was made, Pacula, in her first English-speaking role as the dissident with whom Renko falls in love, was in exile from her native Poland, where Communist authorities had closed the theater where she worked. **AR**

GC For once I agree with everything Anne says, and I *will* mention Hurt's very fine looks. He's a hunk, in his just-trying-to-do-my-job-ma'am, decent-guy way.

CT Hmm, I liked everything but Hurt, who seemed just too damn American to fit into this role convincingly.

HOOP DREAMS
1994. 169 min. Arthur Agee, William Gates. Dir. Steve James

Why is it that many of my favorite movies are documentaries? Maybe because you can't beat them for dialogue, suspense, dramatic tension, and character development. *Hoop Dreams* follows the changing fortunes of William Gates and Arthur Agee, two Chicago teenagers hungry to play with the NBA. The filmmakers show how these two adolescents consumed by the American dream are mere pawns in the money-thirsty sports industry, whose tentacles run all the way down to the junior high school level. You never know where this is going. One minute you think one kid has it made and the other is doomed, and then their fortunes change again, largely due to their determination to succeed despite severe setbacks. They struggle with academics, with injuries, with failure, always knowing the threat of being tossed away as just another ghetto kid if they hurt their knee or fail a test.

Surrounding them are family members who are counting on them for their own validation, like Gates's older brother, who was a high school star but now works low-level jobs, when he can get them, and Arthur's father, who's in and out of the family's life as well as in and out of trouble with the law. The mothers are formidable, memorable women. Have a hankie ready when Arthur's mother gets her nurse's aide degree. This movie will have you on the edge of your seat, break your heart, and give you hope. I could go on and on. *Hoop Dreams* goes on my top ten list. **CT**

AR   Why is it that few of my favorite movies are documentaries? But you got me with this one.

GC   Fantastic, must-see, and everything else Cynthia says.

IN THE LINE OF FIRE
1993. 123 min. Clint Eastwood, John Malkovich, Rene Russo. Dir. Wolfgang Petersen

Eastwood, father of five, the most recent of whom is far too young to read this, once again plays against type, which is becoming type for him, now that he's old enough to play his own uncle, if you know what I mean. As if you *cared!* He is better-looking and far superior an actor in his later years than he was when he was making noodle Westerns in Italy (*A Fistful of Dollars,* the one that started it all, came out in 1964), or running about San Francisco with that large firearm under his tacky tweed blazer.

Here, he's an out-of-breath Secret Service agent who can't shake the awful memories of the assassination of the young president he was protecting thirty years before. And who should pop up to haunt him as he guards the current chief executive but creepy Malkovich as a CIA agent gone really bad? *In the Line of Fire* is a tightly wrapped suspense trip helped out by good acting all around, and by Eastwood's ability, even with his arthritic bones, to dazzle a much-younger Russo. Also sweat-producing are the telephone conversations between Eastwood and Malkovich. Watch, and wonder: Has he, or hasn't he? If he has, who's his surgeon? If he hasn't, who's his trainer? **AR**

GC Eastwood is great. He actually raises a sweat in this movie—and from acting, not just running. Malkovich is over the top, though, and Russo draws the dreaded Stick Chick role—no earthly reason to be there except to prove the old guy can still get it up. Hope they paid her well.

CT Clint doesn't give me any hormone rushes, but with him standing in front of the Lincoln Memorial saying, "Well, Abe. Damn. Wish I could've been there for you, pal," the movie, at least, is irresistible.

MALCOLM X

1992. 201 min. Denzel Washington, Angela Bassett, Al Freeman, Jr. Dir. Spike Lee

Why this movie didn't win the Oscar is an outrage. Why it wasn't even nominated is a sin. It's not your typical Lee flick—an offbeat, radically photographed mood piece and exploration of race issues—but a big-time Hollywood blockbuster movie like they don't make anymore: a grand-scale production with a huge cast, thousands of extras, and a major star. And it's based on a man who played a critical and controversial role in U.S. history.

X has everything: from the search for spirituality and justice to deception and intrigue to exuberant dance scenes and shoot-outs, not to mention the sheer moviemaking spectacle shots in the Egyptian desert. It even has elements of a war movie as X leads his armies of men wearing the crisp suit-and-tie uniforms of the Nation of Islam.

Lee mixes in the actual, sickening news footage of blacks being sprayed with hoses and set upon by dogs in the '50s and '60s, and it all comes together a whole lot better and with more concern for historical accuracy than in any of Oliver Stone's movies. Another interesting tidbit, shown at the end, are newsreel shots of the real Malcolm X, who is virtually indistinguishable from Washington, who should have won the Best Actor instead of Al Pacino for *Scent of a Woman*. **CT**

GC   What planet have you been living on, Cynthia? Did you really expect the Academy to pick an honest, historically accurate portrayal of a controversial black revolutionary over a fictional, blind, irascible but lovable old military vet? Dreamer.

AR   Hey! Pacino was *great* in that role. But, okay, Washington was better. Lee redeemed himself with *X* after the tacky *Jungle Fever*.

A MIDNIGHT CLEAR

1992. 107 min. Ethan Hawke, Gary Sinise. Dir. Keith Gordon

Good war movies don't need much warfare. They need, mostly, young men, innocence, fear, and hope. *A Midnight Clear* has these, a superb cast, and, importantly, vast tracts of sparkling, crunchy-under-foot snow in the Ardennes forest in 1944. The setting is too white and clean to accept death, and the inexperienced American boys dispatched by a crazy commanding officer on a scouting mission can believe they'll escape it. And in fact, the war-weary Germans they discover in the forest greet them with snowballs and Christmas carols. The fleeting relationship between the enemies is so sweet, it almost hurts, and just as heart-hurting is the tenderness the American soldiers feel for one another. They've even given two of their number nicknames that sustain the feeling of family: One is Mother, for his efforts to instill neatness and order, and another is Father, because he wanted to be a priest. *A Midnight Clear* is sometimes painful to watch, but impossible to switch off. There is something almost religious about it, the impression helped by a haunting sound track. When so much goes wrong, as you know it will, the music doesn't alter. It's beautiful, like the snow, and like the souls of the innocent on both sides of war. **AR**

GC   One of my favorite movies, tender and eloquent. It's smaller in scope, but just as moving, as the brilliant 1930 epic *All Quiet on the Western Front.*

CT   I hate to say it, but this really is a war movie for chicks. It emphasizes the soldiers' humanity—even the bad guys'— and it highlights how brutal stupid, power-seeking people can be. Of course, at the risk of being trite, they were all very cute, too, some of them landing big-time TV and movie roles since this came out.

A Real Man in Uniform

That was Jimmy Stewart. He was thirty-two years old and a mere 130 pounds when he showed up at the local draft board at the start of World War II and should have been 4-F, like George Bailey in *It's a Wonderful Life.* But he insisted he had to do something for the Allied cause and, as he said in an interview recounted in the *Los Angeles Times* on his death in 1997, "after they got over their surprise, they told me it was simple. 'We just won't weigh you, and we'll put down any weight you want . . . !' And that's what they did. And I was in." Stewart, who had won the Oscar in 1940 for his performance in *The Philadelphia Story,* was accepted into army flight school (first wrapping up *Come Live with Me, Pot o' Gold,* and *Ziegfeld Girl*) and soon was flying B-24s over Europe. Despite studio entreaties, he made no films while in uniform. He completed twenty-five combat missions and ended up a full colonel with the Distinguished Flying Cross, the Croix de Guerre, and Air Medal with three clusters. Returning to Hollywood, he found the studios eager to put him back to work—though only in films trading on his war experience. He refused to cooperate. It wasn't until Frank Capra, himself a veteran, told him about an idea for a nonwartime story that Stewart agreed to consider making another movie—which turned out to be *It's a Wonderful Life*. "I can't say it took much acting," Stewart said in the interview. "I knew that character that I was supposed to play. He was my father. I just pretended I was him."

twenty-five

DYNAMIC DUOS

"If I'm going to die, let me die with the only friend I ever had."
—*Kirk Douglas, in* Gunfight at the O.K. Corral

Women and men aren't the only pairs who make for charismatic cinematic couples. Sex isn't everything (though you might not believe that while reading this book). Opposites can attract, men fall in love with one another, outcasts find friendship, and the travails of life can create incredible bonds. Often it's the nontraditional relationships that are more fascinating to watch on-screen . . . two strangers from different worlds thrown together and forced to figure each other out, whether it be the lonely women of *Bagdad Café,* the prisoners of *Kiss of the Spider Woman* or the—albeit very different—adult-child friendships of *The Professional* and *Cinema Paradiso.* **CT**

ATLANTIC CITY
1980. 104 min. Susan Sarandon, Burt Lancaster. Dir. Louis Malle

You know those movies that have one unforgettable scene? One that just takes your breath away? This movie has one: It's when Sarandon's character, Sally, stands at her kitchen sink and performs her nightly ritual of rubbing lemons on her hands and arms to get rid of the fish smell from the hotel oyster bar where she works. In the soft lamplight, listening to Bellini's "Norma," she dreams of becoming a croupier and living in Monaco. From his darkened window her neighbor, Lou, watches her, as he does every night. Beautifully captured by Lancaster, he's an aging, small-time hood who pays the rent by looking after, stealing from, and occasionally sleeping with a gangster's widow. He looks at Sally with such regret and longing in his old, red-rimmed eyes, and the whole movie just falls into place and is magic.

Sarandon and Lancaster interact magnificently as two flawed characters among a crowd of less-than-sterling types who are all out for the easy buck, and too bad, sucker, if you get in the way. But Malle, a master at getting to the heart of things, treats them all with great tenderness, including the city itself, which is so powerful a presence that it's like another character, just as seedy and hopeful as the rest of them. And it didn't hurt that the screenplay was written by playwright John Guare.

This was my favorite Sarandon role before she made *Thelma & Louise*. Now it's a tie. As for Lancaster, he was so handsome when he was young that I never thought of him as a great actor. He had to grow old to break my heart. **GC**

CT Intellectually, I know this is a "good movie." But emotionally it left me cold. Lancaster looks like a sleazy corpse, and everybody else in the movie gives me the creeps, except Sarandon, who's, well, you know, Sarandon.

AR *Au contraire.* I found the character played by Lancaster, looking trim, to have such noble-beneath-it-all qualities that I felt deeply for him.

BAGDAD CAFÉ

1988. 91 min. Marianne Sägebrecht, CCH Pounder, Jack Palance. Dir. Percy Adlon

Stuffed into a hot brown suit like a bratwurst—with her plump ankles puffing out of her matronly shoes—a woman who looks like a Bavarian innkeeper arrives at a motel-café in the middle of the desert outside Las Vegas. She shows up on foot with nothing but a suitcase full of men's clothes—including lederhosen. Pounder's Brenda, the frustrated, cranky African-American motel owner who seems to suffer from a case of chronic PMS, is highly suspicious of this German dumpling who's just landed at her doorstep. Who is she? Where is she from? And why is she staying at this place that's just a tiny collection of eccentrics out in the middle of nowhere? This is one of my favorite movies of all time. All the aesthetic elements come together seamlessly: the story, the acting, the photography, the music. The interesting characters are contrary to stereotype, including Brenda's teenage son, who practices his Bach incessantly, much to his mother's annoyance, and a likeable kook played by Palance. In a word: *exquisite*. **CT**

GC In another word: *aimless*. It's got a lot of potential, but nothing happens. There's no plot, no action. I found it ultimately frustrating.

AR I'm a fence-sitter. It's quirky and charming in spots, but confusing and slow-going in others.

BECKET

1964. 149 min. Peter O'Toole, Richard Burton. Dir. Peter Glenville

The adaptation of Jean Anouilh's stage play is essentially a buddy movie, but with highfalutin talk (the characters all sound like GC) you never hear in *Lethal Weapon* or *48 Hours,* and a better denouement, too, especially seeing as it happened in real life eight hundred years ago.

O'Toole is Henry II, and Burton is Thomas Becket, best friends because Henry wants it so and because Becket is allegiant to whatever master he is instructed to serve. This ultimately causes Henry grief, for after he arranges almost on a whim for Becket to be consecrated in 1162 as Archbishop of Canterbury, he learns the man he loves has a sense of duty not reserved for earthly rulers. Becket is basically a good man, and Henry, being kingly, is basically not, and the fatal tale of their relationship is one of the best ever told.

Does this sound depressing? It's not. The script is full of good lines, many of them funny, as when Becket introduces a skeptical Henry to the concept of a fork at dinner, or when Henry, shocking his bishop and various deacons with a demand that the church help him pay for his next war with France, listens impatiently as they complain that "this has never been spoken of before," and roars back, "I've never been this poor before!" Even mundane exchanges sound wonderful because they're delivered by Brits with BBC accents. No one talks better than O'Toole and Burton, anyway. A note of caution: Though the story is full of twelfth-century-style warring and sexual escapades, *Becket* does meander into snatches of dulldom during its two hours and forty-eight minutes (that's too *long* to sit on the couch!), so you might want to keep the remote control at the ready for an occasional FF. **AR**

GC No, don't FF around with this movie. It's too good. Get extra cushions, lie on the floor, take an intermission, call in sick . . . whatever it takes.

CT Henry said the diners would think the forks were new weapons, and they did, those crazy medievalists. I agree with Gabrielle: Recline, relax, and settle in to this one.

CHOOSE ME
1984. 106 min. Genevieve Bujold, Keith Carradine, Lesley Ann Warren, John Larroquette. Dir. Alan Rudolph

In this movie, everybody yearns desperately to be half of a twosome, any twosome. Little details like compatibility and responsibility are steamrollered by the urgency of those two little words: *choose me.*

Product warning: Not everyone can take this movie. I personally find it beneficial, even addictive, but it has been found to cause severe irritation in some viewers. A lot depends on whether you can stomach Bujold. She's not usually my cup of tea, but she's actually endearing in this movie. But then, I find everybody endearing in this movie. It has that effect on me.

Bujold plays a radio sex-talk show host, Dr. Love, also known as Anne, who can only speak to her shrink over the phone. Everybody in *Choose Me* has problems. They're all looking for love, and never in the right places. Eve (Warren) owns a bar and sleeps with her bartender (Larroquette) when she really wants Micky, an escaped mental patient, played by Carradine, who wants her, too, except he sleeps with Anne. Eve needs a roommate, she takes in Anne. Eve has too many men. Anne has none. (You can't really count Micky.

Anyway, he hears voices.) Eve tells Anne, "Why don't you just keep the house and all the men I've collected?" Sounds reasonable.

It's all improbable coincidences, shattered dreams, and fragile hopes for that one connection. Eve to Micky: "Marriage is a sacred thing, isn't it?" "In a beautiful but sordid way," he replies. If you agree, you'll probably like this movie. If not, don't say I didn't warn you. **GC**

CT   Despite some howlingly bad dialogue, I like the way everyone's interconnected, nobody really knows who anyone else really is, and the most honest person in the whole thing may be the pathological liar.

AR   I liked Bujold in *Anne of the Thousand Days* and nowhere else, including here, where she seems half asleep. But *Choose Me* is like *Johnny Guitar* (page 49): so bad, it's good.

CINEMA PARADISO

1989. 123 min. Salvatore Cascio, Philippe Noiret, Jacques Perrin, Marco Leonardo. Dir. Giuseppe Tornatore

I don't understand how American audiences could flock to another Italian import, the beautiful but slow-going *Il Postino,* and not watch this flick in equal numbers. Okay, it's not a love story in the handsome boy meets impossibly beautiful girl and loses his heart vein. It is a love story, though, between a boy and an old man, between the two of them and the cinema, and of the whole Sicilian town and the movie theater. Shot in Bagheria, Sicily, Tornatore's semiautobiographical film plots the friendship of the fatherless Toto and Alfredo, a projectionist who has to snip out all the kisses and fondles in the films under the direction of the town priest. Three out of the four actors mentioned above play Toto as a boy, an adorable little boy, a madly cute teenager, and then a rather unsympathetic adult. (I will say Toto did much better as a boy and a teen than he did as a man.) *Cinema Paradiso* is lush with beautiful imagery, and a lilting score that will remind you of the Sicilian town whenever you hear snippets of it. A cinematic equivalent of a hot cup of cocoa, sweet and warm and nostalgic, and not the thing for someone who needs a double shot of espresso. **CT**

GC   I found the two characters charming, but it didn't quite catch fire for me. Put me down for a cappuccino.

AR   I smiled throughout and even teetered on weepy now and again. I also wrote down my favorite line, which sounds original when spoken by Alfredo: "Life isn't like the movies. Life is much harder."

DEAD AGAIN
1991. 107 min. Kenneth Branagh, Emma Thompson. Dir. Kenneth Branagh

Pop this into your VCR and what you see, after the FBI warning and a few opening credits, is a headline screaming MURDER! It's all uphill from there. Branagh and Thompson—still hitched and the perfect couple when they made this movie—play two roles each, Branagh as a present-day private eye (American accent), and as a composer of operas in 1949 (German accent); Thompson as the composer's dead wife (British accent), and as a woman who's lost her memory in 1990s Los Angeles (American accent). Sound confusing? More's the fun! The flashbacks are in black and white, helping the flustered among us keep track of then and now as the plot transits back and forth. As the contemporary Branagh, a finder of lost heirs, roots about in Thompson's unremembered life, he finds himself poking into the erstwhile murder of the wife who, funny, looks an awful lot like the attractive amnesia victim. Reincarnation? Past lives? Sins revisited?

Hypnotist Derek Jacobi pulls some answers out of secret-revealing trances, and a discredited shrink played by Robin Williams helps Branagh think things through. Eventually, but not too soon, the identity of the murderer is revealed, setting up a boffo ending. The whole thing is delicious. Branagh directed—he did *Henry V* two years earlier—and infuses the work with his theatrical bravado, not to mention his comely presence. Why did Emma divorce him? Oh, right, there was that little matter of Helena Bonham Carter. Don't hold that against him when it comes to art. **AR**

CT *Dead Again* can't hold a candle to other Branagh-Thompson ventures. It has a TV-movie-of-the-week feel to it. I'd rent it, though, if I were in the mood for a whodunit, just because those two are such compelling screen presences (and it's a kick hearing their American accents).

GC So then young Kenneth, bored with Shakespeare, says, "Hey, kids, my dad's got a barn! Let's put on a show! I've seen a lot of Hitchcock and other great directors! We can rip them off! I can do accents! You, too, Emma! Oh, *do* let's! It'll be *such* a lark!" And it is.

HEAVENLY CREATURES
1994. 99 min. Melanie Lynskey, Kate Winslet. Dir. Peter Jackson

This wonderfully bizarre and chilling film is based on the true story of two New Zealand teenagers, Pauline Yvonne Parker and Juliet Marion Hulme, who become obsessively, erotically involved with each other in their private, fantasy world. When the real world intrudes, murder results.

Winslet, as Juliet, and Lynskey, as Pauline, are shockingly effective in their first major roles, and Jackson provides them, and us, with a stunningly realized other world of castles, royal lineage, fantastical beasts, and humanoid creatures. It's a world the girls inhabit more and more fully, until it eventually swallows and replaces their real, schoolgirl world of gym classes and homework.

Most powerful and intriguing of all is that the diaries kept in the movie, a detailed account of both real and imagined events, are the actual entries in Pauline's diaries, kept during 1953 and 1954.

After the pivotal event of the movie, a murder, the girls are separated, never to meet again. In real life, Pauline stayed in New Zealand, and Juliet moved to Scotland, where, years later, it came to light that she had become a best-selling author of murder mysteries, writing under the pseudonym of Anne Perry.

If you ever doubted that truth was stranger than fiction, and infinitely more fascinating, see this excellent movie and believe. **GC**

CT   It reminded me of how intense teenage girl friendships can be, although none of mine led to murder—not that I know of.

AR   I was an airplane-seat fan of Perry's books before this movie came out and her cover was blown, and boy, I read her stuff with a whole new attitude now.

IN THE HEAT OF THE NIGHT

1967. 109 min. Sidney Poitier, Rod Steiger. Dir. Norman Jewison

Don't even *think* about the television show. That worked with *M*A*S*H*—wasn't the boob tube version better than the original?—but the small-screen rendition of this transcendent piece of work held not even the wick of a candle to the Best Picture winner of 1967. That is due almost entirely to Poitier and Steiger (the latter garnered Best Actor honors), whose characters never, ever become as buddy-buddy as did their TV counterparts of the '90s. And thank goodness. I'll bet you know the most famous line, even if you've not yet rented the video. It is declared by Virgil Tibbs (Poitier), a black Philadelphia homicide detective visiting his mother in rural Mississippi who is arrested on general principles after a rich white man is found murdered. Virgil is off the hook once his occupation, and the fact that he earns more than anyone in Sparta, is discovered by Sheriff Gillespie (Steiger) in a scene that I find supremely satisfying every time I see it. The rather discomfited sheriff then says, "Well, you're pretty sure of yourself, ain't you, Virgil. Virgil, that's a funny name for a nigger boy to come from Philadelphia. Whatta they call you up there?" To which Virgil responds, "They call me *Mr.* Tibbs." Old Gillespie has a lot of good lines, my favorite being, "I got the motive, which is money, and the body, which is dead." The relationship between these two men is the beauty of the movie, which was exceptional in the '60s and just as remarkable today. **AR**

CT   Highly evocative of the small-town South in every way—from race relations to the steamy climate. Bravura performances, powerful movie.

GC I hadn't seen this movie in years, so I was curious to see if it would seem dated. It didn't. It's still as powerful. But is that good news or bad news for race relations?

KISS OF THE SPIDER WOMAN
1985. 119 min. Raul Julia, William Hurt, Sonia Braga. Dir. Hector Babenco

The movie that inspired the hit musical is not a musical at all but an intense, claustrophobic, and riveting drama with exceptional performances by Julia and Hurt (who won several Best Actor awards, probably because he played the homosexual part). Confined together in a Latin American jail cell, Molina (Hurt), who's in for corrupting a minor, and political prisoner Valentin (Julia) endure excruciating days of boredom and paranoia. As the flitty Molina wearing a flowery robe, Hurt moans he's locked in a cell with the crabby, depressing Valentin while he might have hoped for a handsome, blond leading-man type to help pass the time. To mentally escape the confinement of the cell, Molina recounts a favorite movie of his for Valentin, who's being slowly poisoned by prison guards and slowly charmed by Molina. Julia exudes a musky, raw masculinity as Valentin and the two develop an unusual, complicated relationship while they serve out their sentences. **CT**

AR I really miss Julia. Wasn't he grand?

GC These two make up one of my all-time favorite duos. And I'm tickled that it was movies that kept Molina going, even tacky movies. I bet *he* liked vampire flicks.

THE MAN WHO WOULD BE KING
1975. 125 min. Sean Connery, Michael Caine. Dir. John Huston

Huston dreamed for decades of making a movie of Rudyard Kipling's short story, and considered pairing Humphrey Bogart with Clark Gable or Burt Lancaster with Kirk Douglas or Richard Burton with Peter O'Toole. We're lucky he couldn't get the project off the

ground until the 1970s, and that it's Connery as Daniel Dravot and
Caine as Peachy Cranahan who enjoy and suffer adventures in Kafi-
ristan. With Christopher Plummer as Kipling himself, there are three
great performances, but Dravot and Cranahan are the duet that makes
this a classic. They spar, they bicker, but they love one another.

India is just too small for these two ex-soldiers, and already ruled
by the British, so they set off for what is now Afghanistan to find
some natives to reign over. And Dravot is at one point mistaken for
a god. But they don't find quite what they expected, and Kipling
offers a few nicely put lessons about imperialism. Even without a
moral, the story is thrilling and silly. For all their woes, why would
these fellows want to return to London? "Home to what?" Peachy
asks. "A porter's uniform outside a restaurant and six-penny tips
from belching civilians for closing cab doors on their blowzy
women?" Speaking of women, there aren't many, but it's a chick
movie nonetheless, with swashbuckling, good-looking guys, and romance of the sweeping vista kind. "Keep looking at me," Peachy
says. "It helps to keep my soul from flying off." Huston's good at
that, too. **AR**

GC   "Three summers and a thousand years ago . . ." is how
       Peachy begins the tale. Great storytelling from a master, and
       great chemistry between the two stars.

CT   Connery and Caine have never been better, and the scenery
       is smashing, too.

PASSION FISH
*1992. 136 min. Mary McDonnell, Alfre Woodard. Dir.
John Sayles*

Soap opera star May Alice (McDonnell) wakes up in a hospital
to learn that she is now a paraplegic. Her new circumstances do not
turn her into a noble, proud, determined character, but rather a bitch,
literally, on wheels. She returns to her childhood home on the bayou
to escape her life, and is so nasty, bitter, and self-pitying that she
runs through just about every home-care worker in the state of Louisiana. Then former crack addict Chantelle (Woodard) shows up.
Chantelle needs to get this job and keep it, but she's willing to

sacrifice only so much of her dignity for it. This sets the stage for your basic "two opposites are thrown together, need each other to survive, and learn to love each other" kind of movie, but it doesn't go there. Well, okay, it kind of does go there, but not in a TV movie kind of way. It's got more bite, and it doesn't hurt that scratchy Cajun music bounces in the background and not some overblown sappy Hollywood wind symphony. Dynamite and memorable performances by both actresses. **CT**

GC   It had all the ingredients to be a great movie, and I kept waiting to get really involved. Never did, and God knows I had enough time.

AR   It does meander toward languid, but it can be pleasant if you're in an easygoing frame of mind.

THE PROFESSIONAL
1994. 196 min. Natalie Portman, Jean Reno. Dir. Luc Besson

Harumph. Highfalutin critics were offended that Besson made a movie about the relationship between a 12-year-old girl and a hit man. Dissolute? I think not. There's a moral to this story, by golly, and great performances by Portman as old-before-her-time Mathilda and Reno as milk-drinking, plant-loving Leon (not to mention a hugely over-the-top Gary Oldman as a drug enforcement officer; he is one weird dude, and I mean both of them).

Portman and Reno are a strange and wonderful team as Mathilda and Leon. Mathilda's family, too screwed up to be worthy of the dysfunctional label, is wiped out in an extremely violent sequence, and she takes refuge with Leon, who lives in the badly appointed apartment next door. Soon, she's wheedling him into teaching her the tricks of his trade. But their alliance is tender and sweet nonetheless. Throw in a bit-o-suspense and what you have is a weird and compelling little flick, though one definitely not for the squeamish. (Besson, by the way, directed *La Femme Nikita*.) **AR**

GC   Sick, sick movie. And all the more disgusting because this is a director and a cast who should know better. To exploit a child to titillate the audience's appetite for violence is

nothing short of pornographic. And, Oldman, get a grip.
You're not fun anymore.

CT   Oldman is indeed cartoonish and unbelievable, but Portman
is stunning and smart, as always, in her film debut, and I'm
glued to anything she's in. "Pornographic"? From the
woman who drools over *Belle de Jour*? Oldman's not the
only one who needs to get a grip.

TRUE CONFESSIONS

*1981. 108 min. Robert De Niro, Robert Duvall. Dir. Ulu
Grosbard*

Go figure. Grosbard directed the tedious *Georgia* (page 178) about
sisters in 1995 and this dandy little number about brothers fourteen
years before. What on earth happened to him in between? The brothers are a Catholic priest played by De Niro and a homicide detective
played by Duvall, who after years of estrangement are thrown together in the aftermath of the murder of a prostitute in Los Angeles.
Based on the book by John Gregory Dunne, it takes us into the
unattractive underbellies of the Catholic Church, the business world,
and the L.A. police force. Along the way, the brothers, each struggling with ethical questions they would rather not face, come to
terms with their difficult relationship. Some of their answers are
disturbing, as are parts of the movie, but that's what makes it compelling. And De Niro and Duvall are tremendous together. A plus: Set
in the 1940s, this movie really *looks* like the 1940s. **AR**

CT   And it really feels like another *Godfather* movie.

GC   Funny, I found *Georgia* dandy and this one tedious. Yes, De
Niro and Duvall are good, but I found their characters too
depressing and cynical to care much about.

twenty-six

THE BEST MEDICINE

"Laugh now, Heathcliff. There's no laughter in Hell!"
—Hugh Williams to Laurence Olivier,
in Wuthering Heights

I seldom agree with the Supreme Court, that merry band of jokesters. But I think their famous definition of pornography serves well for humor: I can't define it, but I know it when I see it. In other words, you're on your own in this chapter. I haven't a clue. My sense of humor was warped at a tender age by multiple siblings, Yorkshire pudding, and socialized medicine. I still find the word *knickers* hilarious.

Furthermore, I've been accused, usually by Cynthia, of laughing inappropriately at things like war, famine, pestilence, and death. True, but only when they're funny. I agree with whoever it was, and I'm pretty sure it wasn't a Supreme Court Justice, who said some things are too serious not to laugh at. **GC**

ARTHUR
1981. 97 min. Dudley Moore, John Gielgud, Liza Minnelli. Dir. Steve Gordon

This is one of my favorite movies of all time, and it's tied on my list with *La Cage aux Folles* (page 67) for the funniest. I just wish they could remix the sound track and remove the dated Christopher Cross score that sits on the movie like a layer of melted margarine ("When you get lost between the moon and New York Ci-ty"). Arthur (Moore) is the world's most lovable drunk. He's a worthless human being worth $750 million. He's good for nothing but having a good time. Gielgud plays Hobson, the long-suffering and infinitely intellectually superior valet, who looks after Arthur with care and comic reserve. Our young millionaire falls in love with Linda Marola (Minnelli), a ditzy broad from Queens. This is a problem, because if he doesn't marry Susan, a dull, sickeningly sincere debutante, he will lose every penny he has. Moore's and Gielgud's characters are so strong and so joyfully acted that Liza can actually fit in without overpowering everybody else. She's sweet as a waitress and wannabe actress who lives with her shaggy-dog father. One of my favorite lines is when Arthur points to a moose head mounted on a wall in his future father-in-law's house and asks, in his sloshed slur and earnest confusion: "Where is the rest of this moose?" **CT**

GC   I liked *Arthur* when it came out, particularly Gielgud. ("I'll alert the media," is his dry response to Arthur's announcement that he's going to take a bath.) But it doesn't wear well. Being drunk isn't that funny anymore—unless you're Peter O'Toole in *My Favorite Year* (page 236)—and Minnelli never was—funny, I mean, not drunk.

AR   Didn't enjoy it even the first time around. Minnelli's annoying, and Moore's, uh, annoying. On second viewing, even Gielgud was annoying.

THE AWFUL TRUTH
1937. 92 min. Irene Dunne, Cary Grant, Ralph Bellamy. Dir. Leo McCarey. b&w

If you could only watch five screwball comedies in your lifetime, this delicious, dizzy romp should be one of them. Director McCarey won a well-deserved Oscar for it, and the movie received six nominations.

Here's how it goes: New York socialites Jerry and Lucy Warriner (Grant and Dunne) suspect each other—wrongly, of course—of infidelity, and have ninety days before their divorce becomes final. They both intend to remarry immediately, she to a hokey Oklahoma oilman, and he to a hoity-toity debutante. But they can't stay away from each other, and spend the ninety days in a hilarious series of plots and scrapes, trying to sabotage each other's wedding plans.

As I was laughing myself silly, it suddenly dawned on me that a big part of my delight in this movie is that Lucy is a complete, terrific individual. She's smart, sexy, lovely, loyal, loads of fun, and secure enough to make an utter idiot of herself, as in the scene where she pretends to be Jerry's loudmouthed, drunken sister to embarrass him in front of his oh-so-proper future in-laws. They just don't make 'em like that anymore. Pity. **GC**

CT   Exactly, and it has one of my favorite movie scenes: when Grant pays a court-ordered visit to his dog and they sing together at the piano.

AR   Extremely silly, and extremely enjoyable. Imagine—Dunne was considered a "serious" actress before this came out.

THE GODS MUST BE CRAZY
1981. 109 min. N!xau, Marius Weyers. Dir. Jamie Uys

A Bushman named Xixo is taken aback when a Coke bottle, tossed from the window of a prop plane, plops down near him in the Kalahari Desert. He carries it back to his village, where members of his tribe discover it has many uses, as a rolling pin, a flute, a children's toy, an implement for cooking. It is so sought after that Xixo's once-peaceable tribesmen and women begin to bicker over it, and he decides that the only thing to do is return it to its rightful owners: the gods. This leads Xixo on a journey that introduces him to "civilization," white do-gooders and Keystone Koppish black rebels.

There is a bit more stupid violence than necessary and a few gags some still see as borderline racist: You judge. I find the movie charming. A South African effort released before the demise of apartheid, it was a smash in Europe in the early '80s and then a bit of a cult thing in the U.S.—it even has its own Web page on the Internet. The best part about it is the rational presence of N!xau, an actor whose name is all but unpronounceable for us Americans—the ! denotes a sort of cluck of the tongue. The director searched for him for months, and he's reason to watch. **AR**

GC   There's no borderline about it. It's tasteless, racist, and patronizing.

CT   I'm going to wimp out and sit on the fence on this one, finding it not particularly funny or racist. It did make me wish for more movies from Africa, though.

IT HAPPENED ONE NIGHT
1934. 105 min. Claudette Colbert, Clark Gable, Walter Connolly. Dir. Frank Capra. b&w

This movie is one of the greats. It was the first to win all five Academy Award biggies—Best Picture, Director, Actor, Actress, and Screenplay (Robert Riskin). Colbert plays the spoiled, imperious heiress Ellen, who is running away from Miami to New York to meet the man she loves. Gable's Peter, a hotshot, rakish reporter, is chasing her, angling for her exclusive story.

Unlike most comedies of this era, this one acknowledges there's a depression going on, and, since Ellen left home almost penniless, we get to see how the poor people live. It's a Capra movie, so it's pretty darn swell to be poor, and hell to be rich. As Peter and Ellen cross the country together, falling deeper in love with every mile, they get to sing along with the other bus passengers, line up for the shower at an auto camp, and wave to happy hobos on passing trains.

Peter's machismo is decidedly dated. He tells Ellen to shut up, slaps her rear, and opines that what she needs is "a guy who'll take a sock at her once a day whether she needs it or not." But, hey, it's a sixty-year-old movie, and it's otherwise so delightful, and these two make such a dynamite, appealing couple, that I'm going to cut it some slack. Hoping you do the same. **GC**

AR   It deserves all the slack we can muster.

CT   It's cute, I'll give it that. But I don't understand its reputation as one of the best of all time. All I could think of looking at Gable's projectory ears was a line I read somewhere about Prince Charles: He looks like a Volkswagen with both doors open.

MY FAVORITE YEAR

1982. 92 min. Peter O'Toole, Mark Linn-Baker. Dir. Richard Benjamin

There is one word for this movie: delightful. Actually, that is *delightful*. I'm besotted with O'Toole, but that goes only a little bit of a way toward explaining why *My Favorite Year* is one of My Favorite Movies. There are so many hilarious scenes, so judiciously few touching moments, such great performances by bit players—oy! I'm laughing as I'm typing!

Here's the setup: It's the early 1950s, back when Sid Caesar was making folks who had those little black-and-white television sets in their living rooms double over with his live *Your Show of Shows*. O'Toole is the aging, famous, boozing, womanizing, matinee idol scheduled to be the big guest on the weekly *King Kaiser* (get it?) *Show*. Linn-Baker (you might remember him from his 1980s television sitcom, but try not to) is the conscientious young fellow assigned by the nervous studio bosses to make sure the feeling-no-pain O'Toole makes it to rehearsals. Does this sound familiar? Mel Brooks was way back when once assigned to chaperone Errol Flynn in the days before his appearance on *Your Show of Shows*. Lord help New York if Flynn in real life was anything like O'Toole in *My Favorite Year*. If so, Flynn should never have tried acting; O'Toole is better *pretending* to be Flynn.

Are you thinking *Lawrence of Arabia*? Don't. O'Toole is incredible here, his comic timing impeccable, and his sloshedness so plausible, you will either want to stir up a martini or take an aspirin. I giggle every time I catch this one on very, very late night TV and curse the commercials. **AR**

GC   My sentiments exactly, Anne. O'Toole can do no wrong for me, although he really pushed it with that dreadful *High Spirits* (1988).

CT   He's boorish, his character at least, and so is the movie.

PRIZZI'S HONOR

1985. 129 min. Jack Nicholson, Kathleen Turner, Anjelica Huston, Robert Loggia. Dir. John Huston

Nicholson is priceless in this black-comedy homage to Mob movies as Charlie, a dim-bulb Mafioso with terrible taste in sports jackets.

At a family (as in Cosa Nostra) wedding, he falls for Irene (Turner), who turns out to be a professional "hitter," a hired killer. The bad part is, she's Polish. As Charlie succinctly puts it, "You ain't no Wop." Now we're about to find out if blood is thicker than love. Or money.

Every convention of Mafia movies is shamelessly and skillfully skewered: the creepily courtly Don, honor besmirched, women defiled, partners double-crossed, and enemies rubbed out, all to the strains of Italian opera. The dialogue is choice, spicy, and satisfying as your mama's meatballs. "Just because she's a thief and a hitter don't mean she's not a good woman." "Sicilians: They'd rather eat their children than part with money, and they're very fond of their children."

Turner is at her wacky, evil best as Irene, wrestling with the conflicting demands of loving wife versus dedicated career woman. Huston, under her father's direction, won a Supporting Actress Oscar for her role as May Rose, a chic decorator who is the black sheep of the family. She is sublime, a Sicilian goddess who personifies all the family virtues—revenge, hatred, suspicion, and treachery. May Rose carried a torch for Charlie until the night he . . . well, I ain't no snitch. Just see this movie if you know what's good for you. **GC**

AR   Oooooo! I thought you were going to give the great ending away. What comes before is a hit, too.

CT   Agreed. Plus, great use of music that contributes to the whole thing instead of detracting from it or being merely invisible.

SLEEPER
1973. 88 min. Woody Allen, Diane Keaton. Dir. Woody Allen

It's amazing that there is anyone on the planet who has not yet seen this movie sans television commercials. It's also amazing that there are people on this planet who were born after 1973, when I was in—never mind. For those of you younger than me, who have not had the chance to watch uninterrupted this hysterical sight-gag-filled masterpiece of political and sexual commentary without any real point, delay not. Forget that Keaton was Annie Hall, difficult an assignment as that may prove. Forget also that Allen is at this writing married to his former girlfriend's daughter.

Set two hundred years in the future, *Sleeper* is sophisticated slap-stick that holds up well. One of the very best of many best scenes is the belated awakening of Allen as a Greenwich Village health food store owner put into the deep freeze after failed surgery for an ulcer—imagine how *you'd* react after two hundred years asleep, and you'll not be able to conjure up anything close to this amusing. (Some of the lines are funnier now than when the movie came out, because they remind us of how very long ago 1973 was, as when Allen's character discovers a copy of *The New York Times* from 1990 and reads a headline: " 'Pope's Wife gives Birth to Twins.' Wow!'') Allen's stint as a robot butler, when he's introduced to the orgasmatron, is also a whoop. Since *Sleeper,* there hasn't been as much hilarity in one hour and twenty-eight minutes. **AR**

GC It's all wonderful silliness, but don't laugh so hard you drown out the great score by New Orleans' Preservation Hall Jazz Band.

CT Sorry, I don't get it. I would have thought one would have to be a teenage boy to think things like orgasmatrons were funny.

SO I MARRIED AN AXE MURDERER

1993. 93 min. Mike Myers, Nancy Travis, Brenda Fricker, Amanda Plummer. Dir. Thomas Schlamme

This is a dizzy, fast-moving comedy about fear of Commitment, the big C. Myers plays Charlie McKenzie, a San Francisco poet who panics as soon as relationships take a serious turn. When he falls for a butcher, played by Travis, his paranoia blooms big time, and he convinces himself she's a husband-murdering psycho.

Actually, with parents like his, a cleaver-wielding maniac might be a refreshing change. Myers, in a second role as Charlie's bel-lowing, haggis-loving father, and Fricker, as his raunchy, blowsy mother, bring us one of the funniest, coarsest couples ever to disgrace the sacred bonds of matrimony. (Dad's shtick with Charlie's younger, cranially challenged brother is a classic.). There are beat-poet send-ups, and Rod Stewart songfests, a bouquet of cameos by stand-up comedians, including Charles Grodin and Phil Hartman, and a huge wink to Alfred Hitchcock for the hanging-by-the-fingernails suspense sequences. It's a great vehicle for comic Myers, and he does it justice. It's all good, gory fun, and there's even a message: Love conquers all. Nice work. **GC**

AR   I really, really, *really* find Myers annoying. But I gotta admit it: I did not hate this movie. Now and again, I caught myself half-giggling.

CT   Okay, I liked it, too. And I found Travis appealing, even though she somehow managed to turn a Russian-speaking, possibly murderous, butcher character into something of a stick chick.

SOME LIKE IT HOT

1959. 119 min. Jack Lemmon, Tony Curtis, Marilyn Monroe, Joe E. Brown. Dir. Billy Wilder. b&w

This movie is sublime. From the opening theme, the manic "Running Wild," to the famous, classic last line, it's a hoot, an inspired, exhilarating ride. Lemmon and Curtis play two musicians who witness the St. Valentine's Day Massacre and escape the mobsters, led by the spats-sporting George Raft, by fleeing to Florida disguised as Geraldine and Josephine, respectively, in an "all-girl" band. Monroe's Sugar Kane, the band's vocalist, welcomes them as bosom buddies, Josephine falls for her, a millionaire playboy (Brown) falls for Geraldine, and the rest of us fall down laughing for the next two hours.

Among all the hilarity, the movie gets in some sly digs at gender and relationship hang-ups, which makes it all the more satisfying. Lemmon and Curtis are magical, and it's poignant to watch Monroe's giddy, breathless Sugar, given her fragile emotional state—she was dead of a drug overdose within three years. When Wilder was asked why he didn't fire her for being difficult and unreliable, he said he had an aunt who would learn her lines and show up on time, but nobody would pay a nickel to see her. What a guy.

Movies as good as this one give me goose bumps. It's awesome that a couple of bucks can buy such talent and give such pleasure. **GC**

AR   Chock full of fun stuff like this: "Have I got things to tell you—I am engaged!" "Who's the lucky girl?" "I am!"

CT   And it's a thrill to see Lemmon in a comedy that isn't based on his boiling frustration, like *The Apartment* (page 203) or *The Out-of-Towners.*

THE TALL BLOND MAN WITH ONE BLACK SHOE
1972. 89 min. Pierre Richard, Bernard Blier. Dir. Yves Robert

French slapstick? But, of course. And very funny. Toulouse, the snooty chief of the French secret service, discovers that his double-crossing second-in-command, Milan, has bugged his flat. Toulouse sets a trap for Milan by making sure he hears that a superagent who will uncover the double-crossing is set to arrive at the airport at 9:30 A.M. the next day. Then Toulouse instructs his aide-de-camp to go to the airport, pick any inconsequential man out of the crowd, and make sure Milan's boys start trailing the poor sap. The aide, for reasons unclear even to him, selects the hapless violinist François, who happens to be wearing one black shoe and one brown. Milan's men pick up the scent and follow François, while Toulouse's men follow Milan's men, and François, of course, remains comically oblivious.

The various agents assigned to the surveillance should be bored silly, but since they think François is a wily spy, they are intrigued by the mundane. Their microphones pick up everything, including François's battle with a broken loo. "Why does the idiot flush the toilet so much? Peculiar," says one, calling his superior to report. Telescopic X-ray camera lenses capture puzzling images. "What's in his violin case?" "A violin." "Hmmmm." Hah! This was such a hit that Hollywood remade it in 1985—badly—with Tom Hanks wearing a red shoe. Note of caution: The dubbed video version strangely loses something in the translation, so rent it with subtitles. **AR**

CT   This looks like a Gene Wilder movie spoken in French, and is about as funny. Take that any way you want to.

GC   So I rented it with subtitles. It *still* loses something in the translation. Mainly, humor.

Some Movies Are Laughable without Even Meaning to Be

GC's   favorites

Striptease (1996): I wanted to hate this movie, but Demi Moore is so hilarious, I just couldn't. It's ego gone berserk: She's hot, sexy, buffed, smart, brave, moral, and a good mother, gets to show her tits, and she even put her own kid in this piece of garbage! All that plus $12.5 mil. You have to laugh.

The Blue Lagoon (1980): Just thinking about it makes me giggle. It's *terrible!* Castaways Brooke Shields and Christopher Atkins are so utterly thick. They swim and laze and eventually make a baby, with no idea where the little sucker came from. It's a great argument for sex education in schools. And her hair keeps getting longer and then shorter. Must be the saltwater rinses.

Blood Beach (1981): Mindless, plotless gore. There's something really nasty under the sand at this beach, and it sucks, really. It devours small animals whole and any human appendages that happen to rest on the surface. We *told* that guy not to lie on his stomach! But it has one great line. "Just when you thought it was safe to go back in the water— you can't get to it."

AR's   favorites

Red Sonja (1985): This swashbuckler has Brigitte Nielsen as a female warrior, and Arnold Schwarzenegger as the fellow who helps her battle an evil sorceress, and a crystal ball that warns Sonja of great danger, and a muscle-bound chick's club that protects the ball, and a ten-year-old prince who falls in love with Sonja, and lines like, "I know you are a brave girl. But danger is my trade." Need I say more?

The Quick and the Dead (1995): A laugh-a-minute, with dust. Grimacing Sharon Stone pretends to be Clint Eastwood, but in tight chaps and strangely '90s-looking sunglasses, and baby-faced Leonardo DiCaprio is a hardened killer named, of course, Kid. It's campy, but not on purpose. It went almost directly to video store shelves, where it's collecting more dust, because it's in "Westerns," not "involuntary comedies."

CT's favorite

Stayin' Alive (1983): In *Saturday Night Fever*'s sequel Tony (John Travolta) has shed his disco gold chains and moved to Manhattan, where he's pursuing a song and dance career. He gets his break in a Broadway show called *Satan's Alley* that culminates in an apocalyptic S&M dance number with fireballs. Even worse than it sounds.

twenty-seven

VILE, VICIOUS VIXENS

"She's a bad little girl and you should have known it."
—Lionel Barrymore, in Calling Dr. Kildare

If there is equality in films, it's in the depiction of wickedness. Moviemakers have a heck of a time ginning up roles for chicks as powerful or brave or complicated or just plain interesting, but when it comes to characters who are the opposite of nice, no problem. Run it through your noggin and see what you come up with: *Mommie Dearest. What Ever Happened to Baby Jane? Misery.* You know the drill. And we're not complaining. The role of a mean and nasty person of the female persuasion is usually meaty, and we're thrilled to see a chick pull out all of the stops on screen, even if she uses wire coat hangers. To boot, it's fun when scary sisters give us the creeps. Yup, women can be just as abominable as men. **AR**

ALL ABOUT EVE

1950. 138 min. Bette Davis, Anne Baxter, George Sanders. Dir. Joseph L. Mankiewicz. b&w

Some of the best lines ever spit, hurled, or just plain spoken in the movies are in Mankiewicz's classic about back-stabbing New York theater life. Mankiewicz wrote the script and directed, and hired the perfect cast to do the spitting, hurling, and speaking. Davis as Margo Channing, in one of her cigarette-voice, bitch-goddess roles, utters several better known than the movie itself, including: "Fasten your seat belts, kids. It's going to be a bumpy night." Cynical Thelma Ritter, as Davis's maid, has two of my favorites: "She re-

minds me of an agent with one client,'' as she observes the obsequi-
ous, conniving, and wicked Eve Baxter making nice to stage great
Channing; and, ''This bed looks like a dead animal act,'' evaluating
the furs thrown down by stylish ladies attending the party during
which Davis warns guests about the rugged ride.

The movie is a lot of unforgettable talk and great theater—on- and
offscreen. One tidbit is that the legendary Davis was looking for
something to jump-start her career when Claudette Colbert broke her
neck and couldn't take the part of aging Broadway star Margo Channing, which today seems impossible inhabited by anyone but Davis.
She's joined by other perfect fits: Baxter, as the villainous hanger-
on; Sanders, as the viperous critic; Celeste Holm, as the understanding friend; and, briefly, Marilyn Monroe, as a breathless starlet in a
role that caught Hollywood's attention. All told, *All About Eve* is
catty good stuff. **AR**

GC　It's all yummy, but I especially love the cynical, world-
weary Sanders: "My natural habitat is the theater. In it, I
toil not, neither do I spin. I am a critic."

CT　A classic that everyone should see at least twice and probably has. An interesting tidbit: Davis was nominated for Best
Actress but lost out to Judy Holliday in *Born Yesterday*
(page 47).

THE GRIFTERS
*1990. 110 min. Anjelica Huston, John Cusack, Annette Ben-
ing. Dir. Stephen Frears*

You'd be hard put to meet three more unpleasant, corrupt characters than Lily, Roy, and Myra, the protagonists in this blood-chilling
tale of connivers and tricksters. Lily, played by Huston, runs a scam
at the track and skims big time from her racketeer boss. Her son,
Roy (Cusack), is a small-potatoes con artist, and Myra, played by
Bening in her first major role, is a high-stakes real estate and jewelry
operator who meets up with Roy. Lily reenters Roy's life after aban-
doning him for years, and meets Myra, who is awfully, and I mean
awfully, like Lily. We have a feeling things will not go well. They
do not.

Adapted from Jim Thompson's novel, *The Grifters* is a brilliant, if nasty, piece of work. Martin Scorsese narrates in voice-over, describing the finer points of all our antiheroes' dirty schemes. What's unusual is that these individuals have not one redeeming social value among them, yet we are riveted. At one point, Lily's boss, played to chilling perfection by Pat Hinkle, confronts her. His sadistic cat-and-mouse game with her is a gut-wrenching masterpiece.

The Grifters is not a pretty picture, in any sense, but it's a bracing, stylish one, beautifully photographed and paced, with great dialogue and plenty of suspense. And let's hear it one more time for Huston, the best practitioner of rotten-to-the-core female roles in current cinema. **GC**

AR   Cynical and mean? Yes. Appealing, anyway? Definitely.

CT   Agreed. I can't ask for change for a dollar anymore without seeing Cusack pull a switcheroo on the bill.

THE MANCHURIAN CANDIDATE
1962. 126 min. Frank Sinatra, Angela Lansbury, Laurence Harvey. Dir. John Frankenheimer. b&w

Twelve years of *Murder, She Wrote* on CBS left a lot of Americans with the impression that Lansbury is a dowdy old broad with a weird New England accent. Actually, she's a British-born, four-time Tony Award-winning dancer and singer with great legs and a lot of acting talent. Though Hollywood didn't know quite what to do with her, she did score a few delectable roles, and this is one of them. She absolutely sends chills down your spine as the power-hungry mother of Korean War hero Harvey and the controlling wife of a nincompoop senator who rails against the Communists he *knows* are in the Defense Department, though he can't get the exact number straight. Sinatra, reminding us that he could act nearly as well as he sang, is Harvey's patriotic and sensible commanding officer, tormented by frightful nightmares about their service in Manchuria and what Harvey did to win the Congressional Medal of Honor. Oddly, Sinatra can't really recall. Was the platoon in fact captured by the enemy and indoctrinated by Russian and Chinese doctors who got into the soldiers' heads and "not only washed but dry-cleaned" their brains?

Is Harvey a programmed Communist stooge? Lansbury's character holds a lot of the creepy clues.

Filmed appropriately in black and white, *The Manchurian Candidate* is part political thriller, part political satire, taking after the left wing and the right wing with equal venom. It's unnerving, shocking, and enthralling. I could keep throwing adjectives at you, but I guess you get the point: This is a great movie. Just don't watch it with Mom. **AR**

GC   I, too, tend to sling adjectives around for this movie. So I'll confine myself to one simple, declarative sentence: It's terrific.

CT   Another one we all agreed on . . . doesn't happen too often. Consistently, entertainingly unpredictable, the movie that is.

REBECCA
1940. 130 min. Laurence Olivier, Joan Fontaine, Dame Judith Anderson. Dir. Alfred Hitchcock. b&w

The master won his only Best Picture Oscar with this gothic thriller, which was produced by David O. Selznick in the wake of his huge success with *Gone with the Wind*. It starts with a famous voiceover by Fontaine as the second Mrs. de Winter: "Last night, I dreamt I went to Manderley again . . ." And you know straight away that this Manderley is to be avoided at all costs. Which, thankfully for us, it is not.

The plain and shy young woman who replaces Rebecca as the wife of Maxim de Winter (Olivier) is up against ominous odds in a pair of wicked women; one of them is the strange Mrs. Danvers (Anderson). The widower de Winter is no walk on the beach, either, but chicks are the ones to watch out for, though de Winter tries to reassure his bride upon arrival at Manderley, "Just be yourself and they'll all adore you. You don't have to worry about the house at all. Mrs. Danvers is the housekeeper—just leave it to her." Mrs. Danvers would like that very much, in fact, and her attempts to rule the roost are chilling. One of the best: As waves crash against the rocks below, she speaks to Mrs. de Winter of her predecessor. "Sometimes, I wonder if she doesn't come back here to Manderley, to watch you and Mr. de Winter together. You look tired. Why don't you stay here and rest, and listen to the sea. It's so soothing. Listen to it—listen." Oooooo! **AR**

GC I love it that the woman who dominates the movie, the woman it's named for, is never seen, not even in photographs. And how about that Mrs. D? The way she caresses the dead Rebecca's fur coat, her underwear . . . very spooky, not to mention kinky.

CT That woman gives me nightmares!

THEY DRIVE BY NIGHT

1940. 93 min. George Raft, Ida Lupino, Humphrey Bogart, Ann Sheridan. Dr. Raoul Walsh. b&w

This is the movie that put Raft, Lupino, and Bogey on the map. It's an intriguing film, one that sticks with you, thanks to a unique story line and some of the best, hard-boiled dialogue of the film noir persuasion. Raft is the star, with Bogey in a lesser role. That would soon change. Lupino plays the quintessential bitch goddess. That wouldn't soon change.

Raft and Bogey play brothers Joe and Paul Fabrini, struggling to establish their trucking business in the face of graft, corruption, and the harsh conditions of long-distance hauling. It's a fascinating window into a little-known world (intimately familiar, however, to Raft, who drove bootleg trucks during Prohibition).

Lupino plays Lana, the grasping wife of an indulgent trucking magnate. She sets her sights on Joe (Raft), who is busy falling in love and spurns her. Bad move, Joe. Lupino puts even Joan Crawford in the shade in the hell-hath-no-fury department. As in: "You road-slob! If it weren't for me, you'd still be kicking trucks up and down the coast. I put that clean collar around your dirty neck, I put that crease in your pants. And you play me for a sucker! I committed murder to get you!" Great. **GC**

CT Great flick. And let's hear it for Lupino, who went on to write, direct, and produce movies herself in the '50s.

AR Lana's not evil, she's *nuts.* Entertainingly nuts. And with very bad hair; that curl on her forehead looks like a croissant.

THRONE OF BLOOD
1957. 105 min. Toshiro Mifune, Isuzu Yamada. Dir. Akira Kurosawa. Japanese w/subtitles. b&w

How could anyone resist a movie called *Throne of Blood*? I couldn't. And the rest of this classic of Japanese cinema is just as good. The legendary director Kurosawa based his story on Shakespeare's *Macbeth,* an inspired choice. That gothic tale of witches, hatred, and murderous ambition adapts perfectly to a Japanese setting. It's the story of a samurai, Washizu, played by the great Mifune, who is egged on by his evil wife, Asaji, to kill his lord for possession of Cobweb Castle. (There's also a Cobweb Forest that looms large in the plot. Can you stand it?)

The visual impact is stunning, with swirling mists, ornately armored, ferocious warriors, and gorgeous brocaded robes. Every frame is like a painting. And Washizu's comeuppance, a famously grisly scene, is unforgettable. But it's Asaji, his wife, played by Yamada, who strikes fear to the heart. She's evil incarnate. No wonder those samurai are armed to the teeth. They're terrified of her. **GC**

AR Yikes. She scared me, too, and I enjoyed it. Kurosawa sets a tantalizing stage.

CT You've gotta be in the mood for this kind of thing, but if you are, it's transporting. And I love the samurais' ponytails that stick out of the tops of their heads like handles.

TO DIE FOR
1995. 103 min. Nicole Kidman, Matt Dillon, Joaquin Phoenix, Alison Folland. Dir. Gus Van Sant

The Hollywood pitch meeting must have gone something like this: Think *Clueless* (page 188) meets Katie Couric meets Lizzy Borden. In candy-colored suits with polka-dot blouses, straight hair, and an American accent, Kidman is the aggressively shallow community college graduate Suzanne Maretto. Obsessed by the idea of making it big on TV, one way or another, she starts out by doing the weather report at a pathetically small cable TV station. When husband Larry (Dillon) starts putting a crimp on her multimedia ambitions, she snares three loser teenagers and charms them into getting rid of Larry. The actors are so convincing as real lowlife teens that it feels like we're watching a documentary (or maybe the *Jenny Jones* show) rather than a movie. As Jimmy, Phoenix has a disgusting Beavis and Butthead laugh that'll make you shiver with disgust, and it would be hard to convince me that Folland isn't the sad, plump lost girl she plays here. Directed by Van Sant (who also did the River Phoenix-Keanu Reeves male hustler flick *My Own Private Idaho*), *To Die For* satirizes the insidious way television invaded our sense of being. It's hard to believe that the cute Pre-Raphaelite Kidman could muster this juicy role, but boy does she. Makes me eager to see what else she can do besides stare blankly out from a cascade of curls on the arm of Tom Cruise. **CT**

GC   What took them so long? Finally, Hollywood skewers our TV-saturated culture, but good. As Suzanne says, "It's nice to live in a country where life, liberty and . . . er, all the rest of it still stand for something."

AR   There you have it: Cruise didn't marry just a pretty face after all.

WITNESS FOR THE PROSECUTION
1957. 116 min. Charles Laughton, Tyrone Power, Marlene Dietrich. Dir. Billy Wilder. b&w

Laughton is Sir Wilfred, a curmudgeonly barrister with a bad heart, a taste for brandy and cigars and, judging by the looks of him, prodigious quantities of red meat. Being perpetually grumpy and irascible, he is, of course, cute as a button. He's attended to relentlessly by a chipper and determined nurse, with whom he has one of those abusive relationships that is tremendously satisfying to both parties. Being the best criminal defense attorney in London, he takes the case of one Leonard Vole (Power), whose good looks aren't enough to hold down a job and who has enough spare time on his hands to hang out with a lonely rich widow he befriended. The widow turns up dead, and Vole is fingered as her killer. It looks pretty bad for him, since he's in her will to the tune of eighty thousand pounds. Sir Wilfred takes the case, convinced the evidence is solely circumstantial and the flighty young man is innocent.

Then Mrs. Vole (Dietrich) shows up, a foreigner with an air of something fishy about her. Mrs. Vole sure seems evil, but is she really, or is there something else going on? The first part of the movie's a treat just for the Wilfred character, then once it gets to the courtroom, it starts twisting and turning just like an Agatha Christie play, probably because it's based on a Christie play. And Dietrich (who was in her mid-fifties when this was made) looks fab, bringing to mind Gloria Steinem's line when told she didn't look fifty, "This is what fifty looks like." **CT**

GC   What a terrific movie! And just a word about that chipper and determined nurse. She was Elsa Lanchester, Laughton's wife and a great character actress, best remembered for her *Bride of Frankenstein* (1935).

AR   The best transfer to film of anything by Christie, better even than *Ten Little Indians*.

Aren't They Adorable? And Don't Forget These

For an exquisitely evil woman, see Mieko Harada in Kurosawa's 1986 *Ran,* a gorgeous epic, ten years in the making, based on Shakespeare's *King Lear*. Kathleen Turner does well being bad, as in *Body Heat* (1981) and the kinky *Crimes of Passion* (1984). But the queen of them all is Barbara Stanwyck. "Do it, Sam! Do it now! Everybody knows he's a heavy drinker!" That's from *The Strange Love of Martha Ivers* (1946). See her pillage and burn in *Double Indemnity* (1944), *The File on Thelma Jordan* (1949), *Ladies They Talk About* (1933), *Baby Face* (1933) . . .

twenty-eight

"HAPPY" DOESN'T ALWAYS PRECEDE "HOLIDAYS"

"I just called you up not to wish you a Merry Christmas."
—*Alan Baxter, in* In Name Only

The very merry *White Christmas* aside, it seems the best flicks that revolve around holidays, of either the religious or secular sort, aren't chock full of good cheer. (Come to think of it, even *White Christmas* blew a brief touch of unhappiness in with the snow, though it was for the most part jolly.) Now, we're not suggesting you rent the likes of *Halloween* or *Rocky IV* (in which the big fight took place on December twenty-fifth). Our recommendations are much more sophisticated. Sort of. So color a few eggs, mold some matzo, fast for a month, and remember what Bruce Willis says in my favorite *Die Hard:* "If this is their idea of Christmas, I gotta be here for New Year's." **AR**

AVALON
1990. 126 min. Armin Mueller-Stahl, Aidan Quinn. Dir. Barry Levinson

This knockout completes Levinson's "Baltimore trilogy," which began with *Diner* and continued with *Tin Men.* The last is the mellifluent multigenerational tale of the Krichinsky family's rise and fall, and it starts in 1915 on the Fourth of July. Why frame the story of

Jewish immigrants with all-American holidays? Levinson offered this
explanation to Gene Siskel of the *Chicago Tribune:* "My family was
not particularly religious. They went to synagogue only on the High
Holidays . . . That's why all of the holidays being celebrated in the
film are American holidays—the Fourth of July, Thanksgiving. I
think the story has more resonance that way, showing how these
people with an Eastern European sensibility dealt with being in
America."

Or how it tried so hard and in many ways failed to deal with the
New World. Levinson places a lot of blame on the widespread avail-
ability of television sets in the '50s, using the boob tube, and the
various Krichinskys' dependence on it, to illustrate the ultimately
ruinous emphasis placed on material success. But the Krichinskys
have a lot of other problems, too, and the story is told by the family's
oral historian, Grandpa Sam (the wonderful Mueller-Stahl), and
through the eyes of his devoted grandson (Elijah Wood), whose father (Quinn) breaks with the family's musical tradition to become a
door-to-door salesman. Bad choice, beautiful movie. **AR**

CT   A movie that's as big and warm-hearted and complicated as
         a big warm-hearted and complicated family. And Quinn is
         at his blue-eyed best.

GC   I think Levinson should have quit while he was ahead. *Ava-
         lon*'s nowhere near as good as the other two. It seems some-
         how muted to me, and a tad too reverent.

FANNY AND ALEXANDER
*1983. 197 min. Bertil Guve, Ewa Froling, Jan Malmsjo, Per-
nilla Allwin. Dir. Ingmar Bergman. Swedish w/subtitles*

If I were fabulously wealthy, I'd want all my Christmases to be
an exact replica of the one in this movie, which is a loosely autobiographical account of director Bergman's childhood in Uppsala, Sweden. It's December, 1907, when we meet Alexander (Guve) and his
younger sister Fanny (Allwin) in their palatial, comfortable home,
celebrating the holidays with their parents, their large, extended family, and the household servants, all of whom adore and indulge the
children and each other. It's a gorgeous, bountiful setting: candles

and lace and greenery, twinkling Christmas trees in every room, magic lanterns, music and laughter. It's the prettiest, warmest holiday scene you could imagine.

Of course, it can't last. Beloved Papa dies, and Mama (Froling) soon marries a dour, penny-pinching bishop (Malmsjo), who tries to break the spirit of the dreamy but headstrong Alexander.

If, like me, you think of Bergman movies as dark and fraught with symbolism—Death walking on the beach in a swirling black cloak— you'll be relieved to hear that *Fanny and Alexander* is warm and accessible. Yes, it's long, but so is a wonderful banquet. It's too detailed and too rich to rush through. It's stunningly beautiful. Is cinematographer Sven Nykvist a god, or what? He won the Oscar, no contest. The movie also won for Best Foreign Film, Costumes and Art Direction. For Christmas, or for any other time of year, *Fanny and Alexander* is a magical gift. **GC**

CT   You can put one in my stocking. A lovely, wintery flick.

AR   It's *very* long, but I hardly noticed. Bergman, avoiding his habitual doom and gloom, paints a magical portrait of life as seen through the eyes of a child.

HANNAH AND HER SISTERS
1986. 106 min. Mia Farrow, Dianne Wiest. Dir. Woody Allen

As you know, there is good Woody and bad Woody, good on display in *Annie Hall,* and bad in *September.* And here we have the very good Woody, the one who mixes humor and tenderness, belly laughs with moral dilemmas. In *Hannah and Her Sisters,* he follows an extended family and its members' failures and successes in love over two years, punctuated by massive Thanksgiving feasts during which many of the various crises come to a head, or threaten to.

It's all sweetly, smoothly rendered. And there are great performances—by Michael Caine, as Elliott, the smooth agent married to solid Hannah (Farrow); by Allen, as Hannah's ex-husband and resident hypochondriac; by Max von Sydow, as the moody lover of Hannah's sensual sister Lee (Barbara Hershey), who falls in love with Elliott; by Wiest, as grandly confused sister Holly, whose rival in befuddled romance is played by Carrie Fisher. And let's not forget

Maureen O'Sullivan (Farrow's mother in real life), as the alcoholic matriarch of the gang. From Thanksgiving to Thanksgiving, carving turkeys and serving up stuffing with smiles all around, the numerous alliances unfold and unravel. And odd as it sounds, it ends up being a very cheery movie. **AR**

GC This movie is as satisfying as one of those humongous Thanksgiving dinners. And it was great to see Caine, a fresh face among Allen's usual suspects, in a role worthy of his talents.

CT Thanksgiving with the Woody Allen family. Almost too scary to imagine

THE REF
1994. 93 min. Kevin Spacey, Judy Davis, Denis Leary. Dir. Ted Demme

Here's the deal: Gus, played by Leary, is a burglar who's just screwed up a heist and is on the run. So he sticks his gun in yuppie Caroline's ribs and demands a ride with her and her husband, Lloyd, to their house, where he's going to hold them prisoner until his dim-as-a-bulb partner shows up. Little does he know that he's in for a worse sentence than life in the pen. He may be armed and dangerous, but he's just no match for the hilariously dysfunctional couple (Spacey and Davis). Their tongues should be registered as deadly weapons.

And it's the holidays, so other equally dysfunctional family members are due to arrive, including a teenage son—who immediately bonds with Gus, recognizing him as a far better role model than his parents—and a mother who's more money-grubbing than any burglar. Gus learns that the average New England family, especially at Christmastime, is a fearsome thing.

The plot's not much of a challenge, but you won't care, because the characters are so juicy. Spacey, relatively unknown at the time, is spot-on as the whiny Lloyd, and Davis's Caroline is a venomous joy. The dialogue sparkles—it's sharp and witty and true, and under all the sniping and feuding there's a generous spirit. Rent this movie for the holidays—or any other time. It's all good, mean fun; richer than eggnog and nuttier than a fruitcake. **GC**

CT *Definitely* rent this movie during the holidays or anytime you're about to suffer from adult-onset-*It's a Wonderful Life*-induced diabetes.

AR When Davis and Spacey were on-screen, I loved it. When they weren't, I was apathetic.

HOME FOR THE HOLIDAYS
1995. 103 min. Holly Hunter, Robert Downey, Jr., Anne Bancroft, Charles Durning, Dylan McDermott, Cynthia Stevenson, Geraldine Chaplin. Dir. Jodie Foster

I'm sure I'm not the only one convinced the filmmakers have stalked our homes to get material for this one. Even if the details aren't exactly the same, it gives a pretty good (not to mention hysterical) portrait of holiday family dysfunction in 1990s America. After all, who hasn't attended a dinner with two turkeys brought by feuding parties? This family includes Claudia (Hunter), who gets fired from her museum job before she gets on the plane to go home and who immediately turns into a resentful kid when her parents pick her up at the airport; her brother Tommy (Downey in an intoxicating and vivacious performance); a control freak sister who casts herself as the family martyr (Stevenson); and Chaplin, as the aunt who gives away lamps and gets embarrassingly looped at dinner. Bancroft and Durning are superb as the archetypal middle-class parents. The only character who seems far-fetched is the seemingly well-adjusted *and* good-looking friend Leo (McDermott). This funny send-up of family life and holidays is also right on target about how amnesia sets in so that everyone actually looks forward to the next visit. As Durning says at grace: "As I was saying, dear lord, before my wife interrupted me, give us those old-fashioned, pain-in-the-ass traditions like Thanksgiving, which really mean something to us, even though goddammit, we couldn't tell you what it is." **CT**

GC Yuck! What a mean-spirited, joyless movie. Let's all join hands and give thanks this family only exists on film.

AR Bancroft and Downey are so magnificent, I barely noticed anyone else.

Stocking Stuffers . . . (In Addition, of Course, to Every Other Video Recommended in This Book)

CT 1) *Harvey:* Don't give it to accountants and quantifiers. 2) *It Could Happen to You:* For my mother, who believes things like this happen. 3) *Personal Best:* For all my lesbian friends. 4) *Driving Miss Daisy:* I'd give this to Gabrielle, but I suspect she'd slap me. 5) *Miss Sadie Thompson:* For fans of Cyndi Lauper, and all girls who just want to have fun.

GC 1) *Tune in Tomorrow:* Peter Falk at his zany best. Not a suitable gift for Albanians or German shepherds. 2) *The In-Laws:* The perfect dose of laughing gas for anyone afraid to visit the dentist. 3) *The Ruling Class:* For the Anglophile. A delicious comedy in which Peter O'Toole plays an English lord who thinks he's Jesus Christ. But don't they all? 4) *Young Frankenstein:* Guaranteed to appeal to pubescents of any age. Brilliant spoof, and Gene Hackman's cameo is a gem. 5) *Scenes from the Class Struggle in Beverly Hills:* See partners of every stripe play musical beds. Perfect for your vulgar, tasteless friends. One of my favorites.

AR 1) *Mister Roberts:* For those who think about enlisting, or who enjoy getting tipsy on cocktails of rubbing alcohol, io-dine, hair tonic, and cola, or who recognize that William Powell got better with age. 2) *Love Story:* For the chick teeny-bopper too young to notice that when Jenny wastes away from a deadly disease, it's unnamed, she doesn't lose her hair or her looks, and she kicks off without a gurgle. 3) *The Sting:* For grown-up females who recognize that, after all these years, Redford in 1973 was at the peak of his good-lookingness and that Newman, who looked even better ten years later, was also quite fine. 4) *Blazing Saddles:* For the sophomoric in all of us. 5) *Fiddler on the Roof:* For lovers of great music, great acting, great sets, and Paul Michael Glaser before *Starsky and Hutch*.

twenty-nine

OLD-FASHIONED LOVE STORIES—

Okay, Well, Maybe Not So Old-Fashioned

"Love is too weak a word for what I feel. I lurve you. I luff you."
—Woody Allen, in Annie Hall

Modern chicks aren't embarrassed to admit that they need a good swoon every now and again (particularly when they're not getting anything else, if you know what I mean). What we secretly desire are princes who will sweep us off our feet and make us laugh until our cherry colas spurt out our noses at the soda fountain. And we know where to find these gallant guys—at the movies. Need I say more? **CT**

BLUE SKY

1994. 101 min. Jessica Lange, Tommy Lee Jones. Dir. Tony Richardson

Bogey and Bacall had it. So did Hepburn and Tracy. And now, in an unlikely but dazzling coupling, Lange and Jones have it in spades. When these two are on-screen together in this movie, the heat just radiates. Carly Marshall, Lange's character, is a blowsy Southern beauty, a bundle of fears and neuroses, oozing sexuality from every creamy pore. Her husband, Steve, is a straight-spined career soldier, moving his wife and two daughters from one dreary base to another in the early 1960s. There's lots of paranoid Pentagon nonsense about nuclear testing and cover-ups of civilian exposure to radiation. Just ignore that stuff. The real story here is the passionate love between this crazy, needy woman and her gentle, over-burdened husband.

There is a fine script, and a slew of solid supporting roles, most notably Powers Boothe as a smarmy superior officer and Carrie Snodgress as his slow-burning wife. And the Marshalls' daughters, Alex and Becky, played by Amy Locane and Anna Klemp, add a satisfying complexity to the story as they cope generously with their loopy mother and tease their uptight dad. "He's blind and she's crazy," says Becky. "Yeah," answers Alex. "They're perfect for each other."

Lange won a well-deserved Best Actress Oscar for her fearless, earthy portrayal of Carly, and Jones should have won one for his Steve. But, hey, maybe what they had on-screen together was reward enough. It sure looked like it to me. **GC**

CT I love a movie that celebrates the love between a dysfunctional human being and a codependent spouse in such a way that the words *dysfunctional* and *codependent* never enter your mind.

AR Can't deny it: I agree with *both* my chick buds. There's enough fire between Lange and Jones that it burns away when he's not on-screen.

FRENCH KISS
1995. 111 min. Kevin Kline, Meg Ryan. Dir. Lawrence Kasdan

If Ryan is cute incarnate, *French Kiss* is her moving picture twin. Of course, you might not appreciate cute. You might not hoot just to think "Kline" and "French accent" together. Did you get up on the wrong side of the recliner or something? This is the best home-on-a-Saturday-night-with-my-cat-I-wish-I-were-in-love video rental of the century.

Ryan is a neurotic engaged to a boring doctor played by Timothy Hutton, who while attending a medical convention in Paris meets one of those French women American women love to hate, and calls off the wedding. The Ryan character flies to Paris to win him back and in the seat next to her on the plane is—*voilà!*—the goofball Kline as a jewel thief who hides a diamond bracelet in his seatmate's carry-on bag. He must then convolute all kinds of words as he tries to get the bracelet back while pretending to help her convince the dull doctor that the French chick really isn't a goddess.

Mon dieu! How long does it take for this mismatched couple to realize they don't really loathe one another? Through how many Paris alleys must they stroll, down how many wine country lanes must they meander, in how many outdoor cafés must they sit, upon how many stunningly blue Riviera waters must they gaze—*mais non,* that is for you to find out. *French Kiss* is romantic silliness at its best. Cute, cute, *cute!* **AR**

GC   Oh, gag me with *une cuillère.* The syrup in this movie plunged me into insulin shock. And it does something I didn't believe was possible: It makes Paris, the City of Lights, look corny. There ought to be a law.

CT   I think the reason Anne likes this movie so much is because she is a lot like Ryan's character. If I needed a fluffy afternoon, I'd watch it. But it's not high-quality fluff, like *Pillow Talk* (page 191).

THE FRENCH LIEUTENANT'S WOMAN
1981. 127 min. Meryl Streep, Jeremy Irons. Dir. Karel Reisz

John Fowles's novel was pretty darn dense—brilliant, but dense, and complicated, too—and Reisz brought playwright Harold Pinter and the versatile Streep onboard to move it successfully, and unconventionally, to the screen. Streep gives one of her impeccable performances, accents and all. Add a dash of dashing Irons, in his first big role, and *voilà:* One helluva movie, and *two* sets of ignitable lovers.

Anna (Streep) and Mike (Irons) are modern-day actors playing the chief roles in a film adaptation of Fowles's book, which tells the tale of Sarah (Streep), who waits in vain by the sea for the return of the French sailor with whom she has had an affair in Victorian England, and Charles (Irons), a gentleman who moves to Lyme Regis from

London and becomes obsessed with her. As they play their parts, Anna and Mike, both married, embark on an affair of their own. There are two points of view, two eras, two endings. It's a dazzling path to take in making a movie of a book, and it works. **AR**

GC   Ditto, Anne, it's a beautiful, fascinating movie. And it was such a relief that Streep's English accent didn't intrude. (I think her Polish accent in *Sophie's Choice* scarred me for life.)

CT   I liked it a lot, even though I was distracted by Irons, who looked like he stepped out of a '70s blow-dryer commercial.

I KNOW WHERE I'M GOING
1947. 91 min. Wendy Hiller, Roger Livesey. Dir. Michael Powell. b&w

The title of this quirky British film with no recognizable stars refers, alas, not to a woman who's going to create a trailblazing future for herself, but to one with a more traditional ambition: to marry a rich man. Our heroine snags one at 25, an industrialist older than her father, and she sets out for the Scottish isle of Kilarin to marry the old guy. But fate-changing winds blow through, tossing up the sea and stranding her on a nearby coast. Also waiting to cross the choppy waters, much to her dismay, is the owner of the castle of Kilarin. He just happens to be not too bad looking in his kilt— actually, he looks a little like Al Gore. He's aristocratic, but broke, and he's smitten by the bride to be, who finds him more distracting than she would care to admit. The two are sort of stuck with each other until the storm blows over. It's billed as a "romantic comedy," but I find that label misleading. Filmed in moody black and white, *I Know Where I'm Going* keeps switching gears, from jaunty to creepy to romantic. Noir fans will love the dramatic photography, and film lovers in general will be tickled by the playful camera that surely must have inspired the likes of Pedro Almodóvar. **CT**

GC   Hiller is, too, a recognizable star. Just not on this side of the Atlantic, more's the pity. And, yes, it is a strange, hard-to-pigeonhole movie, but it's charming, and the scenery is spectacular.

AR   What I liked was the fog and the great big squall that roars around it. Adds to the overall charm, so long as you keep an afghan near the couch.

MISSISSIPPI MASALA
1992. 118 min. Denzel Washington, Sarita Choudhury. Dir. Mira Nair

Usually it's the bad guys who are sexy, but Denzel knows how to use the soft-spoken-gentleman act to bring a woman to her knees, so to speak. Even as Demetrius, in his dorky carpet-cleaning uniform, he could compete on the hummona-hummona scale with Richard Gere in *American Gigolo*. And Choudhury, who plays his lover Mina—and who was looking for a job on the film crew when she got hired as the lead—is equally gorgeous. Directed by Nair, who also brought us the dynamite *Salaam Bombay!* (page 25), this is a beautifully told, all-American tale of immigrant assimilation in small-town Mississippi. It's a love story in the *Romeo and Juliet* vein and is rich with scenes of two family-intensive cultures—from a barbecue at Demetrius's dad's house to a festive Indian wedding attended by Mina's family. When the two lovers are found in bed together, Mina's family reacts violently, causing a rift that they may not be able to overcome. It's a treat to see a movie about middle America made from this fresh and intriguing perspective. **CT**

GC   And a treat with universal appeal. When I saw this movie at the theater, the audience was the most ethnically diverse I'd ever seen in Houston.

AR   Denzel and Sarita are beautiful together.

MOONSTRUCK
1987. 102 min. Cher, Nicolas Cage, Olympia Dukakis, Danny Aiello. Dir. Norman Jewison

Warm, funny, rich, quirky movies like this don't come around very often. So many elements come together to make this one darn near perfect, from the fairy-tale shots of New York, to the goopy "That's Amore" song, the zippy screenplay by John Patrick Shanley, and the extraordinary cast. Cher won the Best Actress Oscar for her portrayal of Loretta Castorini, a widow who's tired of being alone and accepts an offer of marriage from Johnny (Aiello). When he goes off to Sicily to sit by his dying mother, Loretta falls hard for Ronny, a one-handed baker with a passion for opera who also happens to be Johnny's estranged brother. Everyone in the Castorini family has something going on the others don't know about, including patriarch Cosmo (Gardenia) and his sharp wife, Rose (Dukakis, who nabbed the Best Supporting Actress Oscar). As they pause from their individual dramas, they end up in the family kitchen, where secrets are revealed and all the gnarly family business gets worked out. This is one of the few videos I'd buy to watch over and over. **CT**

GC   I like this movie a lot, too. It's full of life and humor. Great fun.

AR   Aiello and Cage are two of my favorites, together, apart, wherever. So of course I love this movie, which makes me tear up *and* laugh out loud.

MY BEAUTIFUL LAUNDRETTE
1985. 94 min. Daniel Day-Lewis, Gordon Warnecke. Dir. Stephen Frears

Working together, writer Hanif Kureishi and director Frears add up to a British equivalent of Spike Lee, using film to tackle tricky social issues. But while Spike deals mostly with class and race, this duo takes on issues of gender, homosexuality, immigration, and generational conflict to boot. It may sound like an awful lot to deal with, but they do so simply and eloquently, in riveting fashion. You don't feel like you're being hit over the head with "the issues," but you're certainly aware of what they are. In one of his earlier roles, the never-to-be-classified Day-Lewis plays Johnny, the once-Fascist punk who reacquaints himself with his boyhood friend Omar (Warnecke). Omar, a Pakistani, employs him to do the dirty work at a laundromat. This is not necessarily an easy arrangement for a post-Fascist to deal with, even if he does fall in love with his new employer. Simultaneously warm and raw, this is not the tea-party Britain we're used to on the big screen. It's a nice break from the Hugh Grant, Merchant-Ivory Britain we usually see (and I say this as a big fan of Hugh and Merchant-Ivory). If you become a Kureishi fan after this flick, check out his hilarious first novel, *The Buddha of Suburbia.* **CT**

GC One of my faves. But what's all this about the usual "tea-party" British movies? Wake up and smell the coffee, Cynthia. Some of the gutsiest, rawest movies around have come from across the pond. *Trainspotting. Naked. The Commitments. Secrets & Lies* (page 126). *Ladybird, Ladybird . . .*

AR Gabrielle's just being sensitive. What I like best about this movie is—big surprise—Day-Lewis.

ROXANNE
1987. 107 min. Steve Martin, Daryl Hannah, Shelley Duvall. Dir. Fred Schepisi

This reworking of the classic *Cyrano de Bergerac* (page 42) has to be one of the most charming movies of all time. Steve Martin, who wrote the screenplay, is Charlie, the jaunty fire chief of a small Pacific Coast ski town. He falls hard for the visiting blond astronomer, Roxanne (Hannah). She likes Charlie, but, well, not *that* way. (His having a nose the size of a ballpark frank might have something to do with it.) She falls for a supposedly buff (I don't see it, myself) fireman who has the intellect of a fire hydrant. She has no idea he's a witless hunk, only that his eyes make her heart go pitter-patter. Thinking only of making her happy, Charlie becomes the poetry-filled voice of the stupefied fireman. (It works, trust me.) *Roxanne* is also filled with wonderful touches, small sight gags, and delicious one-liners. (In one scene, Martin puts a coin into a newspaper box, grabs a paper, looks at it, shrieks in terror, finds another coin, tosses the paper back in the box, and walks on.) Then there's the . . . well, I don't want to give them all away. I could watch this one again and again. **CT**

GC   It's a sweet, pleasant movie, but not outstanding. Once was enough for me.

AR   I confess to a Hannah-phobia so intense that even my Martin-ardor can't overcome it. I find her *grating,* and I'm sure she doesn't think I'm a picnic, either.

THE SHAWSHANK REDEMPTION
1994. 144 min. Morgan Freeman, Tim Robbins. Dir. Frank Darbont

Don't be misled: What we have here is a love story, pure and simple, and based on a novella by Stephen King, no less. Sure there is a cell block full of prison clichés: a corrupt warden, an evil guard, an inmate-rapist who preys on newcomers, a sweet old-timer who loves birds. But at the core is an almost spiritual tale of a devoted friendship developed by two lifers at the fictional Shawshank prison in Maine—almost spiritual and absolutely beautiful and darn near believable. (Folks, this *is* a movie.)

Andy (Robbins) and Red (Freeman) meet after Andy is sentenced to two life terms for the murders of his wife and her lover. Andy's a stuffed-shirt banker, and Red is a veteran, in the joint for decades already. What they discover over twenty years is that even prison can't shackle affection, and that they both are better for the time they spend together, even in hideous circumstances. Oh, there's a plot, too, and it's entertaining, even suspenseful. It's not so important, though. Robbins and Freeman give the kind of extraordinary performances that let us forget we're watching a show. And the conclusion is one of the most satisfying and heartwarming in the movies. **AR**

GC   Yes, great performances, but it's waaaaaay too long. Just because they're serving time doesn't mean we should have to.

CT   I agree with Anne. Sometimes a movie can reach down and touch you way down deep. This is one. I remember seeing Robbins as the dumb-as-a-post pitcher in *Bull Durham* and thinking they must have hired a really dumb actor for the part. Boy, I couldn't have been more wrong!

TO HAVE AND HAVE NOT

1944. 100 min. Humphrey Bogart, Lauren Bacall, Walter Brennan, Hoagy Carmichael. Dir. Howard Hawks. b&w

When you watch this terrific movie, you're watching history in the making—on several levels. It's the movie that made the slinky, insolent newcomer Bacall an instant sensation, that kindled her and Bogey's lifelong passion, and that left us with some of the most-quoted lines in film, from Bacall's first words on screen—"Anybody got a match?"—to "You know how to whistle, don't you? You just put your lips together and blow."

There's not much of a plot. Screenwriter William Faulkner wisely concentrated on the chemistry between Bogey and Bacall rather than on the novel, which director Hawks called Ernest Hemingway's worst. It's a harder-nosed, cheekier version of *Casablanca,* also set in World War II, on the island of Martinique, where Harry (Bogey) and his drink-addled partner, played by Brennan, crew a boat. The war proves bad for business, so the disreputable pair take a job transporting a resistance fugitive fleeing the Nazis. Bacall plays Slim, a singer in Harry's favorite watering hole—which just happens to feature Hoagy Carmichael at the piano.

It's a treat just watching the electricity between these two, their sensuous banter and Bacall's throaty renditions of Carmichael's velvety, sexy music. It's especially remarkable from someone who was born Betty Perske. **GC**

AR   There aren't sufficient superlatives for *To Have and Have Not.* I also like the off-camera story of how Bacall was so nervous, she kept her head down while speaking her lines and created a sensation.

CT   For once, a twenty-seven-year age difference doesn't bother me, those two are so smoky together. And speaking of smoking, no one can do it like Bacall. I spent a part of my youth trying to emulate her—that chick must cause more lung damage than Joe Camel.

THE WAY WE WERE

1973. 118 min. Barbra Streisand, Robert Redford. Dir. Sydney Pollack

If you were in high school or even college in '73, and you're a chick, you'll appreciate the lauding of such a big hit tearjerker as an ace moving-picture love story. Did you not weep hysterically for the entire last half hour when you saw it in the theater? Do you not don large sunglasses and sneak into the video store to rent it on lonely Sunday nights? Yes, you can't quite comprehend Streisand decorating with photos of Lenin. No, you don't really know why Redford's character, a politically-neutral WASP with dreams of being a great writer but not a lot of gumption, would be attracted to Streisand's character, a Jewish leftist who can't shut up. But you *don't care.* This is love the way we've never had it, and the end of love the way most of us probably have, darn it.

So, youngsters, take a tour of the way Katie Morosky and Hubbell Gardiner (is that a great name or what?) were from the '30s through the '50s. Brace yourselves for the predictable finale, during which I typically go through about half a roll of two-ply. Hey, there's some good U.S. history in there, too. Bonus: Redford is at his very best looking. **AR**

CT   And what a gal that Katie is—no succumbing to peer pressure for her, even when it makes her unpopular. Maybe that's why so many young chicks in the '70s fell for this flick. Not so much for Redford, but for K-K-K-Katie.

GC   Redford looks great in that uniform, and Katie is indeed spunky, but ace moving-picture love story? No way. It's a manipulative, schmaltzy, whiny movie with a theme song that only ''Moon River'' comes close to for bathos.

WHEN HARRY MET SALLY . . .

1989. 96 min. Meg Ryan, Billy Crystal, Bruno Kirby, Carrie Fisher. Dir. Rob Reiner

It's a shame there are so few good romantic comedies. This is one of them. When they first meet on a road trip to Manhattan, Sally

(Ryan) is a basically happy person, with Farrah Fawcett hair and ambitions of becoming a journalist. Harry (Crystal) is a wisecracker who obsesses about death. On the trip they bicker about everything, from the ending of *Casablanca* to whether a man and a woman can be friends—Harry insist they can't because the guy always has sex on his mind. "So a man can be friends with a woman he finds unattractive?" she asks him. "No, he pretty much wants to nail them too." Sally drops Harry off at Washington Square Park and they part, then they keep meeting up accidentally every five years or so, bicker for a while, and then disappear from each other's lives again. But when they hook up after they've both been dumped and they decide to give friendship a shot, you can guess what happens then. The chemistry between Ryan and Crystal keeps this movie zipping along, with help from their best friends, played by Fisher and Kirby. This also has one of my favorite scenes of all time, and no it's not the one where Sally fakes an orgasm in the diner, but the one where Harry discusses his marital difficulties at a stadium where the wave keeps coming through. **CT**

GC   Screenwriter Nora Ephron was nominated for the Oscar. She should have won. The dialogue in this movie is priceless.

AR   Yes, it's a very good movie, but it would have been perfect if Ryan had been teamed up with Kevin Kline instead. In France.

A (Bronx) Cheer for Mr. Hays

Incredible but true, the Hays Code reigned in Hollywood from 1934 until 1968, when the G-to-X rating system went into full effect. Named for Will Hays, a onetime Republican Party chairman hired by the studios to help them stop themselves from titillating viewers, the code was written by two influential Roman Catholics and even blessed by the Pope. Mae West, on the other hand, didn't like it one bit—though without the code, we might never have heard her say, "It's not the men in my life, it's the life in my men."

Strangely, the code was pretty easy on violence. When it came to morality, however, it didn't cut slack, and ended production of such movies as *Three on a Match,* with its cocaine-using mothers, and *Red Headed Woman,* with its adulterous leading lady. Movies, the code declared, "shall not infer that low forms of sex relationships are the accepted or common thing." Men of the cloth "should not be used as comic characters or villains." And, though this hardly explains all those twin beds in wedded couples' bedrooms, "The sanctity of the institution of marriage and the home should be upheld."

In her vaudevillian days, the saucy West wrote, produced and directed a number of plays, including *Sex* (which resulted in her being hit with obscenity charges) and *Drag,* about, you guessed it, homosexuals. Once in Hollywood, she had a heck of a time carrying on with her candidly brazen ways, what with Hays and the Catholic Legion of Decency prowling around. *Klondike Annie,* in 1935, in which West played a prostitute, was cut by censors before its release, and audiences never got to see West's character suggestively look a man up and down while saying, "I'm sorry I can't see you in private."

So West became the mistress of the carefully delivered double entendre. It may well be Hays we should thank for such gems as these:

It takes two to get one in trouble.

I'm no angel, but I've spread my wings a bit.

A man in the house is worth two in the street.

Any time you got nothing to do—and lots of time to do it—come on up.

Is that a gun in your pocket, or are you just glad to see me? **CT**

Oscar Likes His Women Dumb—
and Deaf and Blind

I'd always known that about Oscar. He's definitely a sick puppy when it comes to chicks. I didn't start thinking just how sick until I was reviewing *The Piano,* 1993, for this book. That's the role that won Holly Hunter the Best Actress award. She played Ada, who had chosen not to speak since the age of six. Not that I didn't applaud the choice. Hunter was magnificent, as was the movie. It just rang a bell, and I decided to do some checking.

Let's stay with the mutes and deaf-mutes for now: There was *Nell,* about the wild child, in which Jodie Foster grunted and gesticulated her way to a Best Actress nomination in 1994. And how about *Johnny Belinda?* That's the 1948 movie in which Jane Wyman played not just a deaf-mute, but a low-I.Q. deaf-mute who is raped, impregnated, then put on trial for murder. She won the Best Actress Oscar. The Academy should have added at least a purple heart to that one. She makes Marlee Matlin, the deaf, sometimes-speaking-sometimes-signing actress who won the Best Actress award for *Children of a Lesser God,* in 1986, look like a piker. Then there was a shoo-in: not only deaf and mute, but blind, too. How could she miss? That was, of course, Patty Duke, who won the Best Supporting Actress award as Helen Keller in *The Miracle Worker,* in 1948. And who won the Best Actress award that year? Who else but the person closest to the deaf and mute and blind girl—Anne Bancroft, for her Annie Sullivan role in the same movie.

Which leads us to the blind: That Jane Wyman—what a trouper. After all she went through in *Johnny Belinda,* she comes back for more, blind this time, and wins a Best Actress nomination for *Magnificent Obsession,* the 1954 tearjerker. In 1967, Audrey Hepburn was nominated for Best Actress for her role as a blind woman— make that a blind, helpless, terrorized woman—in *Wait Until Dark.* Then there's *A Patch of Blue,* in 1965, which won a Best Actress nomination for Elizabeth Hartman, who played a young blind woman—an abused, browbeaten young blind woman. Shelley Winters, as her prostitute mother, won the Best Supporting Actress award, proving my thesis that Oscar's warped fascination for these roles rubs off on the caretakers, as in *The Miracle Worker,* above, and also in *The Piano,* in which the astounding youngster Anna Paquin won the Best Supporting Actress award as Hunter's daughter, her helper, and interpreter. I rest my case.

There's just one thing that puzzles me about Oscar and his predilections. How come the execrable *Boxing Helena,* in 1993, in which a vengeful surgeon cuts off the arms and legs of the woman who spurned him, didn't catch Oscar's attention? Maybe it was because the hapless—and limbless—Helena could still see and could still mouth off. A chick with a voice and with her eyes open. That's enough to give Oscar nightmares. **GC**

Big Biceps and Gigantic Guns

Girls, you haven't *lived* until you've seen Jean-Claude Van Damme do the splits in his underwear on a kitchen countertop. He performs this feat, and others, while wearing extremely tight pants, in *Timecop,* a futuristic thriller boasting several earsplitting explosions. This and all other all Van Damme movies are, along with such masterpieces as *Lethal Weapon* and *True Lies,* often scorned by misguided chicks who believe that women simply should not be entertained by derring-do involving simulated assault rifles or other weapons of mass destruction.

While I loathe guns of all style in real life, they bother me not a whit in shoot-'em-ups that are clearly fantasy, so long as: 1) the firearms are carried by good-looking guys who sweat a lot; 2) the directors and stunt coordinators really know their stuff; and 3) the screenwriter has a sense of humor. Once those criteria are met, bonus points are awarded to movies that give chicks power roles, as in *Terminator 2* (page 52) and *Lethal Weapon 3,* in which Rene Russo is tougher than the men.

Now, a which-flick-to-rent Q&A:

Q Fond of fellas with ponytails and legs as limber as a ballerina's?

A *Under Siege,* starring Steven Seagal, who looks goofy in a navy chef's hat until the battleship is stormed by Tommy Lee Jones and the kitchen knives start flying.

Q In the mood for a nonsensical plot and one of the most staggeringly inconceivable car cashes ever filmed?

A Jackie Chan's *Police Story,* with the acrobatic Hong Kong marvel himself as star, director, and stunt god.

Q Appreciate men in tank tops who will spare no bogus blood to save their estranged wives from high-rise terrorists?

A *Die Hard,* in which Bruce Willis's brawn fairly glistens with perspiration.

Q Want to see fourteen car wrecks, seven explosions, and Mel Gibson in wet clothes twice?*

A *Lethal Weapon 2,* in which Mel's eyes are almost as dreamy as in the original, Danny Glover is just as cute, and it's not *that* irritating when Joe Pesci says "okay" 108 times.* **AR**

---

*as calculated by *Entertainment Weekly*

Chicks' Favorite Picks

Out of all the movies in the book, here are the ones that we *all* agree are terrific.

Awful Truth, The
Blue Sky
Dead Man Walking
Diabolique
Fanny and Alexander
Fargo
Heavenly Creatures
Hoop Dreams
La Cage aux Folles
Last Emperor, The
Lion in Winter, The
Manchurian Candidate, The
Mary Poppins
My Life as a Dog
Paris Is Burning
Piano, The
Queen Christina
Romeo and Juliet [Zeffirelli]
Sense and Sensibility

Sounder
Thelma & Louise
Thin Man, The
To Have and Have Not
Tree Grows in Brooklyn, A
Wings of Desire

QUIZ ANSWERS

Answers to Quiz p. 7

When Harry Met Sally
Cool Hand Luke
The Caine Mutiny
The Public Enemy
Five Easy Pieces
Tom Jones

Answers to Quiz p. 18

1. *Three on a Match*
2. *What Have I Done to Deserve This?*
3. *Fried Green Tomatoes*
4. *Madonna: Truth or Dare*
5. *Alice Doesn't Live Here Anymore*
6. *Married to the Mob/Gloria*
7. *Broken Blossoms*
8. *Something Wild*
9. *Breaking the Waves*
10. *Truly Madly Deeply*

Answers to Quiz p. 29

> a) *Natalie Wood*
> b) *Tatum O'Neal*
> c) *Shirley Temple Black*
> d) *Jodie Foster*
> e) *Margaret O'Brien*

Answers to Quiz p. 38

1) The Fondas: Grandfather Henry; children Peter and Jane; granddaughter Bridget
2) The Arquettes: Grandfather Cliff; son Lewis; grandchildren Alexis, David, Richmond, Patricia, and Rosanna
3) The Redgraves: Grandfather Sir Michael; children Vanessa, Lynn, and Corin; granddaughters Natasha and Joely Richardson, Vanessa's daughters; and Jemma Redgrave, daughter of Corin

Answers to Quiz p. 45

Peruke	*Wig*
Jade	*Whore*
Pox	*Evil*
Popinjay	*Dandy*
Furbelow	*Ruffle*
Wench	*Maid*
Quaff	*Drink*
Stays	*Corset*
Four-in-hand	*Carriage*

Answers to Quiz p. 92

Cruise—Kidman
Quaid—Ryan
Johnson—Griffith

Coen—McDormand
Pitt—Paltrow
Danson—Goldberg
Banderas—Griffith
Depp—Ryder
Fisher—Taylor
Byrne—Barkin

Answers to Quiz p. 99

1). *I Want to Live!* (1958)
2) *Dance With a Stranger (1985)*
3) *The Bride Wore Black (1968)*
4) *Blood Simple (1984)*
5) *House of Games (1987)*

Answers to Quiz p. 120

Yves Montand, *The Wages of Fear.* Clark Gable, *It Happened One Night.* Daniel Day-Lewis, *The Last of the Mohicans.* William Holden, *Picnic.* Harvey Keitel, *The Piano.* Burt Lancaster, *From Here to Eternity.*

Answers to Quiz p. 177

a) Diane Keaton, *Reds* (1981)
b) Susan Sarandon, *Little Women* (1994)
c) Mira Nair, director of *Kama Sutra* (1996)
d) Katharine Hepburn, *Alice Adams* (1935)
e) Carrie Fisher, *Star Wars* (1977)
f) Ruth Chatterton, *Female* (1933)
g) Doris Day, *Pillow Talk* (1959)

Answers to Quiz p. 184

1. She played Amy, wearing lots of makeup, in the 1949 Mervyn LeRoy production.

2. In all of them.
3. Yes, with Allyson, in 1949.
4. What, are you kidding?
5. In 1933; that she was essentially playing herself.

INDEX